Praise for
10x IS EASIER THAN 2x

"As a 25-year student of Dan Sullivan's, I have experienced firsthand how his teachings have 10x'd every aspect of my life. Dr. Benjamin Hardy has brilliantly captured and taught Dan's 10x concept in this masterpiece. Every entrepreneur must read this book!"

— **Gino Wickman,** author of *Traction* and *The EOS Life*

"This book is not just a call to action, it's also a road map. Dan Sullivan's thinking is essential for your success."

— **Chris Voss,** CEO and founder of The Black Swan Group, author of *Never Split the Difference*

"Dan is the master of 10x thinking. During this upcoming period of disruptive exponential growth, the lessons of this book are not only critical for survival, they are the road map for you to thrive."

— **Peter H. Diamandis,** MD; founder of XPRIZE and Abundance360; *New York Times* best-selling author of *Abundance, Bold,* and *The Future Is Faster Than You Think*

10X
IS EASIER
THAN
2x

ALSO BY DAN SULLIVAN AND DR. BENJAMIN HARDY

Books

*The Gap and The Gain: The High Achievers'
Guide to Happiness, Confidence, and Success**

*Who Not How: The Formula to Achieve
Bigger Goals through Accelerating Teamwork**

Also by Dr. Benjamin Hardy

*Be Your Future Self Now:
The Science of Intentional Transformation**

*Personality Isn't Permanent: Break Free from
Self-Limiting Beliefs and Rewrite Your Story*

*Willpower Doesn't Work: Discover
the Hidden Keys to Success*

*Available from Hay House

Please visit:

Hay House USA: www.hayhouse.com®
Hay House Australia: www.hayhouse.com.au
Hay House UK: www.hayhouse.co.uk
Hay House India: www.hayhouse.co.in

◆ ◆ ◆

10x

IS EASIER
THAN
2x

HOW WORLD-CLASS ENTREPRENEURS ACHIEVE MORE BY DOING LESS

DAN SULLIVAN
FOUNDER OF STRATEGIC COACH

WITH # DR. BENJAMIN HARDY

HAY HOUSE, INC.
Carlsbad, California • New York City
London • Sydney • New Delhi

Published in the United States by: Hay House, Inc.: www.hayhouse.com®
• *Published in Australia by:* Hay House Australia Pty. Ltd.: www.hayhouse
.com.au • *Published in the United Kingdom by:* Hay House UK, Ltd.: www
.hayhouse.co.uk • *Published in India by:* Hay House Publishers India:
www.hayhouse.co.in

Project editor: Melody Guy
Indexer: Joan Shapiro
Cover design: Brad Foltz
Interior design: Julie Davison
Illustrations: Property of The Strategic Coach Inc.

**Cataloging-in-Publication Data is
on file at the Library of Congress**

Hardcover ISBN: 978-1-4019-6995-0
E-book ISBN: 978-1-4019-6996-7
Audiobook ISBN: 978-1-4019-7039-0
10 9 8 7 6 5 4 3 2 1
1st edition, May 2023
Printed in the United States of America

SUSTAINABLE
FORESTRY
INITIATIVE
Certified Chain of Custody
Promoting Sustainable Forestry
www.sfiprogram.org
SFI-01268

SFI label applies to the text stock

**For Babs—
who makes
10x possible.**

"When you shoot for 10 percent better, you're in a smartness contest—you're putting all of your people in a smartness contest with everyone else in the world. They're not going to win. It doesn't matter how much money you give them. . . If you shoot for ten times bigger instead of 10 percent bigger, it's almost never a hundred times harder, and the payoff is a hundred times, so you already know that you've got a better return on your investment. But sometimes it's literally easier, and the reason is because that perspective shift is actually cheap relative to being smarter than everyone around you."

—DR. ASTRO TELLER,
CAPTAIN OF MOONSHOTS AND CEO OF X[1]

CONTENTS

INTRODUCTION

10x Is the Opposite of
What You've Been Told

◆ ◆ ◆

*"What the caterpillar calls the end of the world,
the master calls a butterfly."*

—RICHARD BACH

At age 17, Michelangelo became fixated with secretly obtaining and dissecting human cadavers.

"Violating a corpse" was a crime punishable by death in Florence, Italy, in 1493.

"And if one were willing to risk it? How could it be gone about? Watch the poverty fields for burials?" he asked an elderly friend, Marsilio Ficino, whose father had been a prominent doctor. Ficino could not believe what he was hearing.

"My dear young friend, you cannot conceive of yourself as a grave robber."[1]

But Michelangelo was desperate.

Indeed, he *would* rob graves to get bodies if he could find no other option.

Learning anatomy was essential to his aim.

He'd just begun working on his first life-sized, three-dimensional sculpture: a nine-foot Hercules.

Prompted by the recent death of his sponsor and mentor, Michelangelo planned to do the project to memorialize Lorenzo di Piero de' Medici.

Before attempting this Hercules, he'd done many smaller sculptures. None three-dimensional. And none he'd ever been directly paid for. This was his first major project with a professional mindset. He was no longer thinking or operating like a novice or an amateur.

He convinced the foreman of the Florence Duomo Cathedral to sell him an old block of marble that had been sitting unused in the cathedral courtyard. He used most of his savings from working in the Medici palace the previous two years—five golden florins—to buy the marble.

After Lorenzo's death, Michelangelo had been forced to move back home with his poverty-stricken father, who was skeptical about his son becoming an artist and hoped he'd go into business instead.

In order to earn his father's blessing, he lied about his project, saying he'd been commissioned to make a sculpture and that the commissioner had already purchased the marble. He'd also said he would be paid a small amount each month while completing the project. This was a risky lie—if the project didn't pay off, Michelangelo would likely have to concede to his father's wishes of giving up his dream.

After setting up a spot in the Duomo workshop, Michelangelo began modeling a Hercules out of beeswax. He quickly concluded that he lacked requisite skill to create anything reflecting the true human form.

"How can I establish a figure, even the crudest outline, if I don't know what I'm doing? How can I achieve anything but surface skin sculpture, exterior curves, outlines of bones, a few muscles brought into play? Effects. What do I know of the causes? The vital structure of a man that lies beneath the surface, and that my eye can't see? How can I know what creates, from within, the shapes I see from without?"[2]

He determined that the only way he'd be able to draw and sculpt the human form with living vibrancy would be to study the intricacies and functions of the body directly—outside and in.

Where could he find available corpses?

The dead of the rich were buried in family tombs—he couldn't get those.

The dead of the middle class were surrounded with religious ritual—that wouldn't work.

Which dead in Florence were unwatched and unwanted? Only the very poor, the orphaned, and the beggars. These people were taken to hospitals when they were sick. Specifically, church hospitals with free beds.

Michelangelo now had to take another big risk if he was going to complete his ambitious project. Indeed, getting caught messing with corpses would, at the very the least, get him placed in prison. The worst case was that he could be sentenced to death.

The charity hospital in Florence, Santo Spirito, claimed the largest free guesthouse. Michelangelo began awkwardly sneaking around Santo Spirito to discover where the dead were kept. He found the morgue where bodies were wrapped and held until their burial. He began slipping inside late at night and leaving before sunrise. When his candle began to flicker, Michelangelo knew the monks who baked the daily bread would be nearby soon.

For the next several months, he taught himself human anatomy by dissecting dozens of corpses. He obsessed over the details—how the muscles flexed, the veins pumped, and tendons stretched. He held and cut into every organ. After a while, he became used to the smell of cadavers. He was intrigued that people could be so different, yet their brains looked and felt so similar.

Back home, he sketched what he learned. Anatomy, more than anything else, became Michelangelo's discipline and mastery.[3] To quote a future pupil of his:

> "Through dissection Michelangelo studied every known animal, and did so many human dissections that it outnumbers that of those who are professional in that field. This is a considerable influence that shows in his mastery in anatomy that is not matched by other painters . . . He worked on so many human anatomies that those who have spent their lives at it and made it their profession hardly know as much as he does."[4]

Michelangelo developed the skill and confidence to finish his Hercules. Conceptualizing and planning the design, he sketched version after version, to get a feel for Hercules' posture and emotions.

Rather than creating an outspread figure as was typical of the hero, with wide legs and arms on the hips, Michelangelo designed a closed and compact figure closer to the Greek concept. His knowledge of anatomy inspired him to depict Hercules' power as a uniting force between torso and limbs. Clothed in only a small loin skin, the bare-chested and strong Hercules leaned on his massive wooden club.

Drawing of Michelangelo's statue of Hercules.[5]

Michelangelo built a rough clay model, continually moving the weight and stance to find the best position. Knowing the interaction between mass and tension, he showed flexed back muscles in response to the extended arm on the club. Tendons stretched and contracted as the figure leaned. Ligaments strained. The hips and shoulder pivoted.

All of this the artist could project with conviction and confidence because he understood human anatomy.

He used a flat stick to gauge how deep to cut to reach neck depth, armpit depth, the slope of the torso, the bended knee. He chiseled close to the surface like a plow cutting through a field. After penetrating the weathered outer skin of the Seravezza marble, his chisel found an interior like soft sand, the milky-white shavings disintegrating between his fingers. As he went further below the surface, the marble quickly became hard as iron, requiring all his strength to achieve his desired forms.

He nearly ruined his block of marble. He'd cut too deeply to free the neck, and now his strong chisel on the emerging shoulder muscles sent stressful vibrations into the head. If the marble cracked at the narrow point, Hercules would lose his head.

Luckily, the head held and didn't crack.

To put the level of detail he wanted into every millimeter of Hercules, Michelangelo forged several fine-edged tools. Each blow of his hammer had equally distributed force as though it was his fingers rather than the chisels cutting through the crystals. Every few moments, he stepped back and circled the marble, wiping away the new layer of dust. He examined the work from a distance and then squinted to view it up close.

He made several other mistakes—such as making several blows chipping away the front section of Hercules. But he'd left himself enough spare marble at the back to push the entire figure deeper into the block than he'd planned.

His progress became faster. The anatomy of the marble began matching his clay model: the commanding chest, ripped forearms, and thighs like tree trunks.

He carved carefully yet eagerly, using the hand drill to form nostrils and ears. With his finest-edged chisel, he rounded cheekbones, slowly twirling his hands with the slightest touch to give the eyes a clear, piercing look.

As the project neared completion, he worked longer hours, forgetting to eat, and falling into bed exhausted.

Once finished, word spread about the Hercules.

Michelangelo was offered 100 golden florins—a large sum of money for a common Florentine—by the Strozzi family who wanted it in their palace courtyard.

When Hercules was finished, it was the spring of 1494 and Michelangelo was 19 years old.

To sculpt Hercules at the level he aspired, Michelangelo developed mastery of human anatomy to a degree no other sculptor ever had or would. Aiming for what seemed impossible, he made many mistakes, got serious and focused, took risks, and ultimately completed a tangible project that was beyond noteworthy.

Michelangelo was not born a great artist. He became one and then ultimately reached legendary levels by continually pursuing what I call *the 10x process.*

He set out to do something far beyond anything he'd ever done, and also something innovative and non-linear to the preestablished standard or norm of his field. To complete the project at the level he desired required a full-on transformation of not only his skills and creativity, but also of his commitment, convictions, and identity.

He had to risk a great deal to even attempt his 10x project.

He was required to learn and develop unique knowledge and perspectives, such as the intricacies of human anatomy and how to craft a life-sized and believable human statue.

Completing and selling the Hercules left him a *qualitatively different* person from his former 17-year-old self who began the project.

After selling the Hercules, he was now *mentally and emotionally* a different person, with radically extended skills and more confidence than his former self. But also, professionally, he was *positioned* far differently than his former self. He now had the reputation of having done something significant, which led people to become more interested in him as a person, but also led to others wanting to commission more of his work.

How did Michelangelo achieve such an impossible breakthrough?

In psychology, there's an increasingly crucial concept, *psychological flexibility*, which is defined as the ability to respond to obstacles successfully and in a way that is congruent with personal standards.[6] Essentially, psychological flexibility is moving toward chosen goals even when it's emotionally difficult. You acknowledge and accept your emotions, but they don't control you.

Becoming more psychologically flexible enables you to expand and grow emotionally, and to live a more committed and congruent life, even when it's hard.[7,8,9]

How does this work?

A core aspect of psychological flexibility is *viewing yourself as a context*, rather than viewing yourself as content.[10,11,12] This enables you to not overly identify with your thoughts and emotions, since you're not your thoughts and emotions. Instead, you're the context of your thoughts and emotions, and as you change the context, the content changes as well.

When you view yourself as a context, rather than as content, then you are far more flexible and adaptive. Just as you can change the furniture or remodel a house, you can expand and transform yourself. By expanding yourself as a context—which involves a great deal of emotional development—you're enabled to handle the complexity of bigger obstacles and opportunities without being overwhelmed. You can be humble yet resolved as you innovate new pathways toward increasingly exciting and compelling goals.

Michelangelo was incredibly flexible. He continually envisioned grander and more profound visions, and he evolved himself emotionally and also in skills and abilities to realize his impossible visions. By doing so, he expanded his freedom and agency—*the quality* of who he was and how he lived fundamentally improved with each 10x jump he made, which was continuous throughout his life.

Michelangelo didn't stop at Hercules.

With his new confidence and skills, he began his next 10x jump, which started with the carving of a small cupid statue quickly purchased for 200 florins by Cardinal Raffaele Riario of Rome. Riario was so inspired by the piece that he invited Michelangelo to move into his palace and work for him full-time.[13]

Leaving Florence, where he'd grown up and spent his entire life, Michelangelo arrived in Rome on June 25, 1496, at the age of 21. He quickly located a large piece of marble and began his most ambitious project yet. By the spring of 1497—eight or nine months later—the artist completed a life-sized statue of the Roman wine god, *Bacchus*, holding a vine of grapes at his side with a small child-satyr eating the grapes from behind.

The banker, Jacopo Galli, who lived across the street from Cardinal Riario, became friends with Michelangelo and purchased the *Bacchus* for his courtyard. Galli helped Michelangelo get the commission to carve a *Pietà* statue for St. Peter's Cathedral in November 1497.

A sculpture depicting the Virgin Mary grieving over the body of Jesus, the *Pietà* took two years to complete. Michelangelo wanted this piece to be perfect and he pushed his creative and sculpting abilities to otherworldly heights.

Unlike any of the many other *Pietàs* at the time, he wanted Mary, not Jesus, to be the central figure. Rather than the middle-aged mother of a man in his 30s, Michelangelo reflected Mary as she would have looked as a young and radiant virgin mother. She holds and mourns over her now dead Savior-son. The beautiful body of Christ, mostly exposed, displays Michelangelo's hard-earned mastery of human anatomy.

The completion of the *Pietà* was the culmination of another 10x jump for Michelangelo.

Now 24 when he returned to live in Florence, he was not the same man who had left his hometown three years earlier.

He'd lived abroad, met influential people, and completed two next-level projects—the *Bacchus* and *Pietà*. To this day, the *Pietà* is considered one of the greatest artistic masterpieces *of all time.*

Michelangelo's skills, creativity, and confidence following the completion of the *Pietà* were incomparably beyond where he was after his Hercules. It would almost be insulting to compare the two statues—they are in different stratospheres of quality, depth, and impact. Like comparing fast food to fine dining, or in this case, like comparing fine dining to the best meal *ever* crafted.

In early 1501, Michelangelo began what would be his next 10x jump.

Already four statues into a 15-statue commission for the Cathedral of Sienna, he learned the Overseers of the Office of Works of Florence Cathedral (the *Operai*) were seeking a sculptor to complete their giant David statue.

The 17-foot piece of marble had been sitting in the Florence Duomo courtyard incomplete and baking in the Mediterranean sun for more than 40 years. It had been abandoned and damaged by two separate sculptors decades earlier.

Michelangelo wanted this project more than anything else.

He saw it as a huge opportunity—a *10x opportunity.*

He believed he could do something special with the David. Now 26, Michelangelo convinced the *Operai* that he was the sculptor to complete the David.[14]

Unlike the many other David sculptures of his era—including Donatello's—Michelangelo chose not to depict David standing victorious over Goliath's severed head. He chose not to reflect David as a small and feminine character, as he was often portrayed. Michelangelo reflected on and studied David's interaction with King Saul, in the book of Samuel, when young David convinced Saul that he could go up against the giant, Goliath. Reading about David who *wrested and killed lions and bears,* Michelangelo saw David as the perfect man.

Rather than depict him *after* his great victory over the giant, Michelangelo would depict David *just before* the courageous encounter. His left hand over his shoulder holding his sling and right hand down by his side holding a stone, David's face would express apprehension yet resolution.

For nearly three years, Michelangelo pored over David. And David transformed Michelangelo—*completely.*

When finished in early 1504, David was immediately recognized as a masterpiece. Michelangelo was just 29 years old.

Michelangelo was paid 400 florins for the David statue, his biggest fee up until that point. A council of the most influential artists and politicians of the time came together to decide where the David would stand. It was placed in front of the Palazzo Vecchio—the town hall of Florence. David became the symbol of Florentine independence and liberty. Literally a turning point for the entire city, David renewed Florence's courage and pride, and the people and the city began prospering greatly.

With the completion of the David, Michelangelo's fame rivaled that of Leonardo da Vinci. Having improved his abilities by another 10x level, he was given commissions by leaders of nations and governments.

In 1505 while working on his *Battle of Cascina* painting—which would be paired with Leonardo da Vinci's *Battle of Anghiari* for the council chamber of the Palazzo Vecchio—he was forced to abandon the project. The newly elected Pope Julius II commissioned Michelangelo to build the Pope's tomb.

You don't say no to the Pope.

Michelangelo moved to Rome and got to work.

Three years later—in 1508—the Pope asked him to paint the Sistine Chapel, which he completed in 1512 at age 37.

Throughout his life, Michelangelo continued to take on projects far beyond—*impossibly beyond*—his skill level. Most people are afraid to commit fully to the 10x process because it inevitably requires letting go of your current identity, circumstances, and comfort zone.

Going 10x means you're living based on the most intrinsic and exciting future you can imagine. That 10x future becomes your filter for everything you do, and most of your current life can't make it through that 10x filter.

What got you here won't get you there.

To quote the actor Leonardo DiCaprio, "Every next level of your life will require a different you."

10x Is Simpler, Easier, and Better than You've Been Taught

"But what about the quality of the work? It was in the marrow of his bones to create only the finest he could produce; to create far beyond his abilities because he could be content with nothing that was not new, fresh, different, a palpable extension of the whole of the art. He had never compromised with quality; his integrity as a man and an artist was the rock on which his life was built. If he split that rock by indifference, by giving less than the exhausting best of himself, if he were content merely to get by, what was left of him?"

—IRVING STONE, *THE AGONY AND THE ECSTASY*[15]

History's greatest artists and entrepreneurs understand the difference between 10x and 2x thinking.

You might be thinking: What about people who don't ever make a 10x leap?

Most people reach for just a little bit more—a promotion, a little more money, a new personal record. Going for incremental progress is a *2x mindset*, which at a fundamental level means you're *continuing* or *maintaining* what you're already doing. You're letting *the past* dictate what you do and how you do it. 2x is linear, meaning you're striving to double output by doubling effort. Do more of the same, just faster and harder.

2x is exhausting and soul-defeating.

It's extremely difficult to put the pedal to the metal and grind away for inches of progress.

By contrast, 10x is so big and seemingly impossible that it immediately forces you out of your current mindset and approach. You can't work 10x harder or longer. Brute force and linear methods won't get you to 10x.

10x has become a trendy concept thrown around in entrepreneurial, financial, and self-help circles. Yet, most people radically misunderstand what 10x means and what it can do. In fact, most people understand 10x *literally* and *exactly backward*.

Because most people have it backward, they struggle manifesting 10x in their lives. They get stuck in a 2x mindset. But even more, their quest for 10x leads them to seek the wrong thing, an endless race *for more*.

10x isn't about more. *It's about less.*

Michelangelo understood this clearly. When the Pope asked about the secret of his genius, particularly in regard to the statue of David, Michelangelo explained, "It's simple. I just remove everything that is not David."

Going 10x is the simplification of your focus down to the core essential. Then you remove everything else.

Steve Jobs was the master of *extreme simplification*, which is the essence of innovation.

When designing the iPod, he removed all aspects of owning music that people didn't want and provided technology that made the experience of music *10x better and easier*. Rather than having to go to the store and spend $12–15 for a full album when you really just wanted one song, now you could simply and easily purchase only the songs you wanted and have them all pocket-size in one easy place. No more lugging around hundreds of CDs containing 80 percent or more of songs you don't even like. **Just as 10x isn't about more but less, 10x is also not about quantity.** *It's about quality.*

It's not the quantity of work he did that makes Michelangelo legendary, but the almost unfathomable *quality* of what he did. Each time Michelangelo went 10x, he reached a near godly level of mastery and expression.

Sure, he did a lot. A ridiculous amount, actually. But so do a lot of people. Many are busy yet unproductive. They do a lot but ultimately achieve little.

10x is a qualitative difference from before and after, a wholesale innovation and upgrade.

10x is the equivalent of going from crawling to walking; from not knowing the alphabet to reading; from living in your parent's basement to living on your own; from being awkward and shy to being a bold and emotionally intelligent leader.

10x is tantamount to going from horse and buggy to a car. You may be in the same genre—such as transportation—but you're not comparing apples to apples. A non-linear change has taken place. It's fundamentally a *qualitative shift*, more than a quantitative one. The transformation occurs by operating from a seemingly impossible and imagined future, and takes you in a non-linear and radically different direction and approach than what you (and everyone else) have been doing up to this point.

2x is a focus on quantity. You just add a zero and do more of what you're doing. It's linear and non-creative. It's brute force, not higher intelligence and leverage.

The most fundamental qualitative change is internal, your *vision and identity.* By changing these, everything else you're doing simultaneously changes as well. You take your internal and emotional evolution and externalize that in the form of refined standards and results.

10x becomes your perceptual filter for everything you do. Everything becomes either 10x *or* 2x.

Anything that's not 10x doesn't meet the filter and gets released from your attention. According to constraint theory, the greatest human bottleneck is attention. Our attention is our most finite resource, even more finite and valuable than our time. Indeed, the quality and depth of our attention determines the quality of our time. Most people's attention is scattered, tugged, and seemingly never *right here and right now*.

Going 10x means your attention is directly on *far less*, but it's insanely more potent and impactful because it's focused rather than spread thin.

Finally, 10x is not about any specific outcome. *It's about the process.*

10x is a capability.

It's an operating system you deploy for:

- Dramatically expanding your vision and standards

- Simplifying your strategy and focus

- Identifying and removing non-essentials

- Developing mastery in unique areas

- Leading and empowering others who excitedly share your vision

10x is *the vehicle* for transforming yourself and your life.

Every time you commit to 10x, that commitment takes you on a journey. That journey is the peeling away of more layers of the onion, discovering the essence of who you are. Each layer you peel away is the letting-go of your former self, transforming you increasingly into your truest self.

Committing to 10x and transforming yourself *frees you*.

There are two levels of freedom—surface-level freedom and higher-level freedom. Surface-level freedom is external and more measurable. This is "freedom from"—where you're freed from ignorance, poverty, and slavery. But there is a more abundant kind of freedom that is *internal and qualitative*. This is "freedom to"—which is where you take full ownership over your life.[16]

Higher-level freedom requires commitment and courage. You choose your standard and live based on that standard, regardless of the associated risks or costs. No one can give you this higher-level freedom. A matter of conscious choosing, *freedom to* is purely internal. You could have all the external freedoms imaginable and yet not be free.

10x is the means, and *freedom is the end*.

Every time you go 10x, you consciously choose to live your life at a particular level or standard, no matter how abnormal or seemingly impossible. *You* chose the standard. You commit to it. You live as *you choose*, transforming yourself and your world through your commitment.

The top entrepreneurial coach in the world and co-founder of Strategic Coach, Dan Sullivan, discovered four fundamental freedoms that 10x people seek:

- Freedom of Time
- Freedom of Money
- Freedom of Relationship
- Freedom of Purpose[17]

Freedom is fundamentally qualitative and internal. You must choose it and embrace it. No one can give it to you or take it away.

Michelangelo expanded his four freedoms throughout his life. Freedom was the infinite game he lived, and he played finite games to further expand his internal freedom. Every time he went 10x by committing to and completing a seemingly impossible project, his freedoms expanded.

His time was spent on better things and was valued more by himself and others. Thus, his *Freedom of Time* continually increased.

He got bigger commissions, and those hiring him would give him lodging, pay for his materials, pay for servants, and pay for assistants to help him complete the projects. His *Freedom of Money* grew and stopped being a hindrance to how he lived and what he did.

He became well-known to the extent that the Pope hired him for projects that changed Michelangelo's life and the direction of history and culture. His *Freedom of Relationship* continually expanded with each 10x jump—to the point where he had increasing access to nearly anyone he wanted, and where highly influential people regularly sought him out.

Freedom of relationship facilitates *Freedom of Purpose* because relationships open and close doors. Through a relationship, you can make non-linear and 10x jumps in options and opportunity, such as the person who gets the leadership role because he knows the person who owns the company. Those who despise this reality don't understand the four freedoms and are limited by that fact. Rather than argue with reality, learn the rules so you can shape it to your wishes.

Michelangelo's freedom of purpose reached an almost unbelievable level where he did projects that literally changed the direction of cultures, countries, and economies. With each 10x jump, his chosen and clarified purpose in life became dramatically bigger and more meaningful. How he defined his life exponentially expanded.

Expanding your freedom is the ultimate purpose of the entrepreneur's journey, and there really is no end to how much freedom you can have or create.

Expanding your freedom is what Dr. James Carse would call the "infinite game," which is about continually transforming yourself and the game you're playing, and never getting caught or stuck within any finite game or set of rules.[18]

Being 2x means you're stuck in a finite game—a situation, perspective, objective, identity, etc. You're not expanding your freedom to be, do, and have. You're caught up in fear and paralysis. You're maintaining the status quo of who you now are and what you're now doing.

10x is playing the infinite game of expanding your freedom.

Freedom isn't cheap, though. It requires brutal honesty with yourself and others, which is terrifying yet liberating. There are no half-measures or half-commitments with 10x. To achieve freedom of purpose, you must let go of everything that isn't 10x in your life. This is hard because most of your time is likely caught up in 2x work.

Going 10x is the stripping away of everything that's not "the David" of your core self and highest purpose.

My 10x Journey

This is a book for people interested in 10x level growth and transformation—and how you can achieve that for yourself.

I know this because I've experienced 10x transformations myself.

Many times.

My name is Dr. Benjamin Hardy and I'm the writer of this book, along with my collaborator and primary co-author, Dan Sullivan.

While I was pursuing my PhD in organizational psychology, my research focused on entrepreneurial courage and transformational leadership.[19,20] In my research, I uncovered a radically novel concept, which I called *the point of no return*, that identified a core difference between wannabe entrepreneurs and successful ones. The point of no return is the moment of full commitment, wherein your identity and energy shift from avoiding what you fear to fully approaching what you most want. I also found how the most powerful leaders transform those who follow them, elevating their identity and behaviors to dramatically higher levels.

While completing my PhD program—from 2014 to 2019—in addition to doing my research and getting my education, my blog posts were read by over 100 million people and were regularly published on platforms like *Forbes, Fortune,* and *Psychology Today.* For three years—from 2015 to 2018—I was the number one most read writer on the massive blogging platform Medium.com, based in Silicon Valley. I also published my first major book, *Willpower Doesn't Work,* in 2018,[21] and grew my online training business to seven-figures.

Since completing my PhD in 2019, I've published another five books, three of which are co-authored with legendary entrepreneurial coach Dan Sullivan. Collectively my books have sold hundreds of thousands of copies and are quickly becoming staples in the business and psychology space.

My wife and I have also made several 10x jumps. In 2015 during the first year of my PhD program, we became foster parents of three siblings, ages 3, 5, and 7. Over the next three years, Lauren and I fought the foster system in court, and in February of 2018, we were miraculously granted adoption. One month after the adoption, Lauren became pregnant with twin girls who were born in December of 2018.

Yes, in 2018, we technically went from zero to five kids.

10x transformation.

We've since had our sixth and final child, our epic and smiley boy Rex.

There are many more 10x's I've experienced that I could talk about. But that's not the point. The point is that since the first time I experienced 10x in my life, I wanted to understand the intricacies of the process. Thus, over the past decade, I've excitedly studied the psychology and application of 10x growth and transformation.

My study led me to the work of Dan Sullivan, who over the past 50 years has personally coached more high-level entrepreneurs than anyone living today. His company, Strategic Coach, is the premier entrepreneurial coaching company in the entire world. Over the past 35 years, more than 25,000 high-level entrepreneurs have participated in the Strategic Coach Program.

I started studying Dan's work in 2015 when I was first starting my own entrepreneurial endeavors, and while I was also researching entrepreneurial courage academically. Dan's teaching blew my mind and influenced my own 10x jumps as an author and entrepreneur, enabling me to build a seven figure company from nothing in just a few years.

My love and appreciation of Dan's teachings led me to collaborate with him, which has led to this and our two other books, *Who Not How* and *The Gap and The Gain*.[22,23] As with our previous books, this book is written from my own perspective and in my own words. Using Dan's language, "I'm the 'Who' that wrote this book because no one else could have or would have."

Even still, Dan's teachings form the foundation of this project.

Dan is truly a master.

His ideas and thinking are so unique and counterintuitive that they fly in the face of conventional wisdom. Take for example, the notion that getting 10x bigger results is actually *easier* than going for 2x.

When Dan's entrepreneurs initially hear this idea, they scratch their heads in disbelief. Then Dan unravels radically simple yet profound insights and perspectives, making the truth of this concept so clear it can't be misunderstood.

Between Dan's five decades of working directly with tens of thousands of outlier entrepreneurs and helping them go 10x, and my background in entrepreneurial and exponential psychology, we provide a perspective of 10x in this book that's unlike anything presented on this wildly popular and even more wildly misunderstood topic.

To bring the truth of 10x to you in this book—making it simple, mind-expanding, embarrassingly obvious, and immediately applicable—I delved down countless veins of the psychological literature, interviewed Dan for several hours, interviewed dozens of Dan's top entrepreneurs whose stories have never been seen before now, and transformed my own life inside-and-out to prove the concepts.

When I initiated the collaboration with Dan in 2018, it was an experiment. I believed that by sharing Dan's ideas in the form of mainstream business books, that people's lives could be changed. I also believed high-level entrepreneurs that meet the requirements of Strategic Coach would realize the power and depth of Dan's teachings and join Strategic Coach for continued and systematic 10x growth.

Our experiment worked.

Our initial 10x ambition was explicitly stated in the introduction of *Who Not How*, our first book together. I wrote that our goal in writing that book was transforming the lives of hundreds of thousands of readers in addition to directly leading 500+ growth-oriented entrepreneurs to join Strategic Coach for direct training.

Less than two years since the publication of *Who Not How*, both of those objectives have been achieved. The book quickly became a cult classic and perennial seller in the entrepreneurial space, and high-level entrepreneurs are joining Strategic Coach on the daily in reaction to the liberating gut-punch of Dan's teaching displayed on the silver platter of my writing.

Our collaboration has produced a qualitative 10x transformation in both of our lives and businesses.

At our new 10x level, we've recently re-imagined our next 10x jump, which is publishing dramatically better books that reach millions of readers and directly lead 5,000+ world-class entrepreneurs seeking 10x growth and freedom to join the Strategic Coach program. By joining Strategic Coach, these entrepreneurs receive direct access to the well from which this and our other books were drawn.

How This Book Will Change Your Life

"Anything that is alive is in a continual state of change and movement. The moment that you rest, thinking that you have attained the level you desire, a part of your mind enters a phase of decay. You lose your hard-earned creativity and others begin to sense it. This is a power and intelligence that must be continually renewed, or it will die."

—ROBERT GREENE[24]

I was recently sharing the ideas in this book over a steak dinner with some friends and watched as the scales over their eyes began to fall off. They shook their head in disbelief, realizing how much of their lives were stuck in 2x mode.

It became absurdly obvious they were needlessly maintaining so many situations, projects, and people that were 2x, not 10x.

They were operating out of need not want; scarcity not abundance; security not freedom.

"We have to let go of [so and so client/project]," my friend said to his business partner—who was wolfing down a bite of his 32 oz. tomahawk steak—as he heard me sharing the principles you're about to learn in this book.

Here's the most surprising truth about this book. Counterintuitively, 10x is much, much easier than 2x.

It's much simpler than 2x.

But "easy" and "simple" aren't exactly what they seem. To quote American author T.S. Eliot, "A condition of complete simplicity. . . costing not less than everything."[25]

To go for easy and simple, you'll have to let go of everything in your life that is needlessly hard. More specifically, you'll have to let go of everything you don't truly want.

10x filters-out literally everything that isn't 10x, which is most things in your life.

If you're willing to commit and let *everything* go that you don't really want, then your life will be infinitely easier, simpler, and more successful than it's ever been.

Is this scary?

Yes.

Does it require 100 percent commitment?

Absolutely.

But like ripping off a Band-Aid, the hardest part is thinking about it. The shock factor may be real, but once you make the decision, everything changes. How you do anything is how you do everything. 10x becomes your filter and norm.

In this book, you will learn what 10x is and why it's the most natural, exciting, and powerful way to live. You're going to see yourself and the world entirely differently.

You're going to see your potential and every decision you make differently.

Before you finish reading this book, you'll imagine and clarify highly unique and personal 10x jumps that will transform your life. You'll make 10x your new standard and identity, filtering-out past aspects of yourself that are 2x and holding you back.

There's no end to 10x.

There's no end to freedom.

It's an inside game.

It's an infinite game.

It's a game you can play again and again.

Only you can decide how far you'll go. Only you can decide how much you'll transform into the truest expression of yourself and life's purpose.

If you decide to go 10x from where you are now, your 10x future self will be a different person than you are now. In a short time, you'll have freedoms you can't presently fathom. The 10x value and quality of your time, money, relationships, and purpose will seem *impossible* to you now but will be completely normal to your 10x future self.

Every time you commit to 10x, you'll be required to go through the same process. **In the first chapter** of this book, you will learn the details of this 10x process. You'll begin to see exactly why 10x and 2x are direct opposites, and why 10x is far easier, simpler, and more exciting than 2x. This process is highly imaginative, strategic, and practical.

In the second chapter, you'll learn how to commit to 10x and transform yourself and your identity through that commitment. This is the emotional aspect of the 10x process, which is where the rubber meets the road. Having 10x goals is one thing. But making 10x *your standard*, now that's a different ball game, one that takes pure commitment and courage. That's a game that will transform your entire life if you're serious about it, but it's also the only way to expand yourself and be free. Thus, you'll learn to make 10x your standard and say "No" to increasingly great things, sharpening and refining your filter and identity.

In the third chapter, you'll learn the difference between wanting and needing. To go 10x, you shift all of your energy away from a "needing" perspective of life and the world. You don't need to go 10x, *you want to*. The highest form of freedom is based on want, not need. Choosing what you want takes radical honesty, commitment, and courage. This is how you begin peeling away the layers and getting to the root and core of who you are. The more honest you get with yourself, the more you'll clarify and develop your Unique Ability, which is your superpower as a person and entrepreneur, and it's completely unique to you. Avoiding your Unique Ability leads to a life of frustration and mediocrity. Opening yourself up and developing your Unique Ability takes vulnerability, commitment, and courage—it's like climbing a mountain and jumping off a cliff at the same time. The more layers you peel away by going 10x, the more you become your own version of the David, and the more valuable and purposeful your life will be.

In the fourth chapter, you will be shown a different perspective of your own past, enabling you to better see and appreciate all the 10x jumps you've already made. You'll connect the key dots that brought you to this point and use that throughline to lay out the next qualitative and non-linear 10x jumps your soul is most calling for. You'll learn how to normalize 10x so that it becomes an increasingly natural way to live—seeing and feeling it through both your past and your future.

The fifth chapter will help you shift out of the linear and quantitative model of time that is taught in public education and continued in most of corporate America. This model is based on the industrial factory model of the 19th century and is radically ineffective for 10x growth and transformation. You'll learn the time system Dan has developed over decades to help his entrepreneurs become 10x and often 100x more productive, happy, and successful. Rather than operating in quantitative time, you'll learn to leverage time *qualitatively*, wherein you have far more flow, fun, and transformation. You'll be less scheduled. Your time will be less thinly-sliced and fragmented. You'll have bigger and wider blocks of freedom for deep work, active recovery, and peak experiences.

The sixth chapter takes all the building blocks of the previous chapters and challenges you to create a Self-Managing Company, where you create a culture of freedom. You'll have a self-managing and self-multiplying team to handle *all aspects* of your business. As a Transformational Leader, you'll be *totally free to embrace* the few things that matter most—innovating, strategizing, visioning, collaborating, evolving. Your vision will become so compelling and exciting that the right people will see multiple 10x futures for themselves in your vision. You'll equip everyone around you to be better leaders and evolve beyond their current roles, leading them to bring on new "Whos" and free themselves up for the next stage of 10x growth. This is *Unique Ability Teamwork*. This is how you have an operating system of 10x all around you, while your own personal life gets simpler, slower, deeper, and more powerful.

Are you ready to go 10x?

Let's begin.

PART 1

10x

PRINCIPLES

CHAPTER 1

THE SURPRISING SIMPLICITY OF 10x GROWTH

Why the 2x Mindset Is the Enemy of Results

"The road to hell is paved with the pursuit of volume. Volume leads to marginal products, marginal customers, and greatly increased managerial complexity . . . Hard work leads to low returns. Insight and doing what we want leads to high returns . . . Strive for excellence in few things, rather than good performance in many . . . It is not shortage of time that should worry us, but the tendency for the majority of time to be spent in low-quality ways . . . The 80/20 principle says that if we doubled our time on the top 20 percent of activities, we could work a two-day week and achieve 60 percent more than now."

—RICHARD KOCH[1]

"If you wanted to improve your profits by ten percent, how would you do it?"

I once attended marketing expert Joe Polish's entrepreneur mastermind group, where he presented this and several other questions.

After taking 5 to 10 minutes to think through Joe's questions, we had a group discussion. Dr. Alan Barnard, one of the world's leading experts on constraint theory and decision-making, happened to be in the group that day.

"This is actually a really bad question," stated Dr. Barnard. He then continued:

> "There are literally infinite things I could do to grow my profits by ten percent. The goal isn't big enough to create focus and specificity. If, however, you asked, 'If you wanted to grow your profits by ten times, how would you do it?' that would be a much better question because there are likely to be very FEW, maybe even only ONE way to create 10x growth. Indeed, almost nothing you're currently doing would get you there. To separate the signal from the noise, you need to make the goal big enough to weed-out most paths or strategies. Impossible goals help you identify the ONE or FEW conditions that have the highest possible upside. Those are the areas to focus your scarcest resource - your limited attention on."

To make a goal effective, you've got to test its outer-limits. Push it out as far as you can. Only once you make your goal *impossible* will you stop operating based on your current assumptions and knowledge. You'll be *open to new ideas*, and you'll entertain different paths that you've never considered.[2]

Operating non-linearly based on past assumptions and norms: *2x*.

Operating non-linearly based on an exciting and seemingly impossible vision: *10x*.

Dr. Barnard encourages people to make their goal so big that they believe it's impossible.

For instance, if an entrepreneur wants to make $1,000,000 profits in the next 12 months, Dr. Barnard asks, "Do you believe that's possible?"

The entrepreneur answers, "Yes."

"What about making $10,0000,000 profit in the next 12 months," Dr. Barnard suggests. "Do you believe that's possible?"

"I don't think so," the entrepreneur responds.

"That goal," Dr. Barnard presses, "It would be impossible, unless. . ? What conditions need to be true for $10,000,000 profit in the next 12 months. Then ask yourself how can you create these 'unless' conditions to make the impossible, possible."

The entrepreneur lists conditions that need to be present for that impossible goal to become believably possible.

Dr. Barnard points out those conditions and strategies are where the entrepreneur should focus if they want the highest return on time and energy. Everything else they're doing is noise.

Seemingly impossible or massive goals are highly practical because they immediately separate what works from what won't, illuminating the few paths that have the greatest efficacy.

Small goals are unable to clarify effective pathways because they are too marginal or linear from your current location.

This is a fundamental reason why 10x goals and vision are simpler, easier, and more practical than 2x goals. With a 2x goal, there are too many potential pathways to reach the desired destination. This creates paralysis-by-analysis and makes it extremely difficult to know where to focus your best energy and effort.

Conversely, with a 10x goal, only a limited number of strategies or paths will work.

Take my son Kaleb for example. He's an avid tennis player and wants to play in college. Recently, his coach asked, "Why don't you just go for professional?"

Surprised, Kaleb had never thought that was a possibility.

Driving home from practice, Kaleb and I discussed what his coach had said. "What if you committed to going for professional, would that change anything about what you're doing now?"

"Maybe," he replied.

"Do you think your current trajectory would get you to pro?"

"No."

"If we went for pro, do you think we could find a path for that?"

"Probably."

"Do you think it would be different from a college path?"

"Yeah."

The goal determines the process.

"The only way to make your present better," said Dan Sullivan, "is by making your future bigger."

Chunking-up the goal to its next quantum level up and making it 10x bigger forces you to find different pathways to get where you want to go. You ask different questions to different people.

There are many paths to 2x or linear progress, which is one reason it's ineffective and overly complex to go 2x. There are few paths leading to 10x, making the goal simple and highly effective. Again, *almost nothing* will work for 10x, which is why it's so useful.

There are many coaches in the Orlando area where we live that could likely get Kaleb to the college tennis level.

However, there are extremely few coaches that could realistically guide Kaleb to the pro level.

If we committed to the pro level, we'd have to change Kaleb's training process dramatically.

Ironically, Kaleb's best chance at even reaching his college goal would be chunking-up his goal to the pro level, because at least then we'd start being far more discerning and pickier about everything he's doing. In other words, the easiest way to get 2x growth is by going for 10x, because 10x forces you to stop almost everything you're doing, which is ultimately a waste of time anyway. As the old Norman Vincent Peale quote states, "Shoot for the Moon. Even if you miss, you'll land among the stars."

The same is true of 10x and 2x.

If you're shooting for 2x, you probably won't land much farther from where you are now and you'll exhaust enormous energy grinding inches forward. There's not enough distinction to force clarity about which direction to go. There's also not enough difference to discern what among the many things you're now doing is ultimately a waste.

10x separates the signal from the noise.

Almost nothing works for 10x growth, which means if you take it seriously, you'll have to be a lot more honest about everything you're now doing. You'll also have to be far more choosey about the paths you take forward, because only an extremely limited set of approaches or conditions have any connection or efficacy for such a transformation.

In psychology, *pathways thinking* is an attribute of high-hope people—those who are highly committed to specific goals. These high-hope people are continually learning and iterating their process and path toward their goal. They take feedback from hitting obstacles and not achieving their goals to learn and get better and to adjust their path.[3,4,5,6,7,8,9]

When an objective has a large spectrum of possible pathways or solutions, then it's not a useful tool. Goals are a filtration-tool, filtering the signal from the noise, clarifying where to focus for the highest impact.

10x is simple. Very few paths will get you there.

The higher and more specific your goals and standards become, the fewer options you have—which counterintuitively, actually makes them *easier* to achieve. Bigger and more specific goals immediately axe almost everything you're now doing, making all sorts of space for exploring and scanning much better options.

If you want a really nice house, you have fewer options for furniture. The more specific you get about what you want, the fewer designers there may be who fit your desires. Conversely, if you have "low" or non-specific standards for your house, then there are seemingly endless options for furniture.

When you're trying to solve highly complex and particular problems, you'll need a specialist, not a generalist, to solve your problem. You can't just go to any doctor to reach optimal health.

Almost everything is noise.

Almost everything you're now doing is a distraction from 10x.

The 10x vs. 2x Framework:
Why 10x and 2x Are Literally Opposites

"If we didn't have ambition—some big goal we are after—how would we know what little things, what distractions, to say no to?"

—RYAN HOLIDAY[10]

How could it be that top performing entrepreneurs get better results by taking a simpler, although counterintuitive, path?

Only by living with a 10x frame of reference do you become highly critical of everything you place your time and energy on.

Having a 10x mindset means you know and understand that to accomplish more, you must actually do and focus on increasingly *less*.

You know that working more hours does not equate to better results, but on the contrary, working more hours usually means you're grinding your wheels on not innovating your thinking enough.

Working too many hours means you're living 2x, not 10x. It means you're focused on effort, not transformation.

Economists and statisticians have clarified a crucial and well-understood concept for this exact phenomenon: the *80/20 Rule* or *Pareto Principle*, which specifies that 80 percent of consequences come from 20 percent of the causes, asserting an unequal relationship between inputs and outputs.

Bluntly, 20 percent of your focus is producing 80 percent of your best and most desired results. This "20 percent" consists of the activities you do and particular relationships you have. Just a few things you're investing in are making up almost all the results. Conversely, 80 percent of your focus is producing a mere 20 percent or less of your best results, meaning you're investing lots of time and energy into stuff that's literally holding you back, greatly.

But here's where it gets interesting. There is a crucial distinction that hasn't been clearly spelled-out until now.

The all-important question, if you're someone who wants to live a meaningful and intention life, is: *How do you distinguish the 20 percent that matters and the 80 percent that doesn't?*

There are two things you must do, and most people stop only after the first. However, if you only stop after the first step, then you likely won't be able to separate the 20 from the 80. The first step is necessary, but not sufficient.

So, what is the first step?

In order to clarify what matters from what doesn't, you need to *specify your goal*.

Without knowing your goal, it's impossible to find an effective path forward. In Lewis Carroll's children's book *Alice's Adventures in Wonderland*, Alice asks the Cheshire Cat which way she should go when she reaches a fork in the road.

"That depends a good deal on where you want to get to," said the Cat.

"I don't much care where—" said Alice.

"Then it doesn't matter which way you go," said the Cat.

Without a clear goal, you can't define the 20 percent that will effectively get you there and the 80 percent that's taking you some other direction. Even still, when a goal isn't much different from your current position, then you won't need to change much to get there. Thus, you won't need to separate the 80 from the 20, because when the destination or transformation is minor, then very little needs to change about what you're now doing. This makes it difficult to pin-point where to focus your efforts and change and also stops you from identifying the 80 percent you're still maintaining that isn't serving you.

Small goals don't require 80/20 thinking, because small goals don't require much adjustment from your current approach.

Thus, the second requirement for separating the 20 percent that matters and the 80 that's taking you some other way is setting *much* bigger goals. This goes straight to the research on decision-making and hope we've just covered, including some of Dr. Barnard's crucial insights on impossible goals. Only by stretching your goal far enough out can you parse-out the 80 percent of your current activities and focus that won't get you there.

Only when you make the goal big enough—10x bigger—does it become absurdly and even comically obvious which strategies, relationships, or behaviors won't work (the 80 percent).

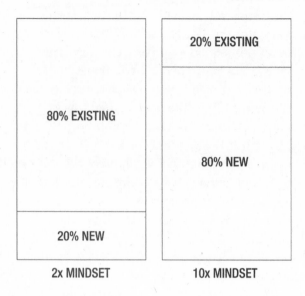

This brings us to the 10x vs. 2x framework developed by Dan Sullivan.

Put simply, if you're going for 2x growth, then you can keep or maintain 80 percent of your *existing* life, or what you're now doing. And in fact, when you're going for 2x or linear growth, that's exactly what you're doing.

2x is operating from the past, primarily continuing the path you've already been on.

2x is linear. You're not doing anything radically different. You're mostly just trying to do more of what you're now doing with as few changes as possible.

10x is the opposite of 2x.

Going for 10x requires *letting go of 80 percent* of your current life and focus and going all-in on the crucial 20 percent that's relevant and high-impact.

Every time you go 10x, this same process will occur. It applies every time you make a 10x jump, no matter how many 10x jumps you've made to this point. This framework is the foundation of 10x or 2x thinking: in order to achieve 10x, you cannot rely on your past self's thinking.

What got you here won't get you there.

To go 10x from where you now are, only 20 percent will scale. The rest will be filtered out. Only by clarifying and identifying with your 10x vision will it become obvious the 80 percent that is holding you back.

10x is *fundamentally and qualitatively different* from what your life looks like now. It's a complete transformation, not simply re-arranging the furniture.

Everything in your world, including yourself, will look different at 10x.

Dan Sullivan has helped countless entrepreneurs double down on their 20 percent and let go of their 80 percent. One of the thinking tools he has his entrepreneurs utilize in Strategic Coach is to identify the top 20 percent of their current clients—the ones that provide 80 percent of the revenue and excitement—and draw a line separating the top 20 percent from the bottom 80 percent.

"What would happen if you immediately eliminated the bottom 80 percent? How long would it take you to get back to your current level of revenue?"

After they consider the question, a common answer from Dan's entrepreneurs is "Between two to three years."

That's not very long.

It's actually crazy how short that is, considering many of these entrepreneurs spent decades building their companies.

A funny and popular meme describes why focusing on the top 20 percent is easier than maintaining the 80 percent:

The $500 client: "I just feel as though with this investment I am about to make in you, that we should understand how our lives are about to change and I need the results and you need to bring them, I am entrusting you with our livelihood and our lives."

The $50,000 client: "Money sent, thanks."

10x people are easier than 2x people.

Take Carson Holmquist, for instance. Carson is the co-founder and CEO of Stream Logistics, a construction transportation company he started in 2012 at 26 years old. Stream Logistics provides transportation and logistics (i.e., trucks and trailers) for construction companies.

From 2012 to 2017, Stream Logistics grew quickly, going from 3 to 30 team members. It was around this time that Carson joined Strategic Coach to further understand how he could help his company go 10x from where it was. One of the first things he learned was that in order to go 10x, he needed to make his company self-managing to free himself up to innovate, strategize, and evolve himself and his thinking.

At that point in time, Carson was working 50 hours per week and was involved *in all aspects of this business.* Admittedly, he was micro-managing and realized he was the bottleneck that literally everything in the business had to pass through.

Carson was busy but non-productive.

Listening to Dan's 10x teachings, he saw how he was holding the team back from effectively growing and working autonomously without him.

He was also holding himself back because his time and attention were too absorbed in the day-to-day details of his business. He was dealing with constant and daily urgent battles such that he didn't have any time to think about the future of the company.

Dan Sullivan sees entrepreneurs falling into this trap all the time, warning them that tightly scheduled entrepreneurs cannot transform themselves.

2x is working *in* the business. 10x is working *on* yourself and working *on* the business.

2x is trying to optimize the horse and buggy, getting millimeters and inches for your efforts. 10x is stepping back and inventing the car, like Henry Ford did, where you're getting miles for the same efforts.

Without transforming himself, his vision, and his thinking, Carson was repetitiously grinding away in 2x-mode.

Carson invested the next 18-24 months into hiring and training a new leadership team to take over everything he was doing. By 2019, Stream Logistics had grown to around 40 team members and was entirely self-managing.

Carson had *nothing* on his schedule.

He entirely freed himself up to begin dissecting his company, evolving himself as a person and leader, and re-thinking the direction of the company.

That year, he joined the highest-level program within Strategic Coach, the *Free Zone Frontier* program, which teaches entrepreneurs how to think 100x bigger by forming unique collaborations and competition-free niches. Carson learned one of Dan's higher-level models, *Who Do You Want to Be a Hero To?*[11] The idea is simple—clarify with precision the exact types of people you want to work with, who also appreciate and value what you do most.

Carson thought hard about this and started reflecting on the different types of clients he had. He dug into the numbers and accounting in his business and realized there were two separate types of clients they worked with at Stream Logistics, which Carson categorized as "Routine Freight" clients and "High Stakes Freight" clients.

At that time, in 2019, the Routine Freight clients made up 95 percent of their clientele. By Routine Freight, these were the projects that were, well, *routine*, meaning there was nothing crazy or unique about the needs of these clients. Mostly, these clients just wanted their equipment moved from point

A to B via a logistics and transportation company. This was where Stream Logistics spent most of their time, working with clients that wanted a simple and ubiquitous service.

Thinking through it, Carson saw the writing on the wall. There was nothing extremely unique Stream Logistics provided to these routine clients. Sure, they provided a very high-quality service—above the quality of most of their competition, which was vast. Yet, these routine clients weren't overly focused on quality. They didn't have specific needs or challenges. Because there was so much competition in the construction logistics space, everything ultimately came down to price. Whoever gave the best price got the business. Thus, it was a constant race to the bottom.

These clients weren't loyal to Stream Logistics. Sure, they liked Stream. But if they found a better deal, they'd take it.

While dissecting his business and thinking bigger picture, Carson also realized that the company's growth would continue being linear with their current model. Although they'd grown fast to that point, their growth had been steadily plateauing, reaching a ceiling or cap for how much more they could do with their particular model.

The company had grown fast because they hired fast. If they wanted to grow their revenue by 20 percent, they'd need to add 20 percent more team members to operate and handle the various projects and workloads. That was the only way they could continue growing with their current model and focus.

The reason for their linear growth became obvious—they weren't providing high-leverage and niche services. Almost all of their service was broad to broad clients.

In reflecting on his High Stakes Freight clients, Carson saw that these made up only 5 percent of their clientele but accounted for 15 percent of the company's profits. These were also the clients that appreciated Stream Logistics services the most, paid the most money, and were the most exciting clients to work with for the team and company.

High Stakes had highly complex, specific, and challenging logistics and transportation needs. With these particular clients, everything needed to be perfect—the shipment had to be at the exact place at the exact time in the exact way. The consequences were "high stakes" if the logistics and transportation wasn't perfect.

Sometimes, these types of logistical situations require more than five oversized load trailers, police escorts to surround the load while traveling on roads and free-ways, etc. It can get dicey and intense.

Carson believed that if Stream Logistics *shifted all of their future efforts* to High Stakes Freight clients, as a company, they could do something unique and special. He also knew that the profitability of working with these clients was asymmetrical and non-linear, meaning that by adding 5 percent more effort, you don't get 5 percent more return but 15 percent or more. For every dollar you invest, you get three or more back. For every minute you invest, you gain five. Thus, by focusing all future energy on these types of clients, he believed the profitability of the company would grow exponentially.

He presented the idea of focusing all efforts on High Stakes Freight clients and putting *no efforts* into adding anymore Routine Freight clients to his team.

Initially, the team resisted the idea.

It made logical sense to them what Carson was explaining. They already knew that the High Stakes Freight clients were their best, most profitable and exciting clients and projects. But the idea of abandoning 95 percent of their clients and 85 percent of their profits seemed too risky.

The sales reps particularly resisted the idea, as focusing on High Stakes Freight clients would dramatically cut their call lists from about 300–400 active prospects down to maybe 30–40. The sales reps couldn't see how they could realistically make a living with so few prospects, even knowing they made more money with each High Stakes prospect.

It took six months for the team to fully buy in and for the company as a whole to make the shift to *100 percent energy and focus* on High Stakes Freight clients. For the first few months, Carson would catch the sales reps continuing to call Routine Freight prospects, trying to get more business there. He'd encourage them to stop and to focus their efforts solely on the High Stakes Freight.

By focusing more of their efforts on High Stakes Freight prospects, a few things happened. First, as an entire team, they realized there were way more of these types of clients than they initially believed. And the specific needs of these clients were more complex than they previously thought.

As the sales reps got more and more High Stakes Freight sales, they saw the power of quality over quantity. For Routine Freight clients, the profit was $260-280 per shipment. With the High Stakes Freight clients, the profit was $700+ per shipment, sometimes multiples of that.

In 2019, *95 percent* of Stream Logistics' clients were Routine Freight.

At the present writing, October 2022, *less than 25 percent* of their clients are Routine Freight.

Over the past 2.5 years, they have put no energy into adding new Routine Freight clients. They maintain the ones they have but won't fight to keep them.

In 2019, Stream Logistics had an annual revenue of $22 million.

In 2022, Stream Logistics will have an annual revenue exceeding $36 million.

But more importantly, Stream Logistics as a company is over 4x more profitable than they were in 2019, and they haven't had to add any new team members.

They still have around 40 employees.

By focusing their energy on High Stakes Freight clients, their team is less spread thin and strapped. Carson told me they can still grow another 50-100 percent in profitability with the current team without needing to add any additional team members.

"We've shifted to a quality over quantity mindset," he told me.

Higher quality, less quantity.

10x is qualitative, not *quantitative*—it's about different and better, not more. The more different and better you are for a highly specific type of person, the more asymmetric the upside in everything you do.

Stream Logistics has far fewer clients than it previously did but is making almost 2x more revenue and almost 4x more profits, in just 2.5 years.

Moreover, the future is enormously bigger and more exciting with their new model and focus.

Back in 2019 when the business was mostly built around Routine Freight clients, the team was getting pretty complacent. By doing mostly routine tasks, they'd reached a level of efficiency and weren't being challenged much. However, when they shifted to High Stakes Freight clients, which are all unique and highly challenging, the operations team was being tested again and learning and growing like they did when they were first starting.

Research shows that in order to activate a flow and high-performance state, a given task requires three things: 1) clear and specific goals, 2) immediate feedback, and 3) the challenge is above and outside the current skill-level.[12,13,14,15]

One of the reasons "flow" has been so thoroughly studied in extreme sports like rock climbing, motocross, and snowboarding is that these activities are "high stakes." The consequences for failure are immediate and sometimes deadly. The challenge-to-skills ratio is insane, wherein the athletes continue pushing the boundaries far beyond what had previously been considered "possible."

Despite being the same size, the whole team at Stream Logistics is qualitatively different and better than they were 2.5 years ago.

Like comparing Michelangelo's *Hercules* with his *Pietà*, you really can't make the comparison. They are in two totally different worlds of quality, focus, and depth.

Since Carson's team is entirely self-managing, and since their team continues evolving and becoming *10x better* and more specific in what they offer to increasingly quality clients, there is constant innovation happening in the company. They're continually learning what their clients need and investing in new ways to provide unique and top-of-line service for these types of clients.

For instance, one challenge with moving huge loads, such as the apartment modules, is getting access to trailers big enough to move the loads. Thus, Carson's team is in the process of having 75 massive new trailers built to alleviate this constraint, making their service even more unique and valuable.

10x simplifies.

2x keeps things complex and muddled.

When you make 10x your target, 80 percent of your current clients and relationships become impediments. Also, 80 percent of your current activities, habits, and mindsets become impediments.

Letting go of the 80 percent *isn't easy*, because the 80 percent is your comfort zone. To go 2x, you can keep 80 percent of your comfort zone. You only need to make minor and subtle tip-toe adjustments along the way to go 2x. Letting go of the 80 percent may feel as extreme as literally killing something you love. As Jim Collins put it in *Good to Great*:

"Good is the enemy of great . . . The good-to-great companies did not focus principally on what to do to become great; they focused equally on what not to do and what to stop doing. . . If you have a cancer in your arm, you've got to have the guts to cut off your arm."[16]

Once you define the 10x jump you most want, you'll quickly distinguish the 20 percent from the 80 percent. When you eliminate the 80 percent, 10x growth becomes organic and accelerated.

Going all-in on your 20 percent makes you and your life 10x better, simpler, and more exciting.

What about you?

- What is your 20 percent that if you went all-in on, you'd become 10x more valuable and impactful?

- What are the few things you do and the few people you work with that produce most of your success and excitement?

- What is your 80 percent that is keeping you grinding away, and ultimately a distraction for your biggest future jumps?

How to Make Continuous 10x Jumps and Create Exponential Freedom

"A 2x goal would involve doing the same things you're doing now, only more of them. But a 10x goal jumps you out of that, beyond that. 10x requires operating in an entirely different way that bypasses the stresses and complications of a 2x goal."

—DAN SULLIVAN[17]

In 1983, one year after getting married, Linda McKissack and her husband, Jimmy, took out a massive loan to start a restaurant similar to *Dave and Busters*. Jimmy had worked in the restaurant business for nearly a decade and felt he could succeed. After a year of running the business, the market crashed, taking the business down with it.

They had to sell it for $600,000 less than they owed on it, and from one night to the next, they went from having no money to now being $600,000 in debt.

Linda was in her early 20s and had zero business background. She didn't even know what the word "economy" meant. But she knew they were in a bad situation financially, and she felt the stress because Jimmy wasn't sleeping at night. He told her, "I don't want to go to bed because bankers call in the morning so when I go to bed, it becomes morning too soon."

Then Jimmy got really vulnerable and honest with Linda.

"I need your help."

"You know I'm a hard worker. In our family, one job isn't enough, we always have two," she replied.

"A mentor of mine once told me a long time ago that if you want to make a lot of money, real estate is the way to do it," he said.

Growing up, Linda had never lived in a home that was owned.

"I don't even know what real estate is. How do I go into real estate?" she asked.

"You take some of your college credits, take a test, and go get a license," he told her.

So that's what Linda did.

She got licensed as a real estate agent and began her business. In the beginning, it started slow and wasn't making much money at all. Her first year she made $3,000 gross revenue. Jimmy said of her $3,000 first year that it was "real gross."

Two years into being an agent, in 1986, Linda started attending real estate seminars in California. Speakers would go on stage who were running real estate businesses that blew her mind. Within a year of going to seminars and advancing her mindset, network, and training, she was doing about 30 real estate transactions and making around $40,000 in commission revenue annually in her business.

One thing she noticed while listening to the successful real estate agents at the seminars was that the top agents in big cities had their own personal assistants. This was intriguing to her because none of the agents in her own city had an assistant.

Within a year of attending the seminars, Linda pulled the trigger and became the first agent in her city with her own assistant. This was both exciting and terrifying. Although her business was growing, she didn't know how she would pay the assistant's $350 per week salary.

Quickly, Linda felt the incredible freedom of no longer doing all the detail work, which she both hated and was terrible at. Her assistant handled all the paperwork, logistics, scheduling, etc.

Linda had freed herself from literally dozens of hours per week of "job work"—her then 80 percent—that drained her energy and wasn't the linchpin of her biggest results. Releasing her 80 percent created a surge of commitment and excitement to go all in on her 20 percent, which was working directly with people who either wanted to list and sell houses or people looking to buy houses.

This surge of commitment and excitement came from a few psychological sources.

Firstly, by making the commitment and hiring her assistant, she now had to figure out how to increase her revenue such that she could confidently pay her assistant. Necessity is the mother of invention. The needed supply always follows psychological demand—when the "why" is strong enough, you'll find the "how."

Dan Sullivan regularly says, "Nothing happens until *after* you commit."

Only after you're committed are you in a psychological position (i.e., felt necessity) to find or create solutions and pathways to higher levels of productivity. This was precisely what I found in my research on *point of no return*.[18] After a person's perceived point of no return—which was the moment of commitment often involving financial investment—their focus, motivation, and insights skyrocketed. As one entrepreneur I interviewed in my research told me, "It's like I become Neo in the Matrix and can dodge bullets."

This also makes sense in light of the growing body of research on hope, described earlier in this chapter.[19,20,21,22] A core aspect of hope is *pathways thinking*,[23] meaning highly hopeful people continually adjust their pathway until they ultimately find and create a way to their goal, even in the direst of circumstances.[24]

The second surge Linda got by hiring her assistant, in addition to the boost she got by committing, was that now her mind and time were freed up to focus on her 20 percent, which excited her. She became greatly relieved from what psychologists call *decision fatigue*[25,26,27] which occurs when you're making numerous decisions and task switches regularly. By outsourcing literally hundreds or even thousands of micro-decisions and tasks each day to her assistant, such as answering and writing emails, writing up contracts, finding specific information, answering calls, etc., Linda's mind and attention both relaxed and expanded dramatically.

Hiring her assistant was one decision that simultaneously freed her from hundreds or thousands of daily decisions that wore out her energy and willpower and bogged down her attention. She could excel in the few areas that excited her and was mentally free of busyness.

Within a year of having her assistant, Linda doubled her revenue.

Her first assistant eventually became overwhelmed with all the tasks required of her, especially with the rapid growth the business experienced that year. Consequently, Linda and her assistant divided up the tasks of the role and had the assistant choose the aspects of her job she loved. Then, they hired another assistant to take over the rest.

With the second assistant, the revenue doubled again the next year.

"Every time we hired an assistant, our business doubled the next year," Linda told me.

Linda continued going to seminars and further found that the top agents specialized even further, hiring other agents to take aspects of the business they didn't love. Linda didn't love working with the buyers but totally loved listing new properties. She decided she'd become a top listing agent and hire a buyers' agent to handle the buyers.

"The listings are where all the leverage is," Linda told me, "Because all my listing could sell in a single day. By working with the buyers, though, I could only do one sale at a time. So, becoming the top listing agent gave me tons of leverage."

She hired a buyers' agent who she passed all her buyers off to, and they split the commission 50–50. This was a huge relief for Linda, because working with buyers took up an enormous part of her day. By hiring a buyers' agent, she immediately freed-up another couple dozen hours per week, which she previously spent working directly with the buyers.

Freeing herself from the 80 percent of detail and busy work with one and then two assistants was a huge jump for Linda.

Freeing herself from the 80 percent working with buyers to delve into the 20 percent—solely listing properties—was Linda's next big jump.

By focusing on her 20 percent and listing more and better positioned properties, her business grew so much that she hired another buyers' agent and eventually another after that. She also hired a marketing person to expand the reach of their business even more.

Linda made 10x jumps by increasingly applying Who Not How.[28] Rather than staying caught in the 80 percent she didn't love, she invested in "Whos" to handle the 80 percent, as well as to organize and manage increasing aspects of her business. Dan and I wrote an entire book called *Who Not How*, which I strongly suggest you read or re-read. Who Not How is a fundamental principle you'll need to master if you want to make 10x a way of life. You can't go 10x by getting stuck in the endless "Hows" of running a business.

You need Whos, not Hows, to go 10x.

As Linda got more and better Whos on her team, and as she focused on an increasingly concentrated 20 percent that excited her, her business exploded. She was leading a powerful team and continually expanding her vision of what she could do.

She began investing in her marketing and branding, and became extremely well-known throughout her city.

By 1992, Linda was the number one real estate agent in her city. Her business had gone more than 10x since 1986. She was now doing over $500,000 in commission revenue.

Despite experiencing rapid growth, Linda was also starting to get frustrated with her current brokerage. Not only did they take a huge chunk of her earnings—*20 percent*, which was now over $100,000—they also continually put roadblocks in the way of the growth she wanted.

Linda wanted to monopolize the real estate market in her city. She wanted everyone in her city to think of her when they thought of real estate. But her brokerage told her she couldn't use her own phone number in her marketing. She couldn't put her own name on the signs in front of the houses she was listing.

Her brokerage was *being 2x* and stuck in the past way of doing things. Ironically, the brokerage also wanted Linda to stay 2x herself. Her 10x mindset was threatening the status quo and her company did everything they could to box in Linda's innovation and expansion.

The term for someone like Linda, who has a 10x mindset in a 2x organization or industry, is *Rate-Buster*.[29,30] This expression originated in factory work when a pieceworker radically outproduced the established norm leading to extreme opposition by fellow workers who feared the rate-buster's high productivity may either lead to a reduction in the piece rate or in a higher expectation of required output.

No one likes the rate-buster because the rate-buster makes them look bad and establishes a new standard and norm.

The rate-buster makes the 2x people around them uncomfortable.

Why do they need to achieve so much?

Why are they always pushing against the status quo?

Why don't they just let things be?

Interestingly, entire organizations and industries, despite claiming they want growth, can get defensive against rate-busters who may be the very linchpin to going 10x. Even still, when you're operating at 2x your objective isn't to evolve but to maintain.

When you're 2x, you don't want to rock the boat. You don't want to face hard truths in the mirror. You're committed to your 80 percent, which is your comfort zone, culture, and habitual way of operating.

That same year, while Linda was bumping her head against the ceiling of her 2x situation, the real estate company Keller Williams was going throughout the United States recruiting all the top agents in each city. They knocked on Linda's door and made a compelling offer that excited Linda.

One of the benefits of shifting to Keller Williams was that they had a cap on what they took from each agent, which at the time was $21,000. Rather than penalizing growth as her brokerage did, Keller Williams incentivized growth.

Linda decided to join Keller Williams despite having to walk away from 52 of her current listings, because those listings were owned by her old brokerage, not her. At that point, Linda was already paying her broker over $100,000 annually in her commissions. She knew she'd quickly make the money back from the 52 lost listing lots more on top by shifting over to Keller Williams.

Even still, 48 of those listings ended up telling the old broker that "if she's leaving, we're leaving with her." She ended up completing those 48 under Keller Williams.

Over the next six years—from 1992 to 1998—the Keller Williams franchise (i.e., single office housing dozens of agents) which Linda worked at went from being insignificant and unknown in her city to becoming the top producing real estate office in the city. Linda also became the #1 agent in all of Keller Williams *throughout the country*, doing 200–300 transactions yearly and making over $800,000 in commission revenue.

That year, in 1998, the woman who owned the franchise Linda worked at decided not to renew her franchise. She wanted to move on to a different company. This led Gary Keller, the owner of Keller Williams, to directly reach out to Linda and Jimmy. He told them:

> "I think you guys are the next likely owners of a Keller Williams franchise. With the previous owner going to Century 21, that frees up this territory to be owned by someone new."

After a few months of temporarily being closed due to the change in ownership, Linda and Jimmy re-opened the same Keller Williams franchise but this time as the owners, not as agents working within it.

By this point, Linda had already gone 10x several times: from growing herself as a solo real estate agent to getting her first assistant, then several assistants, and eventually hiring other agents and a marketing team.

Each time she let go of her 80 percent to pursue her next-level 20 percent, she was going through the process of a 10x jump.

Each time she did this process, she did so by getting more capable Whos on her team while she herself became uniquely skilled in her increasingly niche 20 percent.

Now, being a franchise owner of Keller Williams represented the beginning of a new 10x for Linda. This was a new level with new possibilities. This new context and 10x zone shifted her previous 20 percent of listing properties to her 80 percent, which she'd mostly let go of to reach her next 10x.

Her new 20 percent became recruiting all of the best agents around the city and building a powerful culture in her franchise. Rather than getting commissions solely on her own business, she'd now get commissions for every commission in her franchise. She continued some of her own listing work to be in the trenches and remain a leader-by-example among those led.

Even still, more and more of her time became dedicated to teaching and training other agents her best mindsets and methods and helping them to grow their businesses as she had. She was increasingly becoming a leader and a total giver, and this attracted tons of incredible talent to join her office. Her teaching had validity and relevance because she was teaching from her own experience, not just theory.

Over the next 18 months—from 1998 to 1999—they grew rapidly and even opened a second office 30 minutes from the first office. Growing meant being a rate-buster in the city and altering the perceptions many of the agents held. For example, the average office usually maxed out at about 30 agents. Linda shattered the myth that with more agents there'd be more competition and thus less growth for each agent, showing that with a bigger office the agents got access to better training and resources. It wasn't a zero-sum game. Success is created. Her zest, Transformational Leadership, and culture attracted dozens of new agents and top talent.

In 1999, Linda got another call from Gary Keller. He told her about an opportunity to start a new region up in Ohio, Indiana, and Kentucky, where she'd become an owner of the entire region, which she'd grow to consist of having *dozens* of offices.

Becoming a regional owner would make her direct partners with Gary Keller. She'd split the royalties of every transaction throughout the entire region 50-50 with Gary.

This became Linda's next *10x opportunity.*

But it would require her to start flying up to Ohio, Kentucky, and Indiana regularly to recruit new franchise owners throughout the region, and then help those new franchise owners get their new offices off-the-ground by recruiting solid agents to join the office.

She'd need to let go of her current 20 percent, which became her 80 percent given the next 10x jump. She hired her brother-in-law, Brad, who'd been a successful sales manager for several companies and wanted to be in real estate to manage her businesses.

Linda told Brad, "Hey, how about you join my team and run my company. We will pay you a base salary to run it, plus you'll have incentives and get percentages of what you grow it to. This will free me up to get on a plane and fly up to Ohio, Kentucky, and Indiana."

For the next 8 months, Brad shadowed Linda and watched everything she did, from listing houses to closing deals to recruiting talent and building up the culture of her offices.

They also transitioned the mindset of her clients, helping them get comfortable working with Brad rather than Linda directly. They called him her "Listing Partner." Initially, some of her clients were concerned about working with someone besides her. But over time, they stopped worrying about it because the level of service was the same.

This is a core Who Not How obstacle that causes many people to stumble, whether in real estate or any form of entrepreneurship—believing others can't do your job for you. Also, believing your clients need you and only you to be the one manually performing the job. This is a myth born of fear and ignorance. When you test it, and *let your Who take over and fully own the how,* you re-train both yourself and your customers to see you and your work differently, and better. It becomes less about Whos doing it and more about the end result. Overtime, the 10x clients will love you for evolving and growing yourself and the 2x clients will leave, bothered, because you disrupted their status quo and comfort zone.

Linda fully handed her company to Brad in early 2000 and started spending lots of time in Ohio, Kentucky, and Indiana. Initially, this was a financial step-back, because now she was paying Brad a large salary to run the business.

"It was a step back to step way forward," Linda told me.

Hiring Whos to free-up your 80 percent isn't a cost, but a massive investment in yourself and your business. This is another major Who Not How obstacle stopping many from 10x growth—the belief that hiring talented and capable Whos is a cost they can't afford to make, rather than an investment they can't afford not to make. It's an investment because it frees you up to concentrate on a more high-impact 20 percent, which enables non-linear returns on investment. It's also an investment in you because now the 80 percent gets done by someone who loves the work that has become old to you. The results get done in a more systematic way without you having to think or worry about it.

Getting the first person to open a franchise was a bear. It took Linda *over three years* to get the first franchise up and running in Ohio. Her whole focus during those three years was finding and recruiting the right people to start the franchises with. To do this, she taught classes and seminars throughout the first city she would grow, Columbus, Ohio. She made tons of phone calls to top agents, helping them see the vision and possibilities. She spoke with all of the biggest lenders in Columbus, seeing who were the biggest and best players they were working with.

During those three years, she wasn't making any money directly from her efforts, and was in fact investing large portions of her own income to keep it going. But she knew this was an opportunity worth investing in, and that the long-term payoff would be 10x or 100x bigger than had she remained where she was at. She knew that to succeed at this next level, as with each of her previous levels, that she'd need to evolve herself and her capabilities. She needed to become *10x better and more capable* at her new 20 percent, which stretched her greatly.

Transforming herself through her 10x jumps excited her. It's what she lived for. And every time she did it, she became freer and more expanded as a person, with qualitatively better and more time, money, relationships, and overall purpose.

Once she finally got someone to start a franchise, Linda helped the new franchise owner build out the franchise by recruiting top producing agents to join the office. Linda's primary role from there was simply supporting and encouraging the new franchise owner to go and grow it, since they were now invested and had great financial incentive to succeed as well.

After the first one, Linda became quicker and better at getting more and more franchises started with better-fitting partners. After getting the first three franchises up in Columbus, she moved on to to Indianapolis and then to Dayton. She progressively got better and faster at getting multiple franchises up in a particular city or territory, popping up more and more offices throughout her region.

Her 20 percent was recruiting the right franchise partners, helping them get up and going, and stabilizing the office by helping recruit the initial top agents to support the office. She'd also provide ongoing training and support to all of her franchise owners, helping them overcome challenges, setbacks, and obstacles, and continually raising their mindsets for what they could be and do.

In 2011, Linda hired a regional team to replace her, who would find new people to start and build-up franchises within the region. Since then, Linda's 20 percent shifted to continually expanding herself as a leader and training her regional team, helping them become better leaders themselves. Like Michelangelo, Linda has continually made 10x jumps as a person. Obviously and importantly, no two people's 10x jumps will look the same. Even still, the core principles and process will always be there.

Each 10x jump brings you closer to becoming world-class within that 20 percent. Then, leveraging the growth and freedoms you've now created, you make another seemingly impossible next jump.

Every time you go 10x by letting go of a previous 80 percent and going all-in on a new, more expansive 20 percent, you become more of a master, innovator, and leader. Over time, with enough 10x jumps, you increasingly become the leader to other leaders, wherein you're directly influencing fewer people but the overall impact and ripples of your influence spread exponentially.

At the writing of this book in 2022, Linda's business has expanded to two regions spread throughout Ohio, Indiana, and Kentucky, with 28 active offices and over 5,000 active real estate agents within those 28 offices.

In talking about passing her business to Brad in 1999 and then passing off regional leadership to her regional team, Linda told me, "By letting go of that, and being willing to go all-in on growing and developing regions, I now have an organization that, in 2021, did over $14 billion in revenue."

As a shared owner of both her regions and each of the franchises within those regions, Linda gets a piece of every single one of those transactions.

Fourteen billion dollars in gross revenue is gargantuan when compared to the $3,000 gross revenue she did her first year as a real estate agent!

She's 10x'd the overall revenue of her business more than six times since she started her real estate career.

Each of those 10x jumps first involved a *qualitative shift* within Linda, wherein she expanded her vision and her identity of who she could be. Then, with her elevated vision, she made a qualitative and non-linear shift in her focus and strategy, focusing on her new 20 percent and letting go of her then 80 percent.

Her first non-linear shift and 20 percent focus was becoming a real estate agent and letting go of attending college classes, which she was doing part-time when Jimmy's Dave and Busters-like restaurant went bust.

Then the 20 percent narrowed as she got better and more experienced as an agent, letting go of administrative tasks. Then letting go of working directly with buyers. Then letting go of listing, which had been her bread-and-butter for huge 10x jumps. Then she let go of building out, recruiting, and leading her own franchises. Now, she even mostly let go of going out and recruiting and directly supporting new franchise partners.

As a shared owner of both regions she's built, Linda gets a piece of every single one of the transactions in her business, which now does over $14 billion in revenue!

Her personal annual income has gone up 10x again and again, from four figures, to five, to six, and now to high seven. Not only that, her overall net worth over these years has grown 10x several times as well. Over the three decades of working in the real estate industry, she and Jimmy were also investing in their own properties, which came to include full-on corporate buildings. Her net worth is now approaching nine figures.

Linda made these 10x jumps by following the 10x process. She elevated and expanded her vision to seemingly impossible levels, utilized her vision to zero-in on the core 20 percent that would get her there, and let go of the 80 percent that would keep her where she's at.

She did this again and again, and continues doing so today.

Each 10x jump is non-linear from the last.

Each 10x jump transforms and evolves Linda dramatically, enabling her with more specialized and unique capability and wisdom. Moreover, each 10x jump also enables her to have dramatically more and better of each of the four freedoms: time, money, relationships, and purpose.

Before interviewing Linda for this book, I had her read a really rough initial draft. Here's what she said:

> "When I look at it, I see my whole life's trajectory. I'm like, 'Oh my gosh! I had no idea this is what was happening!' Also, it makes so much sense how you're explaining it, that 2x is so much harder. I tell my agents all the time, 'Why won't you let go of what you have to go get something bigger?' But realtors especially just want to hang on to what they're working on. It's just so limiting. . . . This book is just so good! Because no one really gives you the fundamentals of a path to 10x. They just talk about 10x. And it's a hard concept. Honestly, it's always been a hard concept for me and others to get our arms around. In the real estate world, people are like, 'Oh my, the 2x was so hard! Now you want me to do 10x?!' So they see it like, 'Gosh, you're asking me to do something when this was already so hard.' They don't realize that 10x is something totally different. 2x was just the launching pad to 10x, where you're now doing something totally different than you were before, and you've let

go of what you were previously doing to go all-in on something bigger."

Linda nailed it.

This concept of "10x" has never been spelled-out and distilled in such clear-cut and accurate terms until this book.

In each chapter of this book, you will learn the most simple, clear, repeatable, and actionable path to going 10x in your life again and again.

You will gain the knowledge and tools for continually expanding and clarifying your desired 10x jump, as well as how to hone in on your 20 percent again and again.

You will learn to continually strip away your 80 percent and embrace higher and higher levels of personal freedom, wherein you become the most powerful version of yourself— your own Unique version of "The David."

Chapter Takeaways

- Seemingly impossible goals are more practical than possible goals because impossible goals force you outside your current level of knowledge and assumptions.

- Very few pathways create 10x. With genuine reflection, a 10x target spotlights the few pathways—the high-leverage strategies and relationships—with extreme upside.

- 10x goals enable you to clearly identity the 20 percent of things and people in your life that are producing most of your results, and the 80 percent of things and people in your life that are holding you back.

- Going for 2x growth means you can keep 80 percent of your existing clients, roles, behaviors, and mindsets. Only minor tweaks are needed.

- Going for 10x growth means you must eliminate 80 percent of your existing clients, roles, behaviors, and mindsets. 10x requires a full-scale transformation of yourself as well as everyone and everything around you.

- 2x is linear—to continue growing requires more effort. It's working harder, not smarter. It's quantitatively focused—you're just doing more of what you're now doing without respect to quality, uniqueness, or transformation.

- 10x is non-linear—enormous growth does not require more effort, but often requires less, but better. It's *qualitatively* focused—you've elevated your vision and focus such that you're now transforming the value and impact of what you do for increasingly specific people.

- Every time you make a 10x jump, you do so by letting go of your current 80 percent and going deeper into a more powerful and concentrated 20 percent. Letting go of your 80 percent generally involves hiring Whos to take over your 80 percent, and to systemize and organize what is repeatable so you can innovate what isn't repeatable.

- Every time you go 10x by letting go of the 80 percent and going all-in on your desired 20 percent, you dramatically increase your quality and quantity of your freedoms as a person—which are time, money, relationships, and purpose.

- To get additional resources on clarifying your next 10x jump, visit www.10xeasierbook.com

CHAPTER 2

10x THE QUALITY OF EVERYTHING YOU DO

Shed Your 2x Identity and Relentlessly Raise Your Standards

◆ ◆ ◆

"How you do anything is how you do everything."

—ATTRIBUTED TO MARTHA BECK [1]

Fresh out of college, Chad Willardson was 24 years old when he was accepted into the financial advisor training at Merrill Lynch. Chad was one of 100 trainees in Southern California who started the program and one of two who completed the program successfully.

It was a brutal and intense growth curve.

The purpose of the training was to teach aspiring new advisors how to both invest in and attract new clients, as well as to reach $15 million under management within 18 months. Anyone who did not achieve all the certifications plus the $15 million hurdle was dropped from the program without a job.

Trainees were young and most investors preferred an experienced wealth advisor. Who was willing to let an inexperienced young kid manage their money?

Early in this process, Chad told his manager and some of the senior advisors at the firm that he would aim to only work with clients with more than $100,000 to invest. His manager replied that getting any client willing to invest $100,000 would be literally impossible. No one with that amount of money (this was 20 years ago) would trust someone Chad's age.

Focused on his own standards rather than someone else's, Chad committed to himself that he wouldn't work with anyone with less than $100,000 for him to manage.

For months, Chad was the first person in the office each day, arriving to work before sunrise, and the last to leave. He spent hours studying and passing big exams and certifications, reaching out to countless business owners in the area to build relationships, and reading business, wealth management, and personal development books. While the other advisors and trainees were at the bar drinking and partying on their nights and weekends, Chad was putting in that extra work.

For his first six months he made hundreds of calls every day and experienced nothing but rejection. He didn't land a single new client.

Six months into the training program, Chad received a surprising phone call from a man Chad had cold-called six months previously. Ready to retire, the caller had over $600,000 to roll over into a retirement investment account. Remembering their positive phone conversation and Chad's multiple follow-up outreaches, he wanted Chad to be his wealth advisor.

Chad's *first client* had $600,000, six times more than what his manager said would be an impossible minimum standard. This boosted Chad's confidence and resolve to keep going. During the next several months, Chad took on plenty of clients—all with more than $100,000 for him to manage.

Shortly after his first year in the program, he *raised his minimum standard* for new clients from $100,000 to $250,000.

From that moment forward, he would not take on anyone with less than $250,000 to invest.

He got what he focused on.

He developed mastery at the level of his standard and focus.

By the time the 18-month program ended in 2005, Chad had more than doubled the trainee graduation hurdle and had $30 million under management.

During the next seven years, Chad added another $280 million under management, reaching the top 2 percent of advisors (and one of the fastest-growing) with Merrill Lynch. At that point, companies like Morgan Stanley, Goldman Sachs, and UBS were recruiting Chad and offering more than $4 million cash as a signing bonus!

But Chad sensed the future of advising high-wealth entrepreneurs would not be under the umbrella of any of those firms, including the one he worked for.

Chad's spectacular 10x growth occurred by developing a unique level of mastery in understanding and supporting his entrepreneurial clients. He wanted to 10x this level of mastery even further, with even higher-level clients with bigger challenges to support. He saw that the only way he'd have the freedom to help the level of clients he wanted at the level of service he wanted—offering them options and solutions beyond a specific firm's umbrella—was to open his own private fiduciary wealth advisory firm.

Already in the elite class of a nationwide financial firm after nine years, he summoned the commitment and courage to completely start over and go back to zero. He let go of a cushy and prestigious position that had become 2x, not 10x.

When Chad opened Pacific Capital in 2011, he committed his focus to working exclusively with high-growth entrepreneurs who were millionaires or multimillionaires. He committed to become more niche and specific in who he served and how he helped them.

Starting again from scratch, Chad focused on quality, not quantity.

To provide the best and most nuanced support, he couldn't cast a wide net. He had to clarify the specific whales he wanted to help, and how he would create 10x value for them differently from any other financial firm.

The minimum standard at Pacific Capital's inception was entrepreneurs with a minimum of $1 million to invest and grow.

Chad's goal shaped his focus and mastery. His 20 percent now was radically different and more specific than the 20 percent of his previous 10x jumps that had gotten him here. Rather than cold-calling, hosting seminars, or walking business to businesses as he had before, he joined networks of entrepreneurs who were already successful and leveraged the reputation he had built in the industry.

From 2012–2017, Chad went from starting over to having $300+ million in assets under management. As of this writing, Chad personally manages over $1 billion, with a very strict focus on eight- and nine-figure entrepreneurs. He 10x'd by continually raising his minimum standard and by elevating himself and his value to the level of his rising standards.

In 2021, he rose his minimum standard new client from $1,000,000 to $2,500,000.

In 2022, he rose his minimum standard new client from $2,500,000 to $5,000,000.

In 2023, he rose his minimum standard new client from $5,000,000 to $10,000,000.

His focus and optimization are getting clearer and clearer.

Chad reaches impossible goals by continually eliminating his 80 percent.

Chad doesn't just raise the standard for his clients. He also raises the standard for himself. Each year, he takes on *fewer clients*, but the value of each client is 10x the average of his former clients. Moreover, the value and impact Chad provides these whales is far more unique and precise than when he was working with a broader range of clients. He knows that achieving more does not mean doing more.

Similar to Linda McKissack in the previous chapter, a crucial aspect of Chad's ascension and ability to 10x is his momentum. Unlike many financial advisors, Chad is also an entrepreneur, with multiple companies, ventures, and investments. He's continually 10xing himself such that even his biggest clients are simply trying to keep up with Chad's exponentially elevating lifestyle and financial standards. He's living by example, not offering broad and cookie-cutter theory or products.

All the while, Chad figures out how to do less. Throughout Chad's 10x growth and evolution, he hired a full-time executive assistant and a large team of financial specialists to support him and his clients. His executive assistant took over all of his email, scheduling, phone calls, and all other logistical aspects of Chad's business and personal life. Chad's team of experts at Pacific Capital took over all client meetings, day-to-day operations, investment management, and strategic financial planning for clients.

Chad used to spend over 200 long days in the office each year. Now he doesn't even have his own office inside the Pacific Capital building. He goes in about 30 days per year to connect with the team, share vision, and provide any support he can.

Chad's time used to be spent on literally dozens of different tasks and activities. Now it's invested in a limited few, which he does uniquely better than anyone else in the world.

Higher quality, less quantity.

Yet, despite doing less, Chad's productivity—meaning his *tangible results*—has shot through the roof. He's nearly doubling his business each year while working less. He's published three books in the past three years and taken more vacations in the past few years than he did in the previous few decades.

To quote the 10x thinker, Greg McKeown, "An Essentialist produces more—brings forth more—by removing more instead of doing more."[2]

To go 10x, you simplify your focus by continually letting go of *everything* that doesn't meet your 10x filter. Each time you go 10x, the filter gets finer and finer, letting less pass through.

Most entrepreneurs don't achieve the same kind of growth because they shut down when they encounter resistance. When Chad stopped handholding his clients through the day-to-day, a few of his clients and friends questioned the decision. They wondered why Chad wasn't involved at every touch point and some legacy long-time clients were bothered by the initial changes. They wanted Chad to keep things as they had always been. They didn't like Chad elevating his standards and vision. These clients were 2x, not 10x.

Ironically, Chad had actually made himself *more available* by removing the 80 percent of minutia that kept him absurdly busy and without space to connect and be present. Continually freeing himself from his 80 percent enables him to focus on his highest form of contribution—helping his clients elevate their vision and commitment, and supporting them when they began to falter from that commitment.

Chad's 10x clients recognized and appreciated Chad's evolution because they felt its effects. He was helping them expand their own vision and standards, and they were becoming far more successful and happier by following his example and guidance.

Anytime someone wants you to remain as you are, they do so for their own self-preservation. Your evolution threatens their current security, and they want that security more than the freedom that you seek. It's plain uncomfortable at first. This is one of the most common reasons people and entrepreneurs don't go 10x. They know it will make *those around them* feel uncomfortable for a time. To avoid this discomfort in themselves and those closest to them, people opt for 2x, not 10x.

As you radically evolve through the 10x process, many people in your life won't comprehend the evolution you've experienced. It will defy logic and reality to them, and therefore they will disregard or entirely avoid seeing the changes you've made. 10x can indeed repel 2x.

By embracing the 10x process, you'll evolve internally and externally far more than the average person, although the 10x process is *available to all people* who choose freedom over security.

Most people are afraid to shed old standards and strategies—especially ones that worked. What makes Chad different?

Chad exhibits a quality that only the world's top achievers do: *the ability to rapidly accept a new identity.*

He let go of being the guy who made hundreds of cold calls a day. He let go of being the first in the office and the last to leave. He let go of being one of the top dogs at one of the biggest financial firms in the world. He let go of needing to always be available and look fancy in a suit. He let go of being the guy who answered his own emails, attended client meetings, or even had his own office. He let go of seeing busyness as a status symbol. He let go of trying to please anyone that wasn't in his 20 percent.

None of the things he let go of were bad. Indeed, many of them were crucial aspects in Chad getting where he had gotten. Yet, to continually expand and 10x himself, he had to evolve beyond his then identity (the 80 percent) and embrace a new vision and standard (the 20 percent).

Committing fully to your next 20 percent is embracing a 10x identity wherein you transform yourself and your life through an exciting future.

Holding on to the 80 percent is embracing a 2x identity wherein you avoid major changes and maintain your status quo.

To go 10x again and again, Chad shed the identity that got him here for the identity that would get him there.

Once something became 2x, he let that 80 percent go, passing it off to a capable Who or eliminating it altogether. He further simplified his life down to the 10x standard which most excited him, choosing an increasingly niche and nuanced 20 percent focus and mastery.

Your identity is fundamentally two things: it's 1) the story or narrative you have for yourself, and it's 2) the standards or commitments you hold for yourself.[3] The scientific definition of *identity* is "a well-organized conception of the self, consisting of values and beliefs to which the individual is solidly committed."[4]

Put simply, your identity as a person is *what you're most committed to*. It's the story about yourself you're committed to, and it's the personal standards you're most committed to.

A *standard* is a level of quality and norm you set for yourself. When something is truly a standard, *it's a commitment*. You rarely if ever go outside or below your floor or minimum standard; otherwise it wouldn't be a standard.

We are all committed to standards that we've set for ourselves, even if we don't realize it. Take for example, my friend who is an avid World of Warcraft player. He invests about 16 hours per day playing and is one of the top players on his online server. Recently, he told me he left his guild, the online community he was a part of.

"Why did you leave?" I asked.

"They weren't up to my standard," he replied. "I want to play with more serious players."

Although you may not be interested in online video games, and neither am I, the point is that we all have standards we choose for ourselves. We choose the standards we care about as well as the level we hold those standards to. For instance, two people may be equally committed to tennis though one may be professional and the other an amateur— the pro having much higher standards for their playing than the other.

Elevating and committing to specific standards is how you evolve your identity. Elevating your standards and 10xing yourself involves a process outlined in Dan Sullivan's *The 4 C's Formula*:

1. Commitment

2. Courage

3. Capability

4. Confidence

Nothing happens until you commit.

As you *commit* to a specific standard far above your current capability and confidence, it pushes you outside your knowledge and comfort zone: hence, *courage*.

Through courageously adapting toward your commitment, you experience many "losses" and failures along the way, which you can utilize as feedback and learning. By adapting and applying your learning, you develop *capabilities* and skills you previously didn't have, which you would not have developed without having fully made the commitment.

Commitment leads to mastery, wherein you've *normalized* the new standard. At this level, you have a higher degree of *confidence*.[5]

You're now your 10x self, and it's completely normal to you, despite the fact that both who you now are and your normal life are unfathomable to your past self. With a higher degree of confidence, you now see and attract bigger and better opportunities, which previously weren't available to you, enabling you to start the 4C's cycle anew by making the next level 10x commitment.

Letting go of 80 percent of your identity (including activities, situations, and people) can feel like an enormous loss. Letting go of who you've been, how people have seen you, and how others have related to you can feel like you're losing a big part of yourself.

According to Prospect Theory, humans have an enormous *aversion to loss*.[6] We fear and avoid loss far more than we seek gain. Loss aversion primarily manifests itself in three specific forms—1) continuing to invest in something unprofitable simply because you've already invested in it (i.e., sunk cost bias)[,7,8] 2) overvaluing something you own, believe, or have created simply because it's yours (i.e., endowment effect)[,9,10,11] and 3) continuing to do something you've previously done in order to be viewed by yourself and others as consistent (i.e., consistency principle).[12,13,14]

All of these loss aversion tactics make it extremely hard to let go of the 80 percent. Thus, it's hard to let go of your current or former identity.

Elevating your standards is not easy by any means. It's certainly much, much easier than continuing on a path just because that's what you've been doing (i.e., 2x thinking).

To go 10x, you live based on freedom. You choose the standards *you want* because that's what you intrinsically want, and you're not worried about other people's opinions.

You flexibly evolve your identity, letting go of things that once made up a core component of who you were.

It takes enormous commitment and courage to raise your minimum standard, yet it's how you evolve yourself as a person. As Chad did when he committed to only working with clients with $100,000 or more to invest, for a period of time, you'll struggle reaching and clawing toward your new commitment, with many bumps and bruises along the way. This is the commitment and courage phase of Dan's 4C's. But over time, you'll evolve yourself, your knowledge, and your capabilities until it becomes second nature to you.

Elevating your identity and standards is primarily *emotional* and thus qualitative, which is why *psychological flexibility* is so crucial to 10xing. To be psychologically flexible, you become increasingly comfortable and adaptive to situations and challenges which are initially uncomfortable to you. You see yourself as a context, not the content of your thoughts and emotions. As you evolve and expand yourself as a context, the content of your life—inside and out—simultaneously changes as well.[15,16]

You *commit* to the standards you want, even when it's uncomfortable for a brief time. By embracing your emotions rather than suppressing them, your identity quickly adapts to your new standards and you reach a place of *acceptance*.[17,18,19,20] You've emotionally evolved and expanded as a person, wherein you feel *comfortable and natural* at the new standard. As the prominent and prolific spiritual and emotional teacher and scientist Dr. David Hawkins stated:

> "The unconscious will allow us to have only what we believe we deserve. If we have a small view of ourselves, then what we deserve is poverty. And our unconscious will see to it that we have that actuality."[21]

To make something a new standard, you stop saying yes to the 80 percent—*your now 2x identity and standards*—that no longer fits. You embrace rejection and learning at the new standard until you reach a place of capability and confidence at the new standard.

For instance, if you're a professional speaker and your current speaking fee is $25,000, raise your minimum fee to $50,000 and see what happens. Over the next few months, you may get a dozen speaking inquiries, and all of them but one reject your new fee of $50,000. Thus, you got 1/12 at the new standard. Getting this one yes at $50,000 is *10x more valuable* to your identity and confidence than getting 12/12 yeses at the $25,000 level, even though in the short-run you'd be leaving a nice chunk of money on the table.

Over time, you'll normalize your new standard—first emotionally within, but then externally as your reputation, positioning, and level of mastery. As you do this, you re-train the outside world to see you in a new light. Your standards are the inner-filter through which you operate, but also by which aligned people can know how to operate and collaborate with you.

With Chad's story and your new understanding of shedding your 2x identity by elevating your minimum standards, the remainder of this chapter will deepen your understanding of the next-level application of the 10x process, which is enhancing the quality and decreasing the quantity of everything you're doing.

How you do anything is how you do everything.

What about you?

- What are the standards you hold for yourself?
- Were your standards chosen by you, or adopted by the norms of those outside of you?

- What are your own minimum standards that you're focused on and committed to?

- What would happen if you dramatically elevated your standards? How can you move toward your 20 percent focus and mastery? What 80 percent would have to go?

As you embrace the 10x process, you'll continually be doing and focusing on less. Yet, decreasing the number of things you do will increase the quality, depth, and impact by 10x. By focusing on quality over quantity, such as Carson, Linda, and Chad did, you will experience exponential and non-linear results.

Let's do this.

Set Unreachable Goals and 10x the Quality of What You Do

"Ninety-nine percent of people in the world are convinced they are incapable of achieving great things, so they aim for the mediocre. The level of competition is thus fiercest for 'realistic' goals, paradoxically making them the most time and energy-consuming. It's easier to raise $1,000,000 than it is $100,000. It's easier to pick up the one perfect 10 in the bar than the five 8s."

—Tim Ferriss[22]

Jimmy Donaldson has shed his 2x-identity again and again, never seeming to get stuck or plateaued in one place for too long. Jimmy displays a rare degree of psychological flexibility, in that nothing seems too big or too much of a stretch for him. Nothing seems out of reach.

In 2015, Jimmy was 17 years old. He was living at his mom's house in rural North Carolina. He was a middle-class white kid with few skills who made mediocre YouTube videos in his bedroom. Even still, he had high aspirations for himself, including becoming the number one YouTuber in the world.[23,24]

Fast-forward seven years to 2022 and Jimmy, now age 23, has nearly achieved his goal of becoming the number one YouTuber in the world. Known by his alter ego and brand, *MrBeast*, Jimmy now had hundreds of millions of subscribers across his various social media channels, he's become the fastest-rising Internet sensation in the world, he has a team of over 150 people, and he leads or is involved in an umbrella of businesses which do nearly a billion dollars in annual revenue.

In March of 2022, Jimmy was interviewed on the Joe Rogan podcast. Joe asked Jimmy, "Do you have a lot of guys ask you for advice? like 'Hey, I want to be like MrBeast.'"

The question excited Jimmy. He asked Joe to open his Twitter feed, where he showed the 10x results of someone he'd recently mentored.

> "Before I started mentoring him, he was doing 4.6 million views on YouTube per month, making $24 grand. Probably seven to eight months later, we got him up to 45 million views, and he had a $400,000 month!"[25]

Blown away, Joe asked, "What kind of advice did you give that makes such an exponential change?"

Read Jimmy's next response *very carefully*. It clarifies how he applies the 10x process to achieve exponential results by intentionally doing less. Here's his response:

> "As weird as it sounds, it's much easier getting five million views on one video than 100-thousand views on 50 videos. . . You could upload one great video per year and get more views than if you

uploaded 100 mediocre videos. It's very exponential. To do well on YouTube, you just need people to click your videos and watch them. . . If you get people to click your video ten percent more, and watch your video ten percent longer than mine, you don't get ten percent more views, you get like four-times the views. You have to think exponentially. A ten percent better video gets four-times the views, not ten percent more views. Once you understand that, you funnel your energy better, and really hyper-obsess over these videos. Triple the amount of time you're putting into that video cause you're not going the get triple the views, you're going to 10x the views. So [I help those I mentor] make their videos really good, and also help them build out a team, like an editor. Cause if you're doing five jobs, then you can only put 20 percent of your time into each. If you hire an editor, that editor can put 100 percent of his time into that. You can't spend ten hours per day editing, but he can."

Straight from the mouth of MrBeast himself. 10x is literally that simple. As Jimmy explained, you've got to think exponentially. You can't think linearly if you want 10x results. To think exponentially, you must think *qualitatively*, not quantitatively. It's not about more volume and more effort. That's 2x-thinking, which is linear, slow, and can never produce the exponential results Jimmy is describing.

When you begin thinking in terms of quality over quantity, you funnel your energy better. You stop burning yourself out pumping out more and more, or doing a million different jobs as a rugged individualist.

Instead, you focus on your 20 percent and get really, *really* good at what you do. You build a team around you to handle what would have been your 80 percent. However, for your team members, their role is not *their* 80 percent, since you're hiring pros who love doing the other aspects of the work, whether that be logistics, editing, etc.

Summing up Jimmy's insights on 10x thinking in three bullets:

- Think *exponentially*, which means thinking both much bigger and non-linearly.

- Hyper focus on quality over quantity, and get really good at what you do.

- Build a team to handle everything else so you can focus on achieving quality in your craft.

To go 10x bigger, you focus on getting *10x better*.

To get 10x better, you continually elevate the vision and standards of what you do. You commit to your 20 percent, hyper focusing on quality over quantity. You let go of the 80 percent, knowing that effort alone is not what produces exponential results.

It's crucial to note that being able to do something well, even exceptionally well, doesn't usually translate to the *level of quality* Jimmy is describing, which produces exponential results.

To reach the level of quality that produces exponential results, you need to think exponentially bigger and different. You've got to have a vision and standards big enough, and specific enough, that the quality you're creating is funneled toward that.

If your goal is small, such as 2x, then your efforts will mostly be wasted. You're not being stretched. You may technically be getting more proficient at what you're doing. But you're not evolving or innovating. You're just deepening your habitual grooves, which doesn't mean you're actually getting better.

It's not effort that matters, but where that effort *is directed*.

Whatever you focus on and commit to, you become the master of.

It is for this reason that the proposed "10,000 rule" presented by pop-psychologist Malcolm Gladwell[26] is phony baloney. "It isn't 10,000 hours that creates outliers," said entrepreneur and angel investor Naval Ravikant. "It's 10,000 iterations."[27]

Yes, reps matter. *But only when those reps are directed toward a 10x upgrade.*

Without a 10x goal that your reps are directed to, you'll just be repeating the same form and errors over and over. You'll be optimizing for more of what you've already got, not something of an entirely new and different *quality*.

Most people miss the gold coins around them because they're focused on finding the bronze coins. They're committed to the bronze coins. Their identity is wrapped up in the bronze coins. They're optimizing themselves and their lives for bronze coins.

You get what you're focused on.

You master at the level of your focus and standards.

Does this mean reps and quantity effort don't matter? Of course not.

Jimmy has made or produced literally *thousands* of YouTube videos at this point. That's a lot of reps. The difference between Jimmy and the millions of other people who have also made hundreds, thousands, or even tens of thousands of YouTube videos is that Jimmy's vision and standards are impossibly bigger than anyone else's. Indeed, he was very intent on becoming the number one YouTuber in the world, and he wasn't private about it. To reach that standard, he needed to become uniquely brilliant at creating videos that hundreds of millions of people watched. To do that, he needed a growing team of committed people to help him.

He never got trapped in the 80 percent.

He is laser-focused on his 20 percent, and getting better at what he does.

He's always upping his game, always raising his standards for himself.

The quality of Jimmy's videos is ultimately why we know who he is. If his videos weren't any good, he could have millions of videos with zero views. He developed the ability to produce the quality of videos he does because he commits himself to impossibly high goals and holds himself and the work he does to impossibly high standards.

His transformation and evolution weren't accidental.

They were purposeful.

As Aristotle stated, "It is absurd to suppose that purpose is not present because we do not observe the agent deliberating."[28] The philosophical term for "purpose" is *teleology*, which means that *all* human action is driven toward or *caused by* a specific aim. The word *télos* means "the end or cause of a thing."[29,30]

Everything we do as people is driven by our goals or standards.[31,32,33] You become whatever you're striving for. Your goal shapes your process. Your goal also shapes your personal development and evolution.

Here's where it gets really interesting, though, when you dissect what Jimmy is explaining, and honestly, when you simply break down the core message of this book: despite the fact that all people are driven by their goals, and that we all form a level of proficiency in whatever we focus on, the counterintuitive truth is that massive ambitions are easier than average goals.

In other words, *10x is easier than 2x.*

As Jimmy described, when you think exponentially, it's no longer about the amount of effort you put in. Instead, it's about where your effort is directed, and what your effort is directed toward. When you're thinking 2x, you're actually exhausting far more energy and effort than the person thinking 10x. The 10x thinker is allowing their 10x vision to guide them in radically innovative and different directions, which the 2x-thinker could never consider nor comprehend.

As Dan Sullivan explained, "When 10x is your measuring stick, you immediately see how you can bypass what everyone else is doing."

Furthermore, the 10x thinker is solving a far more nuanced and niched problem. Rather than thinking broadly, they are thinking deeply and narrowly. They're deep in their 20 percent and have freed themselves of the cognitive load of the 80 percent. They aren't trying to do 100 things decently. They're trying to do one thing at a level that's never been seen before.

Taking this idea further—that focusing on exponential goals is easier than linear goals because exponential goals produce a much different and more specific form of quality—Dr. Alan Barnard, the expert on constraint theory referenced in Chapter 1, gave me the following example: if you're trying to make $10 million, rather than solving 100 problems at $100,000 each, it's *much easier* attempting to solve a single $30 million problem.

For multiple reasons.

First, by pouring your attention into the $30 million problem, you develop learning and expertise *at that level*. The level of quality and depth to solve that single problem will be fundamentally different than the quality and depth to solve 100 cheaper and broader problems.

Another reason it's easier focusing on quality over quantity, Dr. Barnard explains, is that by trying to solve a $30 million problem, you don't have to be perfect. You've given yourself a huge margin for error that even if you only achieve one-third of the goal, you'll reach your $10 million standard.

It's easier to find one person to pay you $1 million than to find 10 people who will pay $100,000. It's exponentially easier to find one person to pay you $1 million than to find 100 people to pay $10,000.

In real estate, it's easier to get one property worth $10 million than 20 properties each worth $500,000. Once acquired, the management of the single property is infinitely easier and less time-consuming than managing the 20.

In the 1959 classic book *The Magic of Thinking Big*, Dr. David Schwartz wrote:

> "A personnel selection executive told me that he receives 50 to 250 times as many applicants for jobs that pay $10,000 per year as for jobs that pay $50,000 a year. This is to say that there is at least 50 times as much competition for jobs on Second Class Street as for jobs on First Class Avenue. First Class Avenue, U.S.A., is a short, uncrowded street."[34]

Although the income levels are outdated in Dr. Schwartz's analysis, the concept remains ironclad. In all aspects of life, the competition is highest for average goals.

Not only is the competition highest, but the excitement is lowest and the pathway forward is dramatically more complex and confusing with small and linear goals.

With unrealistic, impossible, or "10x"-level goals, the competition is lowest, the excitement is highest, and the pathway forward becomes simple and non-linear. You stop following the crowd. You shift toward quality rather than quantity and stop competing with anyone.

What about you?

- Are you living exponentially or linearly?
- Are you focused on effort or volume, or are you creating something qualitatively different and better than anything else out there?

- Are you spread thin, doing five or more different jobs, or do you have a growing team of people handling your former 80 percent?

10x Often and Become the Best at What You Do

"In a world that relentlessly races to the bottom,
you lose if you also race to the bottom.
The only way to win is to race to the top. . . .
The only way to be indispensable is to be different. . . .
Expertise gives you enough insight to reinvent
what everyone else assumes is the truth. . . .
You can train yourself to matter. . . .
You are not your résumé. You are your work."

—SETH GODIN[35]

The author James Clear is an outlier at focusing on the 20 percent that will move him toward his 10x future and removing the 80 percent that got him here.

By focusing on his 20 percent, which for several years was blogging, Clear was able to grow a massive email list and become a professional author—which was a major 10x jump for him. Then, after going 10x, he found a new 20 percent, which was spending nearly three years writing his book *Atomic Habits*. Once the book was written and nearing publication, he shifted his 20 percent fully to spreading and marketing the book.

By flexibly shifting his 20 percent focus toward his evolving standards, like Chad and Jimmy mentioned earlier in this chapter, Clear has become a rare master of shedding his 2x-identity the moment it's no longer serving him. He doesn't get stuck or plateaued in any single stage or process longer than is needful. As he stated in *Atomic Habits*:

"Your behaviors are usually a reflection of your identity. What you do is an indication of the type of person you think you are—either consciously or nonconsciously."[36]

Since November of 2018 when *Atomic Habits* was published, it has sold nearly *10 million copies* at the current writing (October 2022) and has been the highest-selling nonfiction book in the world for the previous two years. To put this in proper perspective, out of the *millions of books* published each year, *less than 20* will go on to sell over *one million* copies.[37] The average U.S. book sells less than 200 copies per year and less than 1,000 copies over its lifetime.[38]

In his blogs and book, Clear helps his readers optimize for "the beginning" of a particular objective, such as losing weight, by making the task as basic and friction-free as possible. Rather than doing 500 push-ups, do 5. Rather than writing a chapter of your book, write one sentence. His writing and teachings are designed to help the common man make small changes that compound over time to big results.

But Clear himself is not a common man, and his results are even further from common.

In a world where most people's advice is often superior to their actions, he's one of the few people where you're actually better-off following what he does than what he says.

You won't get 10x results by doing five push-ups.

You won't write a blockbuster book by writing one sentence.

Yes, 10x starts with five push-ups and writing one sentence, but to reach the level of focus, quality, and *mastery* needed to 10x, you must go *all-in*. You can't see yourself as an amateur nor be satisfied with amateurish commitment and outcomes. As the quote just referenced by Clear explained, you must evolve your identity and thus your standards to a higher level or your behaviors will remain mediocre.

When you actually study what James Clear *did* to produce the insane results he has, it's obvious that he himself is a master of *optimizing for "the end"* of a particular objective, more than the beginning. He optimizes for the end of an objective by clarifying and committing 100 percent to his end goal, eliminating the 80 percent, and *refining the quality* of his work—the 20 percent.

More than habits, it's his commitment to holding himself and his work to an unbelievably high standard wherein he polishes his work from 95 or more percent "done" to as close to 100 percent as he can—until it becomes exceptional.

As Clear wrote in a 2021 post:

> "The difference between good and great is often an extra round of revision. The person who looks things over a second time will appear smarter or more talented, but actually is just polishing things a bit more. Take the time to get it right. Revise it one extra time."[39]

Each time Clear reached a significant milestone, he immediately focused on raising the bar even higher for himself. Increasing the quality of his work, constantly and relentlessly, is the secret to his results. First, he continually honed the quality of his blog posts. Then, his book. Finally, he perfected the quality of his storytelling and marketing strategy for his book.

It's helpful to review Clear's process even further to better understand his 10x results. Luckily for us, each year for several years he published an end-of-year review describing what worked and what didn't for him that particular year. You will see in Clear's Annual Reviews an enhanced commitment to his 20 percent, the letting go of his 80 percent, and a consistent focus on quality over quantity.

In his *2014 Annual Review*, after a few years of successfully blogging about habits and growing a sizable email list, Clear discusses his desire to write a book (his next 10x ambition). As he stated:

> "What am I focused on? Going pro as a writer. I've been a full-time entrepreneur for four years now. I've started four different businesses (two of which succeeded) and a number of smaller projects. . .More than anything I've done, I love writing my articles each week and helping people build habits that stick. So, it's time to phase out other projects and turn pro. Mostly, that means finishing my first book. And 2015 is the year to do it."[40]

In his *2015 Annual Review*, he stated that he got his book deal for what became *Atomic Habits*.[41] At that point, writing the book became his number one focus (his new 20 percent). He still maintained his blog and other activities, but those were subtly becoming part of his 80 percent, which he was phasing out to focus on his next 10x jump. He also mentioned hiring his first full-time employee to manage much of his online business while he wrote the book.

In his *2016 Annual Review*, Clear describes the challenge he faced transitioning from world-class blogger to writing a world-class book:

> "What didn't go so well this year? Book writing. Plain and simple, 2016 was the worst year of writing of my young career. I haven't been at this very long, but I've been at it long enough to know that this year was a total disaster from a writing standpoint. . . It all started at the end of 2015 when I signed a major book deal with Penguin Random House. As soon as the book became a reality, my perfectionism kicked into high gear. . . Looking back now, I realize that I spent a

large part of 2016 learning how to create a new style of work. For the three years prior, I was writing a new article every Monday and Thursday. The focus was on creating great work that was usually 1,500 words or less. Now, my writing ambitions have grown and I'm working to create a remarkable book of 50,000 words or more. This transition from rapid work to deep work has been hard for me—much harder than I expected. I'm just now learning what it takes to create something of that scope and do it well."[42]

Each time you go 10x, the quality and magnitude of what you're doing gets higher. Rather than making fast food, you've shifted to fine dining, which requires a much higher degree of mastery and focus. You can't continue juggling as much. You need more time to connect bigger dots.

Inevitably, going 10x requires becoming a leader and hiring Whos to support the 80 percent. 10x requires you to become uniquely masterful in a narrowing 20 percent wherein you produce something innovative, valuable, and of rare quality.

People make the leap of hiring far too late. By hiring even a personal or digital assistant, as Clear did, you can immediately free up space for your 20 percent, which work is higher value and higher leverage than the 80 percent busy tasks. The longer you wait to get a Who, the slower your progress will be because you'll be mired in the 80 percent. This not only keeps you split focused, but slows your mastery of the 20 percent.

In his *2017 Annual Review*, Clear describes lasering almost all of his energy and effort into writing *Atomic Habits* while his business ran almost entirely without him:

> "What went well this year? Okay, here's where I succeeded this year. Book writing. I wrote a book!

(Well, mostly.) Naturally, completing the manuscript became my primary area of focus for 2017. I finished the first draft of the manuscript in November, and we're working on edits now. There are still many improvements to make and, truthfully, a few months of work left, but it feels really good to see literally years of work all coming together... Systems building. Because I spent nearly all of my time writing the book, I had virtually no time to work on the other aspects of my business, which, you can imagine, also happen to be fairly important. Thankfully, my business still had a great year because, with the help of my assistant Lyndsey, we have built a variety of systems that enable the business to run without constant attention from me."[43]

10x requires letting go of increasing distractions.

Every time you go 10x, you become more focused and less broad.

You have higher ambitions with greater and deeper scope, requiring more and better of your attention. To make something 10x better involves deep, *deep* work. Innovation occurs as you break everything down and put it back together in a simpler, easier, and *better* form.

This is what James Clear spent three years doing. He was solving a highly complex problem teaching a model of habits that was compelling, useful, and accurate. He was striving to provide an innovative solution to habits—a universal human challenge he felt to be incredibly important—in a far superior manner than anything currently on the market.

He succeeded.

Innovation happens by *focusing on the 20 percent* that's most relevant to the problem you're trying to solve.

You can't be involved in the great many tasks or decisions you were previously involved in. Your focus must be on higher quality and less quantity. This is why applying Who Not How is essential, wherein you simply enable capable and committed people, like Clear's full-time assistant, to handle everything else in your life and business.

In Chapter 6 of this book, you'll learn the four-stage model every entrepreneur must go through if they want ongoing 10x jumps in their life and business. The third and final stage of this is creating what Dan Sullivan calls a Self-Managing Company, wherein the day-to-day operations and even management of the business is done by someone other than the entrepreneur.

Although Clear only had one full-time employee while writing *Atomic Habits*, he was still applying the principle of the Self-Managing Company. As he stated, his assistant managed nearly all the affairs of his day-to-day business while he wrote his book.

Importantly, your team actually relies on you enabling them to be self-managing, for at least two crucial reasons. First, for your team to operate both at its best and for the individual members to thrive, research shows that autonomy and a sense of ownership are essential (i.e., *self-determination theory*).[44,45] Without feeling and having autonomy and ownership in what they're doing, your team will be handicapped in their own growth and motivation.

Second, your team relies on you enabling them to be self-managing so that you, as the entrepreneur and visionary, can spend most of your time in your 20 percent genius zone. It's essential and crucial for the ongoing success of your business and team that you continually evolve and innovate what you're doing—for you to become *10x better and more valuable* in what you offer. This can't happen if you're overly involved in the 80 percent, either micromanaging or just simply doing it all on your own. Staying in the 80 percent is how you get caught in the mire of mediocrity and quickly race to the bottom of quality and uniqueness. It's how you stay 2x.

In his *2018 Annual Review,* Clear discusses the publication and initial success of his book:

> "What went well this year? *Atomic Habits.* I feel like I've told everyone within earshot at this point, but in case you haven't heard: I published a book this year! . . . I was still working on the manuscript in January and February of this year. If you had tapped me on the shoulder in the middle of my frantic final edits and told me the book would become a bestseller before the year ended, I almost certainly would have cried with relief. As 2018 draws to a close, *Atomic Habits* has been out for 11 weeks (published on October 16, 2018). I did every single thing I could to make this book a success (starting with spending 3 years writing the best book possible), but the reception has outpaced even my high hopes."[46]

With his book now published, Clear's 20 percent shifted to spreading the message as far as he possibly could. He upped his 10x standard and identity again. As he stated in his *2019 Annual Review:*

> "What went well this year? Book sales. *Atomic Habits* launched in October 2018, which meant that 2019 was the first full calendar year it had been available. I came in with big aspirations, but I think it's fair to say that book sales have outpaced my expectations. As of December 2019: Over 1.3 million copies sold worldwide; 12 consecutive months on the *New York Times* bestseller list . . . Speaking. I delivered 31 paid keynote speeches in 2019. This is far and away the most I've ever given in a calendar year. Obviously, this is tied directly to the success of *Atomic Habits.*"[47]

10x is about quality, not quantity.

James Clear understood this, and now he has the most successful non-fiction book in the world.

10x is committing to your ambitious vision and making that vision your standard. You do this by locking into the 20 percent that will get you there and letting go of the 80 percent that got you here.

The completion of each 10x process requires the comprehensive transformation of yourself and your entire life. The whole system and model of who you are and even your very business look unrecognizably different at 10x. The initial 80 percent becomes literally non-existent. The initial 20 percent becomes your new 100 percent—it's now your normal life, identity, and reality.

Just as Jimmy Donaldson (MrBeast) described in making successful YouTube videos, getting 10x or 100x bigger results doesn't mean your video—or whatever you're creating—needs to be 10x better than everything else out there. Rather, Jimmy said your video or product only needs be *10 or 20 percent better* and, importantly, *different,* to get 4-10x the results of even the "best stuff."

Being both *better* and *different* is essential and points directly to the fact that 10x is fundamentally qualitative, not quantitative. 10x means an evolution has occurred, and what you're now doing is actually incomparable to what others are doing, or what you were previously doing.

Because 10x is qualitative and transformational, it's also non-competitive. It's not about you doing or being better than anyone else. Rather, you're being increasingly unique and different from what everyone else is doing. Your work is innovative and distinct from what the masses of 2x'ers are up to.

10x quality and transformation is how you race to the top.

2x quantity and competition is how you race to the bottom.

Atomic Habits isn't 10x better than other similar self-help books, but it is 10-20 percent better and different than the best self-help books. It's a clear qualitative improvement. Consequently, it gets 10x or 100x the results of even the outliers.

Despite not being 10x better than the competition, it is safe and important to say that Chad Willardson, Jimmy Donaldson, and James Clear are all *10x better* than their former selves. They aren't playing a 2x-game of continuing what they'd done before. They aren't competing with anyone else. Instead, they're choosing their own standards for themselves, committing to their 20 percent, and building a team around them to manage the rest.

When you focus on quality over quantity—as Chad, Jimmy, and Clear have done—you can become the best in the world at what you do. By becoming the best at what you do, you get radically outsized returns on the investment of your time and energy.

In the book *The Dip*, Seth Godin explains the importance and benefits of becoming the best in the world at what you do. As Godin explains in *The Dip*:

> "The rewards are heavily skewed, so much so that it's typical for #1 to get ten times the benefit of #10, and a hundred times the benefit of #100."[48]

In order to become the best, you must embrace the art of *quitting*. Those who become the best don't hold on to any 80 percent activity or identity for too long.

Godin explains that quitting the wrong stuff takes huge guts. It's scary letting go of the 80 percent because the 80 percent is your comfort zone. It's your security blanket. It's what you've already mastered and can basically do on autopilot. It's your paycheck. It's your identity and how you're known. It's your story and your habits.

The longer you hold on to the 80 percent out of fear, the slower your 10x transformation will occur.

The faster you let go of the 80 percent out of commitment and courage, the faster your 10x transformation will occur.

Every great leader must face the dilemma of quitting the wrong stuff—even the stuff that's been your bread and butter for years or decades—to become the best at what you do and realize 10x results.

For instance, in the classic book *Good to Great*, Jim Collins describes what he calls *Level 5 Leaders*. These are people so committed to the cause they care about that they courageously yet happily let go of aspects of their business which are good, but not great.[49] An example Collins uses is Darwin Smith, who was the CEO from 1971 to 1991 of Kimberly-Clark Corporation, a multinational company that produces paper-based consumer goods like toilet paper and Kleenex.

When Smith became the CEO, he saw a huge problem for the ultimate success of Kimberly-Clark. The vast majority of revenue came from the traditional coated-paper mills. These produced paper for magazines and writing pads and had been the core business of the company for over 100 years. But Smith and his leadership team had conviction that the best path to greatness for Kimberly-Clark lay in the consumer business, where the company had demonstrated a best-in-the-world capability in its building of the Kleenex brand.

They believed this was the crucial 20 percent, and that the paper mills, which had been Kimberly-Clark's bread and butter for over 100 years, was now the 80 percent.

You can't be great if you're content being good.

You can be good maintaining the 80 percent, but in order to become great, you must go all-in on the 20 percent and commit to greatness. As Collins wrote:

> "If Kimberly-Clark remained principally a paper-mill business, it would retain a secure position as a

good company. But its only shot at becoming a great company was to become the best paper-based consumer company—if it could take on such companies as Procter & Gamble and Scott Paper Co. and beat them. That meant it would have to 'stop doing' paper mills. So, in what one director called 'the gutsiest decision I've ever seen a CEO make,' Darwin Smith sold the mills. He even sold the mill in Kimberly, Wisconsin. Then he threw all the money into a war chest for an epic battle with Procter & Gamble and Scott Paper. Wall Street analysts derided the move, and the business press called it stupid. But Smith did not waver. Twenty-five years later, Kimberly-Clark emerged from the fray as the number-one paper-based consumer-products company in the world, beating P&G in six of eight categories and owning its former archrival Scott Paper outright. For the shareholder, Kimberly-Clark under Darwin Smith beat the market by four times, easily outperforming such great companies as Coca-Cola, General Electric, Hewlett-Packard, and 3M."

The rewards for higher and unique quality aren't linear, but exponential.

10x is easier than 2x.

10x is qualitative and takes you down a totally non-linear pathway of mastery and freedom.

To go 10x requires committing fully to the 20 percent you most resonate with and eliminate everything that can't or won't go 10x with you.

You quit *everything* that can't go 10x *from here*, even if that means eliminating the best of what got you here.

Chapter Takeaways

- Going 10x involves the continuous process of increasing the quality and decreasing the quantity of everything you do.

- How you do anything is how you do everything.

- Shedding your 2x-identity can be difficult, because as people we have the tendency to avoid loss, overvalue what we currently own, and desire to be seen as consistent.

- Your identity is the story you believe about yourself and the standards you hold for yourself.

- Defining and choosing your own minimum standards, no matter how seemingly impossible to yourself and others, is fundamental to experiencing a 10x transformation.

- Evolving yourself to the level of a higher minimum standard requires commitment and courage, which eventually leads to the development of new capabilities and confidence (Dan's 4C's formula).

- Jimmy Donaldson's three ingredients to his 10x process are: 1) thinking exponentially and non-linearly bigger, 2) hyper-focusing on quality over quantity, and 3) building a team to handle the 80 percent so you can focus and improve in your craft.

- 10x goals are easier than 2x goals for many reasons. 10x goals are less competitive. 10x goals require you to focus on very few things rather than many, which improves your brain's ability to focus—research shows that continual task switching makes flow and high performance basically impossible.[50,51] 10x goals promote non-linear approaches which produce novel, innovative, and competition-free solutions. Finally, 10x goals foster leadership and teamwork, wherein you stop doing everything yourself, managing others, or needing to be right.

- Creating 10x results doesn't require you to be 10x better than everyone else. Even being 10–20 percent *better* (and *different*) from everything else can produce 10x bigger results than even the outliers of a particular niche or field.

CHAPTER 3

10x EMBRACES ABUNDANCE AND REJECTS SCARCITY

Get Exactly What You Want, Experience Radical Freedom, and Realize Your Unique Ability

"The world is divided into two types of people: those who are 'needers' and those who are 'wanters.' Needers compete for scarce resources and opportunities, while wanters are involved in the continual expansion of cooperation among abundance-minded individuals."

—DAN SULLIVAN[1]

On August 15, 1978, when Dan Sullivan was 34 years old, he got divorced and went bankrupt *all on the same day.*

This was an insanely low and sobering moment for him. The extreme pain of his divorce and bankruptcy helped him realize that he wasn't taking 100 percent responsibility for his life.

Crucially, Dan realized that he hadn't been embracing or fully owning what he truly wanted. Instead, he'd been opting more for the 80 percent of his life, which he felt he *needed* due to scarcity and loss aversion—including a bad marriage, a busy schedule, low- or no-paying clients, etc.

Near the end of that year—1978—he decided that every day moving forward, he would write in his journal *exactly what he wanted.* He wanted to train himself to live life based on wants not needs, freedom not security, and abundance not scarcity.

On New Year's Eve 2003—25 years later—Dan went to dinner with two close friends and his new wife, Babs. Side note, Babs was one of the things Dan wrote in his journal that he *really* wanted. He told his friends at that dinner:

> "Today I've reached a milestone. I've completed a project. Every day, except for 12 (out of 9,131), during the last 25 years, I've done this exercise of writing down what I want. Twenty-five years later, I can tell you I'm a really powerful wanter."

Dan learned to stop justifying what he wanted. He stopped being constrained by needs or rationalizations. He stopped worrying of others' opinions about his goals.

Instead of chasing what he thought he needed or what others thought he needed, Dan went 10x over and over—from getting his new business off the ground coaching entrepreneurs one-on-one to now having a global company training tens of thousands of entrepreneurs—by embracing only that which he sincerely wanted.

Wanting and needing are two completely different things.

Entrepreneurs who operate out of need won't accomplish 10x goals because no one *needs* to reach them. You can survive just fine living a 2x lifestyle. Rather, 10x achievements are highly personal—they are goals you intrinsically want to reach.

In this chapter, you're going to learn how to let go of scarcity and competition-based needing and replace it with abundance and creativity-based wanting.

By becoming comfortable and unapologetic about wanting what you want—which is a skill you continually enhance—you also learn how to identify and develop what Dan calls your Unique Ability. When you embrace your Unique Ability, you stop worrying about what other people are doing. You stop competing entirely. But also, you realize in the realest sense who you truly are. You carve away everything that's not "The David" and transform yourself into your most powerful, valuable, and genuine self-expression.

Let's begin.

Escape the Scarcity of Needing and Embrace the Abundance of Wanting

A crucial aspect of "wanting what you want" is that you absolutely do not need to justify your desires to anyone.

There is no justification of wants. If someone asks why you want something, you don't need to explain yourself.

You simply want it because you want it.

That's why.

Having a purely wanting approach to life is unthinkable and even incomprehensible for most people because culture and society program people—in school and as employees—to chase a certain set of needs, especially money, as an end in itself. The things we seek are seen as limited and scarce resources which we shouldn't want an abundance of, because if we got more than we "should," then someone else would be left without.

As Dan further said in his book *Wanting What You Want:*

> "When you're in the world of needing, you always have to justify what you need because the needing world is one of scarcity. If you need something scarce, you have to rationalize why you should have it rather than someone else. Not only do you have to justify what you need to yourself, but you have to justify it to everyone else as well. Someone who is a lifetime needer spends a great deal of daily thinking and communication in a never-ending process of justification. But if you cross the line and go into the world of wanting, there's no justification. Ever. . . There's a stand entrepreneurs have to take to not give in to their previous need to justify. Some courage is required here. You have to be committed to living in a world of wanting and not falling back into a life of needing. When somebody asks you, 'Why do you need that?' (because they'll say need rather than want), there's a temptation to slip back into previous language and begin to justify. You mustn't give in to that. Say, 'First of all, I don't need it; I want it.' And then, 'The reason I want it is because I want it.' This is not easily understood by everyone because, for most people, everything in their needing world has to have a justifying reason. When you're dealing with scarcity, you probably are taking someone else's scarce resource. But in the world of wanting, there's no scarcity, because it's a world of innovation—not of taking. Wanters are creating things that didn't exist before. You're creating something new that in no way requires taking something from someone else."[2]

There are two critically important points Dan is making about wanting, which most people don't grasp. Because they don't grasp these two points, people opt for a life of needing, wherein they compete for scarce resources which they must justify seeking. Here are Dan's two core points:

1. **Wanting is about abundance and creation.** Creativity is not a scarce resource and takes nothing away from anyone else. Rather, creativity actually creates new resources and opportunities which previously didn't exist and which would not have existed without someone proactively creating them.

2. **Wanting requires no justification.** When you want something, you don't need to justify that want to anyone else. This will be particularly vexing to the self-righteous needers among us who will attempt to manipulate and guilt you into doing what they believe you *should* be doing, based on their scarcity frame of reference. To go 10x, as well as to live the life you are uniquely suited to live, you can't pay heed to the scarcity-mongers.

I'm going to dissect both of these points in turn. Let's start with the creation of new resources, which shouldn't be confused with stealing limited resources.

In a 2004 essay entitled *How to Make Wealth*, entrepreneur Paul Graham explains the difference between money and wealth. They are not the same thing, but often get confused because money is the typical way of *moving wealth*.

As Graham explains:

"Wealth is the fundamental thing. Wealth is stuff we want: food, clothes, houses, cars, gadgets, travel to interesting places, and so on. You can have wealth without having money. If you had a magic machine that could on command make you a car or cook you dinner or do your laundry, or do anything else you wanted, you wouldn't need money. Whereas if you were in the middle of Antarctica, where there is nothing to buy, it wouldn't matter how much money you had. Wealth is what you want, not money. But if wealth is the important thing, why does everyone talk about making money? It is a kind of shorthand: money is a way of *moving wealth*, and in practice they are usually interchangeable. But they are not the same thing, and unless you plan to get rich by counterfeiting, talking about *making money* can make it harder to understand how to make money." [54]

Money alone is not worth chasing—and if money is all you're after, you will struggle building wealth—which is valuable assets, skills, and creations.

When you view money *as* wealth, then it can be easy to fall for what Graham calls "The Pie Fallacy," which is believing there is a finite amount of wealth available at any one time, and if one person has a lot of the wealth then that takes away from someone else. However, when you realize that wealth and money are *not* the same thing, and that wealth is actually *created*, then you realize there is no finite pie.

Money is an abstraction, it's a finite game.

Wealth is *reality*, it's an infinite game.

There's no scarcity of wealth.

Wealth is the byproduct of choosing freedom, and you can create as much wealth *as you want*.

Graham further explains:

"Suppose you own a beat-up old car. Instead of sitting on your butt next summer, you could spend the time restoring your car to pristine condition. In doing so you create wealth. The world is—and you specifically are—one pristine old car the richer. And not just in some metaphorical way. If you sell your car, you'll get more for it. In restoring your old car you have made yourself richer. You haven't made anyone else poorer. So there is obviously not a fixed pie. And in fact, when you look at it this way, you wonder why anyone would think there was."

In simple terms: wealth is *value.*

Wealth is something that someone *wants*—whether that be a physical commodity, information or knowledge, or some form of service.

Value is *qualitative and subjective*, not quantitative and objective like money is. You can become 10x more valuable and thus wealthy without directly having 10x more money. And indeed, money follows wealth.

The quantitative follows the qualitative.

10x is qualitative. . .

10x occurs as you create more wealth, or value. You do this by creating value that is qualitatively different and better (i.e., innovative) than what currently exists in the market.

The more specific and specialized the value you can create, the wealthier you can become. You're creating things that no one else can or would. You're providing an incredibly useful service that is not only desired but transformative for someone who wants it.

Wealth and freedom are exactly the same thing. Wealth is qualitative and so is freedom.

Wealth and freedom are about *value.*

In his program for high-level entrepreneurs, Dan teaches 4 Freedoms that are about value:

1. The *value and quality* of your time

2. The *value and quality* of your money

3. The *value and quality* of your relationships

4. The *value and quality* of your overall purpose

You can 10x the value and quality of your time, money, relationships, and purpose. *And that's really what 10x is all about.*

10x is the means, freedom is the end.

This is where most people have gotten the entire notion of 10x wrong. They've equated 10x solely with money, making it a finite game with a beginning and an end, with winners and losers.

10x is a *qualitative game* of increasing the value of your freedoms—and to do so by creating the wealth (skills, knowledge, products, etc.) you *intrinsically want* to create, and then sharing that wealth with the specific people who increasingly value and appreciate your value.

When you play 10x as a qualitative game, then you focus on building transformational relationships, not transactional ones. Everything you do is about transforming yourself and the unique value you can bring and providing your increasingly unique value to those you want to form transformational relationships with.

Increasing your value involves becoming more specific and specialized in what you create for specific types of people. As you become increasingly valuable, people will pay you increasing amounts of money in exchange for your value.

To quote Graham again:

> "The people most likely to grasp that wealth can be created are the ones who are good at making things, the craftsmen. Their hand-made objects become store-bought ones. But with the rise of industrialization there are fewer and fewer craftsmen. One of the biggest remaining groups is computer programmers. A programmer can sit down in front of a computer and *create wealth*. A good piece of software is, in itself, a valuable thing. There is no manufacturing to confuse the issue. Those characters you type are a

complete, finished product. If someone sat down and wrote a web browser that didn't suck (a fine idea, by the way), the world would be that much richer."

When you live life based on want, rather than need, you're playing an infinite game. You see that reality is created and chosen—and is based on wealth, freedom, and value. You recognize that each of these things is qualitative, individual, and personal. You're not competing with anyone else. Instead, you're collaborating with other abundance-minded creators.

When you live life based on need, you're stuck playing a finite game. When you play a finite game, you're driven and controlled by external forces. You're competing for scarce resources. You're focused on and worried about what other people are doing. You're not clear on who you really are and you're certainly not peeling the layers of the David away.

Are you a needer or wanter?

Are you playing the infinite game of freedom or are you stuck in some finite game?

Are you building qualitative wealth and value, or are you competing for scarce money?

According to Dan, there are four distinct differences between needers and wanters:

1. **Needing** is extrinsically motivated, whereas **wanting** is intrinsically motivated.

2. **Needing** is security-driven, whereas **wanting** is freedom-driven.

3. **Needing** is scarcity-minded, whereas **wanting** is abundance-minded.

4. **Needing** is reactive, whereas **wanting** is creative.[3]

Committing to what you *want most* is the only way to be free.

If you do anything out of perceived need or compulsion, then you don't feel it is really your own choice, but rather, you feel the choice is being made for you. You're being the victim or byproduct of something external.

When you live based on wants, you're living intrinsically. You're living on purpose—*your purpose*. You're living *without need* to rationalize or justify. You're being, doing, and having what you want simply because you want it, regardless of external opinions or expectations. *You're creating the life you want by creating the value you want.*

This brings us to the second critical point to dissect from Dan's quotation above: when you live based on wanting, you don't need to rationalize or justify what you want, *to anyone.*

You do what you want, because you want to.

That's enough.

Wanting is intrinsic. It requires no justification, even though others (the needers among us) will try to force you to rationalize what you want.

Let's clear this up one more time: you don't need it. . .*You want it.* And you wanting whatever you want takes nothing away from someone else, because you're *creating wealth* and freedom, and that actually makes things better for the world, not worse.

When you operate in the world of needs, you always have to rationalize and justify what you're doing. You can't simply do something because you want to. You may want a new house, or to go on a six-week vacation, or to chase some dream. Yet, if you're operating based on need, you likely won't do any of these things because they can be hard to rationalize.

When you are in a needing frame-of-mind, you can easily be manipulated by other people. Others strive to make you feel guilty for not doing what they think you "need to be" or "should be" doing.

A public controversial example highlights this perfectly.

In a recent interview, Tim Ferriss asked Coinbase co-founder and CEO Brian Armstrong about dealing with scrutiny and criticism. Specifically, Tim asked Brian about his decision to offer severance packages to employees who disagreed with his stance that Coinbase was a mission-driven company and wouldn't over-involve itself in cultural, political issues.[4,5]

Brian explained that during the beginning of the Covid pandemic in 2020, the tumultuous news cycle, mostly dominated by the tragic murder of George Floyd and the Black Lives Matter movement, created a sense of division across the country—and his team began feeling less connected and cohesive as a result.

As division spread internally within the Coinbase team, the employee culture became political and tense. During bi-weekly town hall meetings, Coinbase employees began asking political and social questions that pressured the company to take a stance on issues like police brutality that fell outside the scope of its mission. As many similarly influential companies publicly took bold stances on social issues, Brian and his team knew they had to respond.

During a closed-door meeting with his leadership team, Brian decided to double down on his company values. At first, he decided that while Coinbase's mission is not political, he *needed* to follow the tech trends and make a public statement supporting the BLM movement.

However, after learning more about the organization, he discovered *BLM* had other objectives beyond racial equality, such as defunding the police in America, which he didn't think Coinbase could support.

He realized he had made a mistake, getting swept up in the hype of the cultural moment—at the expense of Coinbase's mission: increasing economic freedom in the world with crypto. This, he discovered, was the mistake of operating from a place of fear, scarcity, and needing. He knew he had to re-focus his and the company's energy and culture on the mission at hand.

A few months after he released his initial statement, Brian released a new public statement informing everyone on his team, as well as the outside world, that Coinbase is a *mission-driven company*. To quote Stephen Covey, "The main thing is to keep the main thing the main thing."[6]

In the Tim Ferriss interview, Brain explained how he broke the news and made the committed clarification to Coinbase:

> "This is the direction we're going in. If you're not okay with that, I totally get it. I didn't make it clear up front, that's my fault. We're going to give this great severance package. Five percent of the company left. It created a bunch of drama for a few months, a couple journalists wrote hit pieces on us and things like that, but afterwards it was better. It was one of the best things I've ever done for the company to be honest. Because now we're fully aligned, we're making faster progress, everybody who joins the company knows what they're signing up for. And it was an incredibly important leadership moment for me because I was terribly scared to do it, I didn't want the controversy, I knew people were going to hate it."

Brian Armstrong did something courageous. He did what he *wanted*, not what others thought he *needed* to do.

Living based on want requires courage.

Living based on want is how you live your life how you want to, not how others want you to.

Wanting what you want is intrinsically motivated. It's doing something for the sake of it, not because you have to rationalize it. Brian simply wanted to make a company that brought forth economic freedom through crypto. He didn't need to rationalize that want. He didn't need any ulterior motives or reasons.

Wanting what you want requires a great deal of self-honesty. It takes making a committed stand about who you are and what you're about, regardless of the repercussions.

Tim Ferriss responded to Brain's story by saying that a "hallmark of good leadership" is making "unpopular decisions."

Eliminating the 80 percent—whatever that looks like for you—will be unpopular for many people in your world. It will certainly be unpopular for the needers in your world—those who don't understand the infinite game of freedom and wealth creation you're playing.

Indeed, as stated previously, a primary reason people don't go for the 10x upgrades they want is because in the end, they're too afraid of making those around them who simply wouldn't get it uncomfortable. They end up buying into the loud agenda of culture and those around them who say they shouldn't want more than they need. They settle for 2x over 10x and, internally, they can't overcome the frustration and suppression this creates. Even more, they fail to realize who they truly could have become, the 10x version of themselves that transformed again and again, the David.

There is enormous external pressure to keep the 80 percent in your life, because the 80 percent represents security but not freedom. Even still, the greatest pressure you'll face is internal.

Freedom is ultimately internal.

Do you have the courage to let go of the 80 percent and go all-in on what you truly want?

Being *free* means you let go of everything you think you need and only choose that which you absolutely want.

Wanting is based on freedom.

Needing is based on security, fear, and worry of other people's judgements.

People don't get what they want because they're too busy seeking what they believe they need. They become busy chasing means rather than directly choosing and living their desired end.

There are two core types of freedom:

1. **Freedom from**—which is *externally escaping* from what you don't want, and is avoidance-motivated.

2. **Freedom to**—which is *internally committing to and courageously choosing* what you most want, and is approach-motivated.[7,8]

You could have all the external freedoms in the world but not be free. Similarly, you could *be free* even if all of your external freedoms are taken. As Viktor Frankl said in *Man's Search for Meaning*, "Between stimulus and response there is a space. In that space is our power to choose our response. In our response lies our growth and our freedom."[9]

Freedom is ultimately an internal choice and commitment, regardless of the finite game you find yourself in any particular moment.

Freedom and wanting both transcend context. They operate above context. They aren't defined by the rules of a given context. Instead, they utilize a higher plane to transform the context and game (i.e., reality) entirely.

You know internally whether you're free. You're free when you choose what you want and you go for it, rather than accepting what you think you need.

Nothing happens until after you commit, and it's only *after* you commit that you know what freedom feels like. As the popular saying goes, "Everything you want is on the opposite side of fear."[10]

An obvious challenge people face is that they *don't know what they want*. They're far too busy justifying what they think they need. They haven't learned to be brutally honest with themselves and others. They're still living in fear.

Learning to clarify what you want without justification or apology is vital to going 10x since 10x is based on want, not need. Indeed, no one *needs* to go 10x.

Elon Musk doesn't need to go to Mars, *he wants to.*

Martin Luther King Jr. didn't need to rally for racial equality and freedoms, *he wanted to.*

You don't need that new car, you want it. Or you don't. *It's okay either way.*

Wanting is based on freedom and abundance.

Wanting is based on honesty with yourself and the whole world—you're no longer trying to pose and posture based on what others think. You're living your life how you want, and you're being yourself.

As the *Alcoholics Anonymous* founder Bill W. stated, "All progress starts by telling the truth."

To be free, you can't keep lying to yourself.

Living in a world of needs and rationalizations is prison. It locks you into relationships and situations you don't want but maintain out of fear and perceived security or obligation.

To be free, you must first be completely honest with yourself. Being honest with yourself starts by admitting to yourself what you want most.

Not what you think you want.

Not what you think you need.

But what you truly—at your core—want.

Until you can admit and commit to what you want, then you're not free.

When you live based on freedom and want, then your life starts transforming in qualitative and non-linear ways. You stop operating in the finite-minded world of other people's goals and rules.

You stop being like anyone else entirely.

You start fully embracing the *uniqueness* that is you. And *you are* unique. No one else is like you and no one else *can* or *truly wants* to be like you. The best thing you can do is embrace and value your uniqueness. Then live that out in the world in your highest and purest form by helping others in the way only you can.

You develop your unique mastery by going 10x again and again, choosing freedom over security, and going all-in on the 20 percent that both excites and terrifies you. You peel away the 80 percent and become your own David, which is unique and like no one else.

It all boils down to wanting what you want.

What do you truly want, more than anything else?

What would excite you more than anything else to be, do, and have?

What would you be and do if you weren't afraid of what others thought or the repercussions?

How would it feel to be more honest and real with yourself and the world?

The highest and Fourth of Dan's 4 Freedoms is *Freedom of Purpose*—doing what you most want to do, which is the highest and purest expression of yourself—your purpose for being.

As you continue evolving as a person, your sense of vision and purpose for yourself and your life will expand to unbelievable levels. You'll progressively want to give more and more of yourself and your resources to the betterment of the world, in your own unique way.

Clarify and Define Your Unique Ability

"Unique Ability requires you to determine what you personally like and dislike doing, and decide that others' opinions about it are irrelevant. The basis of Unique Ability is to continually be conscious of the activities and

the settings you like and that energize you—and the things that don't. This is where freedom starts: with the understanding that your own judgments about your own experience are 100 percent valid... Unique Ability is really amazing. And I have to tell you, it never is a lot of different activities. It's only a few activities. People say, 'Well, I have a Unique Ability in 10 different areas. And I say, 'Well, that might be good for the next 90 days. But you're going to notice at the end of 90 days that seven of those someone else could do. There's just 2–3 that are really yours.' I've been on this now for 25–30 years and it's interesting that you think you've gotten to the end of it. But I find, because I'm always doing new things, that what I thought was my Unique Ability before I started taking on a bigger challenge and producing a bigger result, you can fine-tune it even more."

—DAN SULLIVAN[11]

In May of 2014, Nike released the "P-ROD 8," American skateboarder Paul Rodriguez's eighth signature shoe.

When the shoe was released, Nike informed P-Rod that he was only one of four athletes to ever release eight unique signature shoes. The other three athletes were Kobe Bryant, Michael Jordan, and LeBron James . . .

Having a signature shoe with *Nike* is an extremely rare feat. Over the company's 40-plus-year history, less than one percent of Nike's athletes have received the coveted honor. To have a Nike shoe that carries your own name or nickname on it, though, that's even rarer still. Consider the football legend Bo Jackson, whose signature Nike shoe was called the Air Trainer SC. It wasn't called The Bo.

Back in 2005, Nike was making its second attempt to succeed in the skateboarding market and subculture. The

21-year-old P-Rod was one of the world's top skateboarders at the time, and Nike made P-Rod an amazing offer to join the Nike team. Despite being an incredible opportunity, P-Rod had long dreamed of having his own signature skate-shoe, and Nike did not make him that offer.

In his 2022 interview—*20 and Forever*—reflecting on 20 years of skateboarding and his career as a whole, P-Rod stated:

> "My dream when I started skateboarding was to have a signature board and a signature shoe. To me, that's wholly completing the pro skater dream. So, if I didn't get a shoe, I feel like my dream would be incomplete. My manager was talking to [Nike], negotiating, and said to me, 'Okay, here's what they want to offer. Here's what the terms of the deal are.' And I was like, 'That all sounds good, but what about a pro shoe? What about a signature shoe?' She's like, 'They didn't mention anything about it.' So, she went back to Nike and called me back, 'They're not planning to do signature shoes.' I was literally like, 'Nope! I'm perfectly happy where I'm at.' I wasn't planning on leaving [éS, his previous shoe sponsor]. I was just young and stubborn and stuck to my guns."[12]

Looking back, P-Rod is sometimes freaked out by the implications of that moment in time. In 2022, he released his tenth signature shoe with Nike, and his shoes have been among the top selling of *all skateboard shoes* since 2005, selling millions of pairs. He says,

> "I literally think about that story and can't believe it. What if they had just come back and said, 'Okay, nope.' What would have happened? I'm just grateful they came back and believed in me that much. And there we went, 10 signature shoes later."

P-Rod is one of the best skateboarders to ever touch a board. He's unique and technical. His style precise and powerful. He's innovated and transformed what "skateboarding" means to hundreds of thousands of skaters.

P-Rod is a 10x person that has had an extremely long career for a skateboarder. He's never plateaued or gotten stuck but has continually evolved and innovated himself, his focus, and his craft.

At age 14, after just a few years of skating, P-Rod submitted his first "Sponsor Me" video to Andy Netkin, the manager of a local skateboard shop named One Eighteen in Los Angeles. Netkin immediately saw P-Rod as a future superstar.[13]

At age 16, P-Rod got sponsored as an amateur by the skateboard company City Stars, and two years later premiered in their long-awaited skate video *Street Cinema*.[14] He even got the closing part of the video, which is usually reserved for one of the most esteemed pros on the team.[15]

At 19, P-Rod was featured in the prestigious Transworld Skateboarding 2002 video *In Bloom*. In the beginning montage of his video part, there is commentary from skateboarding legend Eric Koston, who describing P-Rod stated:

> "His whole deal is natural, like it's hard for him to fall. He's just manufacturing tricks out like a conveyer belt. Cause it comes way too easy for him. He's got something going on that's pretty good. That's for sure. Cause it works. He learns so fast. Whatever it is he does, it looks like he was meant to anyways. Beware of the flare. Just watch out."[16]

A crucial reason for P-Rod's continued evolution and success is that he's been operating within his Unique Ability.

Your Unique Ability is the purest and most honest expression of yourself. It's the center of who you are—"the David". . . the "20 percent" of any particular 10x jump.

Your Unique Ability is *how you create value and wealth that is unique and specialized.* It's your radically unique way of doing what you do, such that no one else can compete with you even if they wanted to. Your Unique Ability is also your unique vision and purpose—your "why" for what you're doing.

After coaching tens of thousands of entrepreneurs for nearly 50 years, Dan Sullivan has seen that those who take their Unique Ability seriously, meaning they take *themselves* seriously, are the ones who make the biggest 10x leaps.

The reason is simple: Unique Ability is qualitative and individual, it's extremely unique value that *only you* can create. It's not just what you do, but *how* you do it. P-Rod doesn't just skateboard with an extreme degree of skill but also an extreme degree of *uniqueness*—which is actually a core component of mastery.

Your Unique Ability is where you have superior skills, where you're completely intrinsically motivated and thus energized and engaged, and it's also where you see neverending possibility for improvement.

When most entrepreneurs begin working with Strategic Coach, they find that far less than 20 percent of their time is focused within their Unique Ability. Instead, they're investing their time, energy, and focus all over the place. They're caught up in the 80 percent where they may be good or even excellent, but they're not in their Unique Ability.

As someone takes their Unique Ability seriously and shifts the majority of their time to developing it, 10x and non-linear jumps follow.

An obvious and important question that comes up with Unique Ability is whether it's nature or nurture. The not-so-satisfying answer is that it's *both*.

We all have a Unique Ability—the purest and freest expression of our self and our purpose—but not everyone commits to and develops their Unique Ability.

Your Unique Ability is personal and internal. Therefore, it takes being honest with yourself about what you most want.

What you most want and your Unique Ability are connected. You must embrace that you yourself are a unique individual. You've got to value your own uniqueness, which also means valuing and appreciating the uniqueness of everyone else.

Committing to your Unique Ability—the thing you want to do and which excites you most—takes extreme commitment and courage. It takes not worrying about what anyone else thinks about what you do and how you live.

You've got to fully bet on yourself.

Although Unique Ability may come "naturally" to you, that is misleading. Committing to your Unique Ability is the hardest and most intense thing you will ever do.

It's pure commitment and courage.

It's never-ending.

It's freedom and how you build your most unique value, which the right people will immediately recognize and appreciate beyond what you can presently imagine.

The more you commit to your Unique Ability—which is the 20 percent of a chosen 10x jump—the more you and your life will transform.

You're not being inhibited by what other people think.

You're not avoiding what you ultimately want to do.

This is why things come *easier* for you when you're in your Unique Ability than they come for other people. It's not that things are "easy" for you. It's that you're going all-in on what you most want to do, and because you're all-in, you grow and transform at non-linear and exponential levels.

You learn 10x faster than most people.

You progress 10x faster than seems normal.

You make leaps in your progression, skills, and results that are otherworldly.

When you embrace your Unique Ability, work becomes play. As you follow your curiosity and interests, you become open to new potential and possibilities.

You reach outside and above your current skill-level, which enables greater flow and higher performance. You're continually elevating your standards within your domain, making them higher and more nuanced and unique. No one else is competing with you. You're in your own world of creativity and innovation.

For you, because you're continually pushing your boundaries, it's intense and hard, but it's also extremely *liberating*. To not be free is much harder than being free. Despite being excruciatingly scary and hard, *it's much easier than the alternative*. And the freedom, wealth, and benefits of embracing your Unique Ability are 10x or more than the grind of just doing something because you can, or because you believe you should.

When you're operating in Unique Ability, you're always raising the stakes and attempting things you've never done before. You're always seeing how far you can possibly go. Because you're in flow and beyond your current capability and confidence, you're courageously elevating beyond where you've previously been.

You're continually letting your most exciting future dictate what you commit to, and you go all-in. You don't become complacent and content with what you've done in the past. You don't settle for 2x.

As Robert Greene explained in *Mastery*:

> "The great Masters in history. . . they excel by their ability to practice harder and move faster through the process, all of this stemming from the intensity of their desire to learn and from the deep connection they feel to their field of study. And at the core of this intensity of effort is in fact a quality that is genetic

and inborn—not talent or brilliance, which is something that must be developed, but rather a deep and powerful *inclination* toward a particular subject. This inclination is a reflection of a person's uniqueness. This uniqueness is not something merely poetic or philosophical—it is a scientific fact that genetically, every one of us is unique; our exact genetic makeup has never happened before or will never be repeated... With those who stand out by their later mastery, they experience this inclination more deeply and clearly than others. They experience it as an inner calling. It tends to dominate their thoughts and dreams. They find their way, by accident or sheer effort, to a career path in which this inclination can flourish. This intense connection and desire allows them to withstand the pain of the process—the self-doubts, the tedious hours of practice and study, the inevitable setbacks, the endless barbs from the envious."[17]

Your Unique Ability is not linear or static. Just as the 20 percent of each 10x jump will be different, the expression and focus of your Unique Ability will also be different in each 10x jump. Just because something was a Unique Ability activity in the past doesn't mean it still is.

Your Unique Ability is always evolving and directed at your most exciting future.

It's always taking you to the core of who you are and your highest purpose—the David.

There's no end to peeling away the layers.

Each 10x jump you make will non-linearly and qualitatively transform you as a person.

Each 10x jump will take you and your life in surprising directions. Take for example, Michelangelo, who went from drawing human bodies to sculpting the 17-foot David to painting the Sistine Chapel to becoming the lead architect of the massive dome of St. Peter's Cathedral.

None of these 10x jumps were linear, but each were completely intrinsic and intuitive to Michelangelo. Each 10x jump he made required him to renovate the foundation he'd built in his previous 10x cycles, often in a lateral or non-linear direction that only made sense when "connecting the dots backward."

As P-Rod stated in his *20 and Forever* interview:

> "The one saying that my dad told me when I was younger was, 'What got you there will keep you there.' He was trying to prove the point that just because you think you've made it, doesn't mean it's time to take it easy. It means it's time to keep it going."[18]

Your life's objective is to *develop mastery in* and *fully express* your Unique Ability. There's nothing more important to master. There's nothing more important to dedicate yourself to. It's *your* work. Your life's work, and if you don't do it, no one else will.

A simple, profound, and somewhat comical story highlights the importance of dedicating yourself to your Unique Ability and purpose above that of anything else. While working on his seminal research on "flow," Dr. Mihaly Csikszentmihalyi, the originator of the concept, emailed the management master Peter Drucker, seeking to interview him about creativity. Drucker's response blew Csikszentmihalyi's mind so much that he included it in his book:

> "I am greatly honored and flattered by your kind letter of February 14th — for I have admired you and your work for many years, and I have learned much from it. But, my dear Professor Csikszentmihalyi, I am afraid I have to disappoint you. I could not possibly answer your questions. I am told I am creative

— I don't know what that means. . . I just keep on plodding. . . I hope that you will not think me presumptuous or rude if I say that one of the secrets of productivity (in which I believe whereas I do not believe in creativity) is to have a VERY BIG waste paper basket to take care of ALL invitations such as yours—productivity in my experience consists of NOT doing anything that helps the work of other people but to spend all one's time on the work that Good Lord has fitted one to do, and to do well."[19]

The more you explore and refine your Unique Ability, the more you're doing your work, not someone else's. You'll reach a level of *unique mastery* that becomes increasingly obvious and impactful to yourself and those around you, the more your life's work begins to feel like a *sacred calling*. Your Unique Ability defines and clarifies your *Mastery*—what you and you alone are uniquely suited to do.

Research shows that when someone subjectively feels their work is a *calling*—meaning they have a *sense of purpose*, and that they're *doing what they are meant to do*—that they experience greater overall subjective well-being or happiness as well as greater career success than those who view their work as a *job* or *career*.[20] Viewing your work as a "calling" need not be tied to any religious belief system, though it can be.

Research has found a consistent link between feeling a sense of calling and heightened levels of career maturity, career commitment, work meaning, job satisfaction, life meaning, and life satisfaction. These links appear most robust when people are actually living out their calling at work.[21]

Other research shows that individuals who have a sense of calling are more likely to ignore career advice from mentors or advisors, particularly advice suggesting more secure or mainstream options.[22] This doesn't mean they don't listen or take advice, but that in the end, they ultimately trust their inner voice and make their own decisions.

At the end of the day, no one can make your decisions for you. No one is you.

No one has your unique vision or way of approaching life.

No one has your Unique Ability.

Thus, other people's advice can only take you so far.

This reality hit me hard while writing this book. I was experiencing a great desire to go 10x in various areas of my life and work. But in order to do so, I had to have some difficult and uncomfortable conversations, which were high-stakes and had huge consequences. Many of my greatest mentors and advisors suggested I don't have these uncomfortable conversations, but instead, to play it safe.

I was told by multiple people that I'd lose my greatest opportunities, current and future, if I went forward with what I felt in my heart I *wanted* to do. In the end, I listened to myself and made important adjustments in various relationships and situations, and rather than destroying the relationship, my honesty built greater trust, commitment, and freedom for all.

Trusting yourself and forging your unique path is actually what Robert Greene calls the "X factor" of *mastery*. As he explains:

> "Mastery is not a function of genius or talent. It is a function of time and intense focus applied to a particular field of knowledge. But there is another element, an X factor that Mastery inevitably possess, that seems mystical but is accessible to us all. Whatever field of activity we are involved in, there is generally an accepted path to the top. . . But Masters have a strong inner guiding system and a high level of self-awareness. Inevitably, these Masters, as they progress in their career paths, make a choice at a key moment in their lives: they decide to forge their own route, one that others will see as unconventional,

but that suits their own spirit and rhythms and leads them closer to discovering the hidden truths of their object of study. This key choice takes self-confidence and self-awareness—the X factor that is necessary for attaining mastery."

Mastery is not just the ability to do something well. It's the ability to do something *uniquely well*. If it's not unique, innovative, and uninhibited self-expression, *then it's not true mastery*. Mastery and uniqueness are inseparable.

Thus, for you to reach your highest level of mastery and personal calling, you do so by taking your Unique Ability seriously and fully developing and expressing it. You develop your Unique Ability by:

1. **Being increasingly honest with yourself and other people about what you most want for yourself and your life.** Don't justify your wants to anyone. No one else is you. No one else wants what you want. No one else has your Unique Ability and your unique vision and desires.

2. **Expanding your vision and thinking exponentially bigger for yourself about what you can be, do, and have.** Continually hone your Unique Ability—that which excites you, energizes you, and which you see potential for never-ending improvement—and utilize your Unique Ability to bring forth your 10x vision. Become increasingly clear on who you are and what makes you unique and different from everyone else on this planet.

3. **Clarifying your ideal future self and what they would be doing.** Be very specific about this. What context are they in? What mission are they fulfilling? What is the cause they

are about? What Unique Ability does your future self have, which they are utilizing to dramatically impact and advance what they most care for? What are the unique standards your future self lives by and has normalized, even though they may seem unfathomable and unrealistic to current you?

4. **Clarifying the 20 percent** that if you develop greater mastery in, you'll experience your desired 10x jump in freedom of time, money, relationships, and overall purpose.

5. **Letting go of the 80 percent** and allowing yourself to explore your curiosities and interests.

Each time you go 10x and transform yourself and your life, you'll be clearer on your Unique Ability.

For example, I could say, "My Unique Ability is to learn, understand, and distill complex ideas in a compelling, simple, and useful manner." However, I could be even more specific than this, defining my Unique Ability to position the highly nuanced value I provide to highly specific people. For instance, I could say, "My Unique Ability is to clarify and conceptualize highly complex ideas in the form of compelling, story-driven, and science-based books."

A word of warning when it comes to defining your Unique Ability. It's much, much bigger than anything you specifically do. More directly, your Unique Ability is the unique way you approach what you do when you're living at your best. It's not tied to any specific activity, although you can frame it that way strategically and thoughtfully if you'd like.

There's danger in defining your Unique Ability based on a specific skill, such as writing. 10x jumps are often require a great evolution in your Unique Ability, so you want to avoid putting yours in a box.

As decision-making expert Annie Duke stated in her book *Quit*: "When your identity is what you do, then what you do becomes hard to abandon, because it means quitting who you are."[23]

It's best to chunk your Unique Ability beyond any finite game to the higher and more infinite game—which is beyond context or any specific activity. This is you at your essence, and what you're ultimately doing beneath any specific activity. In this way, I may define my Unique Ability as, "Connecting with truth, internalizing and being transformed by it, and teaching it in such a way that it transforms those who hear it."

Given that Unique Ability is at the core of who you are and thus highly personal, it requires extreme commitment and courage to connect with, develop, and utilize your Unique Ability.

If it doesn't feel like you're radically exposing yourself, then it's not Unique Ability.

If it's not transforming you rapidly, it's not Unique Ability.

If it doesn't feel like play and raw creativity, it's not Unique Ability.

If the rabbit hole doesn't go far down, it's not Unique Ability.

If you're not innovating, breaking rules, and changing boundaries for what "reality" means in a particular discipline or craft, then it's not Unique Ability.

The scariest and most exciting thing you'll ever do is be your truest self, holding nothing back, and with no apology. This is how you develop mastery in your Unique Ability.

What about you?

- What is your Unique Ability?

- What is the unique value you provide to others, which no one else can?

- What is the 10x jump that excites you most, which requires you go all-in on your Unique Ability to realize?

- What's the 80 percent of your life keeping you busy but unproductive, because it's keeping you outside your Unique Ability?

Create Transformational Relationships Where All Parties Are "The Buyer"

"The only man I know who behaves sensibly is my tailor; he takes my measurements anew each time he sees me. The rest go on with their old measurements and expect me to fit them."

— GEORGE BERNARD SHAW

When P-Rod was offered the initial sponsorship with Nike, he knew what he wanted. He wanted to have a signature pro-model shoe as part of the deal.

Even though getting a highly lucrative opportunity with Nike was a life-changing opportunity, if P-Rod didn't get that signature shoe as part of the deal, *he was happy to walk away.*

P-Rod knew what he wanted.

He wasn't desperate.

He was operating out of want, not need.

He was clear on the standards he held for himself, which *he* himself chose, irrespective of what anyone else thought or suggested.

Because P-Rod's Unique Ability as a skateboarder and artist was becoming so valuable, he was confident calling the shots in his life. He had that confidence. He knew what he brought to the equation. He knew what he could do. He knew there was no competition.

He'd gone 10x multiple times before.

He'd transformed himself and his life again and again—watching his Unique Ability become profound, undeniable, and exciting.

He was playing his own game.

He was playing the infinite game.

He was free.

He continually applied the 10x process to transform his life, evolve his Unique Ability, and expand his freedom. As a result, he could be increasingly "choosey" and selective about what worked for him and what didn't. He wasn't desperate to be in any partnerships or relationships, because he understood the value of his Unique Ability and he was operating based on want, not need.

This takes us one level further into Dan Sullivan's strategic mindsets, which he teaches only the highest level of entrepreneurs. This next concept is one Dan calls Always Be the Buyer.[24] There is a fundamental and crucial distinction between what Dan calls a "Buyer" or a "Seller."

Being the *Buyer* means you have clear standards for yourself, and you know what you want. The opposite is being a *Seller,* where you're desperate to be in a particular situation because you think you *need it.*

As the Seller, you'll twist yourself into uncomfortable shapes to be accepted. You're unclear on and uncommitted to your intrinsically crafted standards. You continually lower or change your standards to "get the sale."

In every social situation, you're either being a Buyer or a Seller.

The difference between a Buyer and a Seller is *the Buyer can walk away.*

The Buyer is not desperate to be there.

The Buyer is the one who does the rejecting, whereas the Seller is the one who gets rejected.

P-Rod was totally willing to walk away from Nike if he didn't get exactly what he wanted.

P-Rod was the Buyer.

Together, he and Nike formed a *transformational relationship* and collaboration that has now spanned 17 years, 10 signature shoes, and millions of sold pairs. Together, both P-Rod and Nike have innovated and evolved many times, expanding far beyond what they initially considered or planned when the partnership was formed.

The only reason they've continued to evolve and expand so much is because P-Rod was the Buyer. Had he been the Seller, he would have lost his confidence and conviction toward what he most wanted. This would have impacted everything he did, even his skating. Since how you do anything is how you do everything.

Once you allow yourself to be the Seller, then you're selling yourself short. You're letting some finite game define who you are and what you can do. You're being externally, not internally, driven. You're operating based on perceived need, not want.

To go 10x, you must be the Buyer.

Then, as the Buyer, you form transformational collaborations with other Buyers—wherein the whole becomes infinitely different and better than the sum of all parts.

As Dan Sullivan explains:

> "When you have a *buyer mindset,* you continually use your best learning from all of your experiences to create standards about what will be useful to your future and what won't be. You always want to be

upgrading your present based on the best standards you've created. There are always a lot of possibilities, and you have a bigger and better future plan, and that's why you have to use the standards you've built to determine the best opportunities, including who will be useful for you to collaborate with. Potential collaborators have to be resonant with where you've determined you're going and with how you're developing yourself out of higher levels of capability. Your bigger commitments are going to require courage, and while you're going through a stage that requires courage, you'll want to be in relationships with people who are also committed and in a courage stage— people who are always growing."[25]

In transformational relationships where everyone is the Buyer, payoffs are not necessarily equal for all parties, but the payoffs are uniquely exciting and 10x *from the perspective* of each person involved.

These types of relationships are "compelling offers" for all parties involved.

If being in the relationship isn't a compelling offer, one that offers 10x transformation and growth, then it's a no-go for a Buyer.

All participants bring different and unique value to the table. They are positioned differently and ultimately want different things from the collaboration. Trying to make the payoffs equal or "fair" is a transactional approach and fails to appreciate the uniqueness of each participant's individual context, vision, and desires.

You know a relationship is transformational when neither party feels they are losing, and neither party feels they are getting the "upper hand" in the deal.

When someone feels they are "losing," they're being a Seller.

In transformational relationships, *there are no losers.* Everyone wins in the ways they want, and no justification is required for what each party wants.

In these types of relationships, everyone wins *if the relationship continues* transforming from 10x jump to 10x jump. Everyone loses *if the relationship ends* because one or both parties shift from 10x to 2x. When momentum shifts to keeping things status quo, 10x transformation halts.

To requote Dr. James Carse in *Finite and Infinite Games*:

> "A finite game is played for the purpose of winning, an infinite game for the purpose of continuing the play. . . Finite players play *within* boundaries; infinite players *play with* boundaries. . . Only that which can change can continue."[26]

When you're in a finite game, you're *playing* the game.

When you're in the infinite game, you're continuously *changing* the game.

Being an infinite-player means you're striving to *continue playing* and transforming the game.

Only that which can *continue* can compound and grow exponentially.

Only that which can *change* can continue.

Only that which *effectively adapts* can successfully evolve and not be filtered-out.

Evolution and compounding go hand-in-hand.

If something comes to an end, then so do the compounding effects. The only way for something to continue, and thus experience compounding and transformational results, is by effectively evolving.

If something stops evolving, it will eventually stop compounding.

As Naval Ravikant said, "Play long-term games with long-term people. All returns in life, whether in wealth, relationships, or knowledge, come from compound interest."[27]

This is why the infinite game is so crucial.

Infinite players are continually transforming and elevating themselves and their Unique Ability based on want, not need. They then form 10x or 100x synergistic and compounding relationships that transform and elevate all parties in desired ways.

Chapter Takeaways

- Society trains people to believe freedom and creativity are scarce resources to compete for. This is not true because money is a finite resource, while wealth is an infinite resource.

- When you choose freedom over security, then you embrace a life where you choose exactly what you want, rather than vying for what you think you need.

- Living a life based on intrinsic wants enables an abundance mindset that allows you to create the wealth and life you want, without needing to justify to anyone why you want what you want.

- Living a life based on external needs enables a scarcity mindset that causes you to compete for the limited resources you believe you need. People who live based on need feel they have to justify their actions so that others will accept them.

- You must make a choice here and now: Will you continue living in the "needing" world where you must compete for scarce resources and justify everything you do, or will you embrace the "wanting" world where you freely choose, create, and get what you want?

- You can only go 10x by embracing a purely wanting approach to life, because 10x isn't inherently something anyone needs, but only something you can have if you choose the freedom to want and create it.

- Your Unique Ability is a central and core aspect of who you are, which can only be uncovered and developed by embracing what you most want.

- Your Unique Ability is the way in which you provide the most value for other people, which no one else could ever replicate even if they wanted to.

- Your Unique Ability is more valuable and exciting than any specific industry or skill, though it can be utilized effectively toward specific activities such as teaching, leading, strategizing, etc. Overly linking your Unique Ability to any single activity, such as teaching, will inhibit your ability to evolve both yourself and your Unique Ability to higher levels. Your Unique Ability is what drives your best and most exciting performance.

- Being in a flow state occurs when you embrace your Unique Ability because you're not overly editing yourself based on external approval, attachment to outcomes, etc. Instead, you're just purely free to be and do and create as you want and in the way you want. You're completely free and energized as a result and the byproduct is inspired creativity. This is also why and how you transform and expand your Unique Ability to otherworldly levels, wherein you become uniquely skilled and *masterful* at what you do.

- To become a true master at what you do, you can't merely be an expert at something. Expertise is the ability to do something well. *Mastery* is the ability to do something *uniquely well*. A master is someone who can never be replicated, they can only be learned from. Embracing your Unique Ability is how you develop Mastery as a person, and become the highest and most genuine version of yourself.

- When you embrace and take your Unique Ability seriously, you immediately remove yourself from ever competing with anyone again. You appreciate the truth that you and everyone else are unique individuals who can never be replicated. Rather than trying to be like other people, your objective becomes to peel away the layers impeding you from being the most expansive and evolved version of yourself—the "David."

- Your Unique Ability is never a finished product and evolves dramatically with each 10x jump you make.

- Letting go of the 80 percent and fully embracing the 20 percent that most excites (and most scares) you will take you much closer to your Unique Ability.

- As you develop your Unique Ability to profound levels, you'll have increased freedom to dictate the situations and opportunities in your life.

Rather than desperately being in situations you don't truly want, you only embrace the situations and opportunities where your Unique Ability *is valued*, but also, where your Unique Ability *can be most transformed and expanded.*

* To get additional resources on clarifying and developing your Unique Ability, visit www.10xeasierbook.com

PART 2

10x
APPLICATIONS

CHAPTER 4

UNCOVER YOUR 10x PAST TO CLARIFY YOUR 10x FUTURE

You've Done It Before and You'll Do It Again

"You can't connect the dots looking forward, you can only connect them looking backwards. So, you have to trust that the dots will somehow connect in your future. You have to trust in something: your gut, destiny, life, karma, whatever. Because believing that the dots will connect down the road will give you the confidence to follow your heart, even when it leads you off the well-worn path."

—STEVE JOBS[1]

While writing this book, I asked my friends, family, and clients to read the early drafts.

One friend, a relatively small entrepreneur, mentor, and dear friend of mine, told me that he loved the concepts but ultimately, he didn't believe the book was for him. "I'm not looking for the level of transformation and commitment you're describing in this book, Ben. I guess I prefer 2x over 10x as a way of life."

I saluted this dear friend of mine, agreeing that this book is *not for everyone*. And that's completely fine. 10x as a way of life may not be for you. If you've made it this far into this book, you're probably clear whether 10x is for you.

Or maybe you're still on the fence.

If the idea of 10x perplexes or discourages you, continue reading. This chapter will help.

Another one of my friends who read the first 100 pages while the book was still a rough draft was both inspired and frustrated by what he read. It's not that he disagreed with the premise. On the contrary, he said the concept of 10x was actually incredibly clear and simple.

The concept frustrated him because he realized he wanted to live a 10x life—but to do so, he'd need to make some serious changes. He'd need to completely alter the trajectory of his career.

Here's what he said when I asked what he thought of the book:

> "I come at it from two different places: my personal life and my career. For me personally, the concept of 10x is inspiring and I feel like something I could really get behind to improve my life and my relationships. I particularly appreciate how you frame it as qualitative rather than quantitative. It's not about the numbers but how you fundamentally transform. But from the view of a middle manager at a Fortune 500, publicly traded company, I can't help but be completely frustrated. Not by your writing or

the 10x concept itself, but from the complete imprac-
ticality of actually trying to implement it from where
I sit. There are so many layers of bureaucracy that
make change in a large organization so difficult. So
really what I take from reading those first 100 pages is
another nudging that I need to make a career shift. I
just haven't been able to figure out what I would like
to shift to. Coming full circle, I need to better define
what I want."

To be clear, this book was written with *high-level entrepreneurs* in mind, who not only have a great deal of freedom in
their lives but also who continually seek and create greater
freedom in their lives and trajectories.

10x is fundamentally about freedom.

The freedom to be, live, and create what you want and
how you want.

Freedom obviously isn't free. It requires extreme self-
honesty, commitment, and courage. It requires peeling away
the layers of fear and attachment that would keep you 2x
and living a life based on need, not want. It takes owning
the consequences of your wins and losses, as well as the
consequences of not being understood by many of those
around you.

Therefore, my friend, who is not an entrepreneur, isn't
the directly intended audience of this book. That said, my
response to him is the same as if I was talking to a high-level
entrepreneur: *Wherever you are now, going 10x from here will
require a total remodeling of both yourself and your business.*

You can't go 10x with the same model you have now.
This includes not only your business and strategic model but
also your mental models and identity as well.

Going 10x will transform everything in your life if you
fully embrace it.

If you want to 10x, you have to radically change 80 percent of your life. This is a scary thought.

How could you mentally survive such a sacrifice?

In our book *The Gap and The Gain*, Dan Sullivan and I present a counterintuitive mindset shift that makes letting go of your 80 percent not only possible, but fun.

If you stay stuck in what Dan calls "the gap," 10x won't be an enjoyable experience for you. 10x will actually be detrimental to your mental and physical well-being, as well as all of your relationships, if you say in the gap.

You may be able to go 10x a time or two while in the gap. But frankly, you'll be a shell of who you could have become, because the gap keeps you living for external rewards, rather than your intrinsic desires. It keeps you chasing, not living. It keeps you feeling awful about yourself, not confident and with momentum.

Only by learning to live and embrace "the gain" will 10x become a truly enjoyable and ongoing journey for you. But not only that, by being in the gain, you'll also take far more from *every experience* you have in life—the good, bad, and ugly. You'll learn to take every experience and *turn it to your gain* such that you're constantly and quickly getter *better and wiser*, and never plateauing.

After helping you more fully understand the difference between the gap and the gain, and why being in the gain is vital for living a 10x life, this chapter will help you recontextualize your past from a gain perspective. Specifically, you'll learn a simple technique for better seeing and appreciating the 10x jumps *you've already made* as a person and entrepreneur to get where you are now.

After helping you frame your previous 10x jumps, we will then dive into two powerful models that will help you clarify, in extreme specificity and excitement, the next 10x jumps you want to make. By clarifying your next 10x jumps, you'll also clarify where you want to more fully develop and transform your Unique Ability.

Let's begin.

The Gap and The Gain

"Your level of capability in the future depends upon your measurement of achievements in the past. You can't move forward and grow until you've acknowledged how far you've come and have properly measured your gains."

—DAN SULLIVAN[2]

While leading a Strategic Coach workshop over 25 years ago—in the mid 1990s—Dan Sullivan made an important realization. He noticed that despite having objectively achieved a lot over the previous 3–12 months, many of his entrepreneurial clients *de-valued* that progress. Said another way, they were dissatisfied and even emotionally negative toward what they'd accomplished.

One client in particular was so negative that Dan came up with a model that became *The Gap and The Gain*. Dan was asking the group of entrepreneurs to reflect on and discuss the progress they'd made personally and as a business the previous 90 days, since their last workshop.

This client was insistent that *absolutely nothing* positive had occurred since they'd last met.

"Nothing?" Dan asked.

"Yes, absolutely nothing," the man replied.

"Well didn't you say you'd gotten a new client, and that your team was working on some important projects?"

"Yes, but that stuff doesn't matter because we missed a lot of opportunities we should have had. We should be a lot further along than we are now."

This man was in the gap.

The gap is a lens by which you measure *what is* against what *could be*. In the gap, you're measuring what is against what you believe *should be*.

When you're in the gap, you're measuring yourself or your situation against an ideal.

This happens so much that it's the conventional mode of operating for most people. Take for example, my children, who come to the dinner table when it's time to eat. Sometimes they'll get to the table and let out a huge sigh of disappointment that dinner isn't something else.

Rather than appreciating the meal mom worked hard to make, and the fact that they have a nice home, a nice family, and a warm dinner to eat, they *devalue the whole experience* because they're measuring it against some arbitrary ideal in their mind.

Now, let me be really clear, because this is a highly nuanced yet simple idea, which can be easily misunderstood.

Being in *the gain*—which we will go into more in a moment—isn't simply about being grateful for what you have and where you are. Despite not *being* gratitude, being in the gain does trigger an enormous amount of gratitude among other things, including confidence, wisdom, inspiration, and excitement.

The gap and the gain aren't about gratitude or lack of gratitude.

Being in either the gap or the gain is purely about *how you're measuring* yourself and your experiences. I'll detail the effects of measuring yourself in the gap first, then explain the positively transformative effects of measuring yourself (and everything else) in the gain.

Dan's client was measuring himself, his life, his wife, and his business against an ideal in his mind. He was upset and frustrated that he wasn't where he thought he *should be*. By measuring himself against his ideal, not only was he devaluing where he currently was, but he was also devaluing his entire past.

When you're in the gap, then your past becomes a problem. It becomes a nightmare because your past isn't what it *should have been*.

You're not where you "should" be as a person.

Having a problematic past doesn't support creating a bigger future. On the contrary, having negative energy, emotions, and created meaning about your past only perpetuates the fact that your future won't be any different.

Not surprisingly, this client's gap mindset ended up corroding and destroying everything he claimed mattered to him, leading to his inevitable divorce and loss of ambition. Eventually, chasing ideals stops being fun when you've made it your habit to measure yourself against them, feeling the burden again and again (and again. . .) of never being enough.

When my children were upset about the dinner on the table, they were *measuring their experience* against an ideal in their mind. As a result, they not only devalued the benefit they'd just received, but they were also worse-off emotionally for having gotten dinner.

That's the disturbing part of being in the gap. You've technically made progress but you feel worse as a result, because of the framing you've placed on that progress— measuring it against what it *should be*.

You can be in the gap about *anything*, and usually people who tend to be in the gap are in the gap *a lot*. Perhaps the most destructive form the gap can take is when you're in the gap about other people, wherein you only see where those who support you—like your employees—are not *measuring up*.

While writing *The Gap and The Gain*, this point particularly hit me hard. I'm a father of six kids and I realized how often I'm in the gap about my kids, especially the ones we adopted a few years back through the foster system. When I'm in the gap about my kids, I'm measuring them against ideals for where I think they should be. Most sadly, though, when I'm in the gap about my kids, I'm not seeing all the ways they've actually grown and progressed—either short-term or long-term—which are substantial.

By putting my kids in the gap, not only do I devalue them, but I teach them to devalue themselves. I teach them that their success and happiness are an unreachable ideal, which they can forever pursue but will never indeed realize.

Measuring yourself against ideals is a losing battle, even for the most positive and idealistic among us. The reason is simple: ideals aren't stable. They're constantly changing based on where you're presently at.

Ideals are like the horizon in the desert.

No matter how many steps you take toward the horizon, it continues extending out ahead of you.

When you're measuring yourself against ideals, it's like measuring yourself against the moving horizon and then being mad at yourself for not being at the horizon.

News flash: *You can't ever reach the horizon.*

Similarly, you can't reach your ideals because no matter how far you go, your ideals will always stretch way, way beyond where you're now at.

This doesn't mean you shouldn't have ideals. It doesn't mean ideals aren't useful. On the contrary, ideals are incredibly useful for providing direction to set spatial and specific goals to progress toward.

However, even after you've set clear, specific, and measurable goals, it's still easy to go into the gap. You can go in the gap if you *didn't* hit the goal, measuring your progress against the target and feeling like a loser for not having "succeeded." You can also go into the gap if you *did* hit the target, measuring your progress against some different ideal beyond or different from the target itself.

Both are destructive.

Both are painful.

Both corrode the joy you could experience by being in the gain.

Fundamentally, the gap is an *unhealthy need* you've placed on something outside of yourself to avoid facing the truth within.

When you're in the gap, you think *you need* the ideal—you *need* that new car, *need* that deal, *need* that new client, *need* the weather to be better, that bestseller, etc. etc. etc.

No matter how much you achieve or consume, if you're in the gap, your endless "needing" won't go away. It will only get worse. The gap can never be satisfied externally even though you may spend your life chasing that mirage.

Take, for example, the actor Matthew Perry who starred as Chandler Bing in the television show *Friends*. In his memoir, *Friends, Lovers, and the Big Terrible Thing*, Perry describes his lifetime of chasing fame, women, alcohol, and drugs to ultimately fill a gap inside. As he describes:

> "I was pretty sure fame would change everything, and I yearned for it more than any other person on the face of the planet. I *needed* it. It was the only thing that would fix me. I was certain of it. . . But the magic never lasts; whatever holes you're filling seem to keep opening back up. (It's like Whac-A-Mole.) Maybe it was because I was always trying to fill a spiritual hole with a material thing."[3]

Being in the gap, like any addiction, is a sickness. Entrepreneurs may experience a lifetime of achievement, yet their self-confidence will decrease with every win. Many successful people who adopt this mindset take extreme measures to numb their pain.

Spoiler alert: *The gain is the antidote.* But we'll get to that in a second.

If you stay in the gap, going for 10x will be traumatic. Instead of being motivated by your goals, your goals will burn you out.

Hilariously, many gap-minded entrepreneurs rationalize their mindset, saying it's *the reason* they're successful. Because they're "never satisfied," they're always stretching and reaching for more. All the while, they miss the point that they're missing the point. Usually not until after it's too late do they realize they paid too heavy a price to continually chase their ideals, missing this moment *right here and right now*.

Does this mean you shouldn't go for 10x?

Does this mean you should let go of all ambitions and goals?

Although that's the knee-jerk reaction and conclusion many come to—that you should just let go of goals, dreams, and 10x altogether—that's not what being in the gain is about.

Letting go of your dreams isn't the answer.

Your life will be bleak and purposeless without massive and stretching 10x goals and meanings to fulfill.

So, then what does it mean to be in the gain?

And how can you possibly have both—where you're stretching and transforming toward huge dreams yet fully happy and satisfied with where you now are?

Again, it all comes down to how you measure yourself and your experiences.

The gap is a reactive and external approach to measuring yourself and your experiences.

The gain is a proactive, creative, and internal approach to measuring yourself and your experiences.

When you're in the gain, you're never measuring yourself against anything external. You're only measuring yourself against yourself. More directly, you're measuring yourself against where you were before.

While in the gain, you have ideals as well as clear and specific goals you're stretching toward—*even 10x goals*. But you're not measuring yourself against those ideals or even against your goals. Instead, you're *only measuring yourself backward* against where and who you were before.

As Dan states:

> "The only way to measure the distance you've traveled is by measuring from where you are back to the point where you started, not from where you are toward the horizon."[4]

By measuring yourself backward, you're actually seeing and appreciating your progress, which is your own. By seeing and appreciating your progress, you feel enormously better and clearer on who you are and where you're at.

This feeling of confidence and momentum is essential to going 10x. It helps you keep proper perspective of where you're at and what's going on. The truth is, you're making far more progress than it sometimes feels like. Regularly reflecting on, appreciating, and measuring that progress immediately *lightens the weight* of 10x. It boosts you forward on your best and worst days.

But there's something deeper than merely recognizing and measuring your progress regularly. By regularly measuring yourself backward, you begin to view your past differently. You begin to see "wins" and gains you normally wouldn't consider "progress." You start to glean more from your experiences, the good and bad. You squeeze more juice out of your experiences because while in the gain, you're the one defining what your experiences mean.

While in the gap, your experiences are driving you. If things aren't how you ideally want them to be, then you're the victim.

In the gain, you're antifragile. Everything happens for you, not to you. Every experience has something to offer. Every moment you learn and become better, not bitter as a result.

Regularly refencing your own progress also helps you truly embrace your own game in life. You're not competing with anyone. You're on your own unique path. You're having your own unique experiences and converting those experiences into new insights, standards, and growth.

Loads of research in psychology and neuroscience backs up Dan's gain concept. I'll list just a few:

- **Research shows that happiness and positive emotions—especially gratitude—lead to more creative thinking, better decision making, higher performance, and self-determination.** [5,6,7,8,9,10,11,12] Being in the gain radically boosts positive emotions, gratitude, and appreciation. The emotional signature of the gain is *dopamine* (i.e., happiness, motivation, and excitement). The emotional signature of the gap is *cortisol* (i.e., stress and frustration) which hurts performance.

- **Research shows that confidence is the byproduct of past successes, more than the cause of future success.** [13] Being in the gain continually boosts your confidence by allowing you to reference your progress. While in the gap, you don't and can't appreciate the progress you've already made. You can't see where you're now at because you're referencing yourself against continually adjusting external criteria. Only by measuring backward against a clear starting point can you see not only how you got to where you're at but also where you're now at. By clarifying and appreciating your progress, your confidence increases, which boosts your imagination and motivation to see and create more gains.

- **Research shows that highly hopeful and motivated people continually take feedback from not achieving their goals to iterate**

or adjust their pathway forward.[14,15] High-hope people take *every experience* they have as a learning opportunity—no matter the experience. Everything happens *for* them, not *to* them. They utilize every experience to improve how they live and approach life. This is pathways thinking, which is taking every experience you have and using it for learning and iteration. Every experience is a perpetual goldmine filled with more and more lessons.

Practicing a gain mindset is very simple. At the end of each day, you could write down three "wins" you had that day. Those wins could be things you learned (even from things that didn't go well). They could be literal progress you made toward your goals, even if it was minor progress. It could be experiences you had, such as spending time with your kids.

Whatever you focus on expands.

Whatever you see, you create more of.

By focusing on the gains in your life, you'll begin to feel like you're always winning. You'll begin to see and create more gains from every day and every experience. Consequently, you'll be able to create more gains from every day.

You can measure your gains for all different timeframes. Here are a few questions you could reflect on simply to get yourself into the gain:

- How have you grown as a person over the past three years?

- What are the biggest things you've learned in the past 12 months?

- What are 10 important things you've accomplished in the past 12 months?

- What meaningful experiences have you had in the past 90 days?

- How are you clearer on your goals and vision than you were 90 days ago?

- In what ways is your life different and better than it was 30 days ago?

- What important progress have you made the past seven days?

- What progress have you made in the past 24 hours?

No matter where you're currently at in your 10x process, you're making gains. You're making more gains than you actually realize. Regularly referencing your gains enables you to see and feel that progress. Taking ownership of your experiences also enables you to transform your experiences into more gains. By learning more from every experience you have, you'll stop repeating needless errors. You'll never plateau as a person.

Even if externally it appears you've gone backward, like Dan going bankrupt and getting divorced on the same day, you can turn any experience into a gain. In the gain, rather than being the victim to your experiences and situations, you gratefully learn from every experience and get better.

Even something truly terrible could happen—you get hit by a car and become paralyzed. You lose a loved one. Or like the Biblical prophet Job, you seemingly lose everything. All of these things can be for your experience, profit, and learning.

Turning seeming losses into gains is how you grow and evolve as a person. Once again, humans have an extreme aversion to loss. It's why we hold on to our 80 percent far longer than we should. Rather than feeling a "loss" whenever you proactively let go of the 80 percent, whatever that may be, now you can better recognize it *as a gain*.

You're letting go of something that once brought you value but no longer does so you can now make room for something better.

Every time you let go of the 80 percent, *you're gaining massively.*

A friend recently told me that he'd let go of alcohol as part of his 80 percent that no longer fit his 10x future self. He didn't see letting go of alcohol as a loss, but a *huge* gain.

I believe this perspective of "gaining" by letting go is important because I've often seen people overly dramatize and ritualize the letting go of their past identity, past successes, certain activities, or even addictions.

Instead, just embrace the reality that you're taking a *major step forward* by letting this thing go—even if it's something amazing, like a lucrative aspect of your business. It's literally holding you back at this point! Go forth, my friend, into your 20 percent and let's see how insane your 10x transformation can be!

When you're in the gain, *everything* happens for you.

You become antifragile.

Every experience is valuable.

You continually learn from every experience.

You're always getting better, always learning, always taking nuggets from even the most mundane.

You've Gone 10x Before: Review Your 10x Jumps and the "20 Percent" of Those Jumps

"Time travel backward to the point in your life where you made only one-tenth of what you're making now. Looking back, could you ever have imagined being where you are right now? Probably not. Just as you probably can't imagine going 10x in the future. But look at your past, and you can see that you've already done it at least once. And you can do it again."

—DAN SULLIVAN[16]

Now that we've laid out some of the groundwork of the gain, it's time to review and reframe your past to better appreciate all the times you've gone 10x before.

By seeing 10x more clearly in your own past, you'll also be able to more clearly see it in your future.

You've gone 10x many times.

Anytime you've committed to something you wanted and transformed through that commitment, *you went 10x*. You made a fundamental and qualitative upgrade that permanently expanded your freedoms and agency.

When you went from crawling to walking, *you went 10x*. You committed and transformed yourself. You can look back and see that at one point, you weren't able to do something and then you made the transformation.

When you learned how to speak, *you went 10x*.

When you learned how to read, *you went 10x*.

When you learned how to make friends, *you went 10x*.

Anytime you committed to something beyond what you'd done and transformed through that commitment, *you went 10x*.

Learning to drive a car (or fly a plane) is a 10x jump.

Becoming an entrepreneur is a 10x jump.

Anytime you go 10x, you no longer operate as the same person you did prior to the 10x. You've altered your identity, mental models, and way of being. You've expanded your Unique Ability.

As a powerful exercise, take some time to reflect back on your previous 10x jumps. Also, reflect on the *core 20 percent* of each of those jumps—the things that remained when you were one-tenth of where you're at now. Also reflect on the 80 percent you let go of in each jump you made.

By clarifying the 20 percent in each stage, you'll see how you've continually refined your Unique Ability to create 10x freedoms in your life.

I'll provide a few of my last 10x jumps as an example.

Committing to serve a two-year church mission was a 10x jump for me. I left on that mission in 2008, and it took almost two years to get myself to a place where I was ready to go.

My 20 percent for this 10x jump of getting on my mission was letting go of the trauma and pain of my past, connecting with my own future, connecting to God, and living my life based on my own standards and decisions rather than succumbing to my current situation or peer group.

My 80 percent for this 10x jump was anything and everything that took me away from that 20 percent. Specifically, my 80 percent was holding on to the grudge and anger against my parents for decisions or mistakes they'd made, many of my high school friends, and all other addictions or distractions that were keeping me 2x at that stage in my life, such as video games.

After returning from that mission, which transformed my life forever, my next 10x jump was getting into Brigham Young University. Given that I'd barely graduated high school before my mission and had no college credits, this was an unrealistic or "impossible" goal, just as getting on my mission was unrealistic considering what I went through in my childhood. BYU is as competitive as many Ivy League universities. You need straight As and elite test scores. I started at Salt Lake Community College in 2010 with the commitment of attending BYU.

My 20 percent for getting into BYU was becoming an excellent student, taking full responsibility for my results and grades, learning how to navigate systems and politics, and increasing my commitment to my own goals and standards, rather than getting stuck and content with where I was, which is 2x.

My 80 percent for this 10x jump was defaulting to old habits, not taking my work and grades seriously, letting my friends dictate my direction, and peer pressure from my employers and others to stay where I was at.

When I got to BYU in the Fall of 2011, my next 10x was getting married and getting into a PhD program to better my understanding and mastery of psychology—advancing my life and career.

The 20 percent was becoming the type of person who could identify and attract my 10x life partner, Lauren, as well as learning psychology and philosophy at an extremely high level. It also became important to learn how to write and research at a PhD level.

The first time I applied to graduate school, I got rejected by 15 different programs. I turned this into a major gain by looking in the mirror and committing to get better, rather than being bitter as a victim.

My commitment to learning and getting better enabled me to find a young professor who became one of my greatest friends and mentors, Dr. Nate Lambert. Nate taught me how to research and write with confidence—skills I'm still using to write this book. Together, Nate and I submitted over 15 academic papers for publication, which easily enabled me to get into the best PhD program for me—organizational psychology at Clemson University.

Once at Clemson in the Fall of 2014, my next 10x was growing our family, completing my PhD, and becoming a professional author. Specifically, I committed to getting a six-figure book contract from a major publisher. This was my *keystone goal*—the one outcome I believed would create much of the freedom and opportunity I wanted. Achieving this one goal would enable me to provide for my family doing what I loved.

The 20 percent of this 10x was overcoming my fears and anxieties of sharing my ideas and writing publicly, learning to write effectively, learning to write virally, and learning how to build a massive audience and email list of people who wanted more of my writing.

I started blogging online in Spring of 2015 and wrote hundreds of blog posts. Over the next 18 months, my blogs were read by tens of millions of people and I grew my email list to over 100,000 people. In February of 2017, I got a $220,000 book deal from Hachette, one of the Big-5 New York publishers. *Willpower Doesn't Work,* my first major book, was published in March of 2018. One month earlier, in February of 2018, Lauren and I were granted adoption of the three children we'd been fostering the previous three years. Lauren also gave birth to twin girls in December of 2018. In April of 2019, I completed my PhD.

I'm writing these words near the end of 2022 and have gone 10x again since completing my PhD three and a half years ago. Since completing my PhD, I've published five bestselling books, including three with Dan Sullivan. I've 10xed the amount of money I invest toward retirement. Lauren and I have 10xed our emotional development and maturity toward our children.

My 80 percent of the past three and a half years has been letting go of people-pleasing, saying "Yes" to opportunities or situations I already know aren't interesting to me, and needing to be right. I've also let go of needing to always be productive. I've embraced recovery and relaxing, and slowing time down.

That brings me to the *current 10x jump I'm still in the middle of,* which I've been in the past year or so. My 10x process right now is focused on becoming an amazing and loving husband and father to my six children, writing 10x better and more impactful books that sell millions of copies, and 10xing my financial freedom.

This is what I personally want.

Other people's opinions of my 10x goals don't really matter.

This doesn't mean I don't listen. It doesn't mean I'm locked-in and inflexible, or unchangeable. It simply means that I want what I want.

The same is true for you.

You get to choose the 10x process and focus you most want in your life, based on the standards and freedoms you want to experience for yourself.

You don't have to justify your 10x dreams.

At every 10x stage, there is a 20 percent you're to focus on and master and an 80 percent that will stop at nothing to keep you where you're at.

At each 10x stage, the 20 percent will stack and build upon each 20 percent of your previous 10x stages. Your Unique Ability will continue to develop, often in non-linear and surprising ways.

At each 10x level, your life will get better and freer, yet the 80 percent will not go away, it will only be different. You'll be tempted and even pressured to shift from 10x to 2x, wherein you allow the continually spawning 80 percent to distract you from going all-in on the next 20 percent.

Now it's your turn:

- Identify five of your past 10x jumps.

- Give each of your previous 10x jumps a name and a timeline. For example, mine could be named: Getting on the mission (2006-2008), getting into BYU (2010-2011), getting married and into a PhD program (2011-2014), growing my family and becoming a well-paid professional author (2014-2019), 10xing as an author and evolving emotionally as a person (2019-present).

- Clarify the 20 percent of each of your 10x jumps, as well as the 80 percent that you let go of at each level.

- As you reflect on the 20 percent of each 10x jump you've made, reflect on how that 20 percent helped you further develop your Unique Ability.

Make mapping your previous 10x jumps a habit. Review and further contextualize them regularly. As you study and expand your past, you'll learn more and more from it, which will better enable you to clarify your 10x future.

Staying in the gain is essential fuel, perspective, and happiness that will not only carry you forward on your 10x quests, but it will also ensure you're making the *right* 10x jumps moving forward. By "right" 10x jumps, I mean the 10x jumps that you *most want*, rather than seeking what society, culture, social media, or anyone else has trained you to think you want or need.

Being in the gain supports living the life you want, and it helps you appreciate where you are now. You can continue advancing 10x as you want, but you don't need 10x to be happy or worthy.

You're in the gain. You're already happy and worthy.

Continuing to go 10x and transform your Unique Ability will simply enrich the happiness you already have.

As Thich Nhat Hahn said, *"There is no way to happiness— happiness is the way."*

Take a deep breath.

Exhale.

You're in the gain.

You're making amazing progress.

You're exactly where you should be.

Measuring your gains enables you to frame your past effectively. It also enables you to make your past more concrete and measurable—where you can actually see and appreciate all the progress and growth you've made. You're not the same person you were even last week.

By reflecting on your gains and valuing your progress, you're now in a better place to *think forward* about the next 10x jumps you want to make. For the remainder of this chapter, we will dive into two specific ways you can begin conceptualizing your next 10x jump.

The first is a concept known as "fitness function"—which helps you get hyper-clear and specific about who you want to become.

The second concept is a classic tool Dan Sullivan uses to help his entrepreneurs envision 10x, which is imagining your "Dream Check." Both of these applications—fitness function and Dream Check—will help you better clarify your next 20 percent focus, and where you will use your Unique Ability.

Define Your "Fitness Function"— You Become What You Focus On

"The biggest understanding and capability you gain from transforming your past experiences into lessons is being able to define your standards. You know what's acceptable and what's unacceptable, and this knowledge is what matters most. You create powerful filters of high personal standards by which you determine which ongoing experiences are best for growth."

—DAN SULLIVAN

In computer and evolutionary sciences, *fitness function* means clarifying the qualities and measurement of a specific objective. Put simply, fitness function clarifies *what you're optimizing for*—your chosen standards—and the "fitness" or developmental path required to live those standards.

This is vitally important, and understanding fitness function will enable you to better clarify your 20 percent and next-level Unique Ability. It helps you get highly specific about *what you want*, as well as the specific growth and value you'll experience.

Fitness function is similar to looking at the direction and destination of an airplane. A slight tweak in direction—even a few degrees different—over a long enough period of time leads to massive differences. Even being *one degree off* for a long enough period of time will lead you hundreds or thousands of miles away from your desired destination.

The famed German pilot Dieter Utchdorf has explained this principle with the tragic 1979 plane crash in Antarctica. It was a large passenger jet with 257 people on board that left New Zealand for a sightseeing flight to Antarctica and back. As Utchdorf explains:

"Unknown to the pilots, however, someone had modified the flight coordinates by a mere two degrees. This error placed the aircraft 28 miles (45 km) to the east of where the pilots assumed they were. As they approached Antarctica, the pilots descended to a lower altitude to give the passengers a better look at the landscape. Although both were experienced pilots, neither had made this particular flight before, and they had no way of knowing that the incorrect coordinates had placed them directly in the path of Mount Erebus, an active volcano that rises from the frozen landscape to a height of more than 12,000 feet (3,700 m). As the pilots flew onward, the white of the snow and ice covering the volcano blended with the white of the clouds above, making it appear as though they were flying over flat ground. By the time the instruments sounded the warning that the ground was rising fast toward them, it was too late. The airplane crashed into the side of the volcano, killing everyone on board. It was a terrible tragedy brought on by a minor error—a matter of only a few degrees."[17]

Similar to airplanes, but with even greater implications, your fitness function points in the direction you're ultimately going and simultaneously who you're ultimately *becoming*. Even a slight tweak in direction and destination will lead you to become a radically different person than you would have been.

The details matter here.

Your own fitness function will be unique to you, because what you most want and the specific standards by which you define success are also unique to you.

By defining your fitness function, you'll know where to focus your energy. You'll know the 20 percent to go all-in on. And you'll know when you're being successful.

No one else has the exact same goals or standards you do. Therefore, measuring yourself against someone else's results or standards is a losing game because you're not ultimately optimizing for the same thing. You're not playing the same game . . .

Your standards aren't the same as anyone else's.

Your objective isn't the same.

Your Unique Ability and calling aren't the same.

There is no external competition.

Therefore, measuring yourself against someone else's results and standards is a sure path to becoming average or good, but never uniquely great, one-of-a-kind, and world-class. You can't beat someone else at being them, just like someone else cannot beat you at being you.

The scariest and most courageous thing you'll ever do is to be yourself.

I'm still learning this lesson, as I often find myself measuring and comparing myself with other authors. Yet, in a recent conversation with my friend and artificial intelligence expert and entrepreneur Howard Getson, I was reminded that *my* fitness function (what I'm optimizing for—my Unique Ability and calling) is radically different than those other authors'. What they're going for and what I'm going for are totally different, especially in terms of who we're becoming.

Sure, we may use similar metrics like book sales to measure our progress. But if "book sales" was purely the fitness function of what I was going for, I'd most certainly be writing different books. So, number of books sold *isn't* my primary fitness function, though it's certainly part of what I'm optimizing for.

My fitness function is different from anyone else's and highly specific.

So is yours.

What are you ultimately going for?

What are you "optimizing" for?

What level of capability and results do you want to develop and master?

What are the standards you want to refine and actualize?

Defining your fitness function is as simple as defining the specific standards or criteria you want to grow into. The criteria you feel called to and want to create.

The more specific your fitness function, the more specialized, nuanced, and valuable you will become.

Your agency as a person is based on what you choose to develop yourself into.

We all will become someone.

It's your responsibility to define what you want and to direct your focus and attention toward that.

Your fitness function is your filter. It filters not only what's important and what's not important. It also filters *what you see* and what you don't see—your *selective attention.*[18,19]

As you clarify the specific 10x transformation you want, that 10x becomes your filter of the world. Over time as you get more committed to it, you not only become more optimized and specialized for that particular thing, *but you also begin filtering everything else out.*

The economic term for this is *opportunity cost.*

The evolutionary or biological term for this is *atrophy.*

You *will* atrophy and become increasingly unaware in the areas outside your filter.

By getting committed to something specific—a chosen fitness function—you become an increasingly specific and unique type of person. You stop seeing, noticing, and paying attention to anything that isn't relevant to your perceptual filter.

Whatever you focus on *expands*.

Whatever you focus on, *you create more of.*

Whatever you focus on, *you become*.

Whatever you focus on, you develop a finer, more nuanced, and more specific understanding of. As author Robert Kiyosaki stated, "Intelligence is the ability to make finer distinctions."[20]

"Finer distinctions" describes a finer and more nuanced understanding of a particular thing. The more you pay attention to and focus on something, the finer the distinctions you develop for that particular thing. Take football, for example. Someone who is merely a casual fan watching a game isn't watching the same game as someone who really understands the game.

The person who understands the game will see far more nuance and meaning—*finer distinctions*—within every facet of the game than the casual watcher. They'll recognize important subtleties that the casual observer won't notice, such as whether or not the left tackle on one team is the starter or the backup. The implications of even the seemingly smallest details will be gargantuan to the person making finer distinctions. The person with greater understanding sees and understands the situation more systemically, recognizing that even small tweaks to even small individual parts can create massive and non-linear changes to the overall whole.

The scientific term for this level of systemic thinking is the *Butterfly Effect*, a concept initially developed by mathematician and meteorologist Edward Norton Lorenz, who used the analogy of the exact time and path of a tornado being influenced by minor vibrations such as a distant butterfly flapping its wings several weeks earlier.[21,22,23,24]

Seeing finer distinctions is the difference between high definition and low definition—the difference between mastery and excellence, or less. One has far more detail and precision. But also, one has unique angles and connections made through study and commitment, whereas the other person only has a surface-level perspective.

Consider driving: When you first learn, your conscious mind is required to pay extreme attention to each little aspect, such as signaling when changing lanes. But as you drive more and more, you group multiple aspects of driving together in your memory such that you can unconsciously perform literally hundreds of individual tasks at the same time. The parts have integrated into a new whole.

When viewing a particular situation—such as a car accident—the experienced driver has a better understanding of what may have occurred than a newbie driver who will have a surface-level and likely inaccurate understanding of the what and why of a particular situation.

The author and learning expert Josh Waitzkin describes this idea of finer distinctions and developing a more granular and systemic level of mastery in his book *The Art of Learning.*[25]

Josh grew up a chess prodigy and went on to become a chess champion. He then shifted his interests to various forms of martial arts, wherein he also went on to become world champion.

"Making Smaller Circles" is how Josh describes cultivating finer distinctions—which is a process of zooming further and further into something. The better you understand and experience something, the more your brain chunks your understanding together with other things. The psychological term for this is *automaticity* and it's how you go from consciously doing something to mastering it on the unconscious level.[26,27]

As Josh describes:

"Most people would be surprised to discover that if you compare the thought process of a Grandmaster to that of an expert (a much weaker, but quite competent chess player), you will often find that the Grandmaster consciously looks at less, not more. That said, the chunks of information that have been put together in his mind allow him to see much more with much less conscious thought. So he is looking at very little and seeing quite a lot. . . Now think of me, Josh, competing against a less refined martial artist. Let's say I am in the process of instigating a throw that involves six technical steps. My opponent will experience an indecipherable flurry of action, while for me the six external steps of the throw are just the outer rim of a huge network of chunks. Our realities are very different. I am 'seeing' much more than he is seeing. . . Experientially, because I am looking at less, there are, within the same unit of time, hundreds of frames in my mind, and maybe only a few for my opponent (whose conscious mind is bogged down with much more data that has not yet been internalized as unconsciously accessible). I can now operate in all those frames that he doesn't even see."

What does all of this have to do with 10x and clarifying your 20 percent?

Put bluntly, as a person, *you are now in the process of becoming someone specific.* You are optimizing for *something*—whatever your standards are—even if that something isn't well defined or intentioned. You're making finer distinctions and developing expertise in whatever you're focusing on. In our world of distraction, many people are developing finer distinctions and expertise in random things like celebrities' lives, video games, etc.

Whatever you focus on expands.

Whatever you focus on, you develop finer distinctions in.

Whatever you focus on, you create more of.

Whatever you focus on, you become in an increasingly specific way to the exclusion of all else.

The number one goal of life is developing mastery in your Unique Ability and thus living out your unique calling and purpose at the highest possible level. There is no end or ultimate "arrival" to this process. It's a continuing process of developing higher value and quality of freedom in all key areas, and doing so in your own unique way.

The more specific you get in what you want, the clearer will be the 20 percent rabbit hole you go down.

Whatever you pay most attention to becomes your filter to the world. Your attention filters what you see and what you don't see. It also reflects who you will *eventually become.*

Your continued focus develops extremely fine distinctions and expertise in whatever you commit yourself to. Thus, in defining your 10x, you want to be as specific as possible about how you define and measure success (i.e., your "standards").

Your standards will be your own.

Your 10x transformation will also be your own.

Who you become will be incomparable and unique to anyone else.

Your 10x transformation will become highly specific. It will also make you into someone more specific—and more valuable and unique.

What about you?

- What are you optimizing for?

- What do you ultimately want to be and do?

- What standards do you want to create
  and realize?

- What *minimum standards*—such as the level of client you work with or time it takes to run a marathon—will help you adapt and evolve to where you want to be?

- What is your fitness function—the capabilities and results you want to be able to produce and master?

Define Your "Dream Check"

"To get rich you need to get yourself in a situation with two things, measurement and leverage. You need to be in a position where your performance can be measured, or there is no way to get paid more by doing more. And you have to have leverage, in the sense that the decisions you make have a big effect . . . I think everyone who gets rich by their own efforts will be found to be in a situation with measurement and leverage. Everyone I can think of does: CEOs, movie stars, hedge fund managers, professional athletes. A good hint to the presence of leverage is the possibility of failure. Upside must be balanced by downside, so if there is big potential for gain there must also be a terrifying possibility of loss. CEOs, stars, fund managers, and athletes all live with the sword hanging over their heads; the moment they start to suck, they're out. If you're in a job that feels safe, you are not going to get rich, because if there is no danger there is almost certainly no leverage."

—PAUL GRAHAM[28]

Despite growing up so poor that for a time his family lived in their Volkswagen van on a relative's lawn, Jim Carrey believed in his future. Every night in the late 1980s, Carrey would drive way up into the Hollywood Hills that looked down over Los Angeles. He would park his car, look down over the city, and visualize directors valuing his work. At the time, he was a broke and struggling young comic.

One night in 1990, while looking down on Los Angeles and dreaming of his future, Carrey wrote himself a check for $10 million and put in the notation line "for acting services rendered." He dated the check for Thanksgiving 1995 and stuck it in his wallet.

He gave himself five years *to become the type of person* whose Unique Ability was valued at that price.

Just before Thanksgiving of 1995, he got paid $10 million for *Dumb and Dumber.*

Jim Carrey was highly specific in the standards he set for himself. His wasn't a random evolution but a highly conscious and specific one, based on the fitness function he chose for himself.

As a person and actor, he went 10x many times.

He transformed himself and his Unique Ability over and over through full commitment to his dream and calling.

He became a true master of his craft. No one else could do what he did.

One way Dan Sullivan helps entrepreneurs clarify their next 10x, and thus illuminates where to develop their Unique Ability further, is what he calls the "Dream Check." Jim Carrey applied this principle—writing a Dream Check of $10 million to do a single movie—to become one of the most unique and successful comedian actors of his time.

There is good money and bad money.

Freedom of Money is about *quality money*, wherein you're making money in the most exciting, energizing, and trans-formational way possible—by utilizing and further mastering your Unique Ability.

Think about the largest check you were ever paid to do something that you felt was exciting, and ultimately *play.*

You got paid to do something you would have done for free.

Being paid for your Unique Ability *is* living your dream. It's also increasingly important if you want to make bigger 10x leaps, individually and as a business. If an entrepreneur doesn't 10x the value and impact of their Unique Ability, the whole business will falter and struggle. Moreover, the whole team will follow the entrepreneur's lead and be caught-up in the busy 80 percent that isn't energizing and isn't where they can be their best.

The more you develop your Unique Ability, the higher the value the right people will place on it.

The more you invest in your Unique Ability, the more 10x transformations you will make. Your Unique Ability is how you transform yourself again and again into the most unique, valuable, and true form of yourself. Unique Ability is how you create *unique wealth and value*, which others will happily pay increasing amounts of finite money for.

Your Dream Check can point the way to what you focus on and optimize yourself for. It clarifies your 20 percent that you'll go all-in on. By going all-in, you'll become 10x more capable in that 20 percent, which is highly specific and nuanced, not broad.

Having a Dream Check also gamifies 10x, making it a fun adventure.

Your Dream Check shows you exactly the Unique Ability you are to develop, such that being paid the seemingly unrealistic or absurd amount of money is actually not crazy at all. With the level of Unique Ability you acquire, it actually feels *totally normal and natural* to be paid at that level, even though right now it seems and feels unfathomable.

What is your Dream Check?

Michelangelo continued getting bigger and more exciting commissions to do projects that not only resonated with his Unique Ability, but were a profoundly challenging yet exciting opportunity to further develop and expand it.

For me, my dream check would be being paid $15 million to write a highly niched and specialized book with the right collaborator. Fifteen million dollars is almost exactly 10x the check I've been paid to write a book that excited, scared, and energized me.

Here's the key question I'd have to ask myself to take my Dream Check seriously:

> "What kind of value would I need to provide wherein it would be a total no-brainer and extreme bargain to the right person to pay me $15 million to write a book for/with them?"

Just being honest about myself. If I were to legitimately be paid $15 million to write a book, a few things would need to be true. For it to make sense, the value would need to be 5–10x the price, so it would need to translate to at least $75–150 million in value. To do that, the book would need to bring that level of positioning and business to the person or organization I'm collaborating with.

If I was collaborating just with a book publisher, that would mean I'd need to sell 5–10 million copies of the book, since each book provides only a few bucks profit for the publisher. This is why celebrities like the Obamas can get a $60 million book deal.[29] The expectation is that millions of copies will be sold and thus it's a no-brainer for the publisher.

If I was collaborating with a high-end business leader, I might only need to sell a few thousand of the *right* copies. This particular business may charge hundreds of thousands or even millions of dollars for their specialized service, and thus, they only need dozens or potentially hundreds of "sales" to make the $15 million investment a no-brainer.

This brings us back to fitness function.

It also begs a question Dan encourages you to ask yourself: *Who do you want to be a hero to?*

Ask yourself your own version of this question, for it illuminates your fitness function, 20 percent, and the focus of your Unique Ability development.

First, you define your Dream Check.

This Dream Check should be ballpark 10x what you've been paid to this point for a Unique Ability project. This is a massive, even absurd, amount of money to be paid for something that would ultimately be extreme play and transformational for you to do.

Then you ask yourself these two questions:

1. What specific value would I need to provide such that my Dream Check would be a no-brainer and extreme bargain for the person who would happily pay me?

2. What would need to be true of my Unique Ability to be valuable enough that someone would see it as a no-brainer and extreme bargain to write and pay me my Dream Check?

In order to provide *that* level of value, you would have to become *10x better and more specific* in your Unique Ability. You'd have to be able to produce *10x value* for the person who wants it—whatever specific results those are.

Who do you want to collaborate with?

Who do you want to create specialized value with and for?

What kind of Unique Ability would you need to have for you to get that Dream Check?

What specialized skills and abilities and results do you want to create and develop?

10x is about *better*, not bigger.

Hence, to get your Dream Check, you'd *become 10x better and more valuable* in some unique and specific way to *whomever you want to be a hero to.*

What would your 20 percent be—where you'd go all-in to further master your Unique Ability and transform yourself into the kind of person where getting that Dream Check isn't just crazy, but feels completely natural?

If the idea of "Dream Check" doesn't resonate with you— then think of some specific mountain top or peak experience that does. For example, maybe you want to have some year-round family trip, or finish an ultra-marathon in a particular time, or complete some other massive achievement or adventure that is far more relevant and important to you than money.

The point is: Is this a 10x adventure that would also develop your Unique Ability and transform your life?

Is this what you most want to do, regardless of what other people think?

Chapter Takeaways

- Many high achievers are prone to being in "the gap," wherein they constantly measure themselves and their experiences against unreachable ideals. This makes them feel terrible and unsuccessful, regardless of what they've achieved.

- Ideals are like a horizon in the desert. They provide illumination and direction but are unreachable. No matter how many steps you take toward the horizon, it will continually move out of reach. Ideals are the same. They are useful for direction, but you shouldn't measure yourself against them.

- Being in the gain is a twofold concept that enables you to effectively measure your progress and transform every experience you have into greater learning, meaning, and growth.

- To be in the gain, you only measure your progress backward against where you were before. You never measure yourself against anything external—whether that be your own ideals or other people.

- If you're living in "the gap," then going for 10x growth will be a nightmare for you and everyone around you. Firstly, you won't recognize, value, or appreciate the progress you're making along the way, since you'll be measuring yourself against continually moving and unreachable ideals. Secondly, being in the gap alienates you from those around you, making life a drag and "success" an impossibility for them and you. Third, without transforming every experience you have along the way into learning and growth, you won't continually get 10x better and more unique, which is what 10x is fundamentally all about.

- People tend to have an inflated aversion to loss, which can make letting go of your 80 percent feel painful. However, when you see it properly from a gain perspective, you realize that letting go of your 80 percent—whatever that may be—is actually a huge gain! Letting go of something that's no longer serving you is a massive step forward!

- One application of a "gain" mindset is reviewing your previous 10x jumps. In so doing, you can also clarify the 20 percent of each stage, as well as the 80 percent you powerfully let go of.

- By reflecting on your previous jumps and "connecting the dots backward," you'll firstly see that you've gone 10x many times before. This will normalize 10x for you, helping you see that you can continue going 10x in the future, as you have in the past. Additionally, in examining the 20 percent of each 10x jump, you'll be able to see and appreciate how you've been developing your Unique Ability to this point.

- Accurately and powerfully measuring your progress backward enables you to more fully understand and appreciate your own past. This also helps you better clarify and contextualize your future—the non-linear 10x jumps you now feel most excited and ready to make.

- In reflecting on your next 10x jump, one helpful concept is called fitness function—which asks the question: What are you optimizing for? Fitness function clarifies the *qualities you want to develop* and the *standards by which you measure* progress and success. Whatever you focus on you become.

- Think about your "Dream Check"—a 10x level opportunity that someone in the future will happily pay you because you've become that uniquely valuable.

- What would your Unique Ability need to involve—in terms of capability and results—to attract your *10x Dream Check*?

CHAPTER 5

TAKE 150+ "FREE DAYS" PER YEAR

Escape Factory Time and Open Your Schedule for "Kairos" Flow, Fun, and Transformation

"If we want to live a Wholehearted life, we have to become intentional about cultivating sleep and play, and about letting go of exhaustion as a status symbol."

—BRENÉ BROWN[1]

In the knowledge working and digital world we now live in, the traditional 9 to 5 workday is poorly structured for high productivity. Although this may be obvious given people's mediocre performance, addiction to stimulants, lack of engagement, and the fact that most people hate their jobs, it's impossible to ignore the evidence.

The entrepreneurs who make the fastest and biggest 10x jumps escape the soul-sucking corporate or bureaucratic model of time.

This bureaucratic model of time is how children are trained in the public education system of the 21st century and is based on the organizational and factory systems of the early 20th century. When students come out of the 9–5-style public education system, most of them are then funneled into corporate jobs that are based on the same premise of time. The emphasis of a quantitative model of time is filling time with menial tasks and effort. The emphasis is not on creativity, innovation, and *results*.

As Seth Godin explains, "Every year, we churn out millions of workers who are trained to do 1925-style labor."[2]

To go 10x, you approach time *qualitatively*, not quantitatively. This is actually what Einstein's relatively theories are based on and it's a more accurate view of time than the outdated and mechanical Newtonian models.

Newtonian time, which is inaccurate, views time as *abstract, fixed,* and *linear*—the past is behind us, the present is now, and the future is in front of us. Newtonian time also views time in *absolute* terms, meaning time is the *same for everyone,* everywhere, and in every situation. Twenty-four hours for you is the same as 24 hours for me.[3]

Einstein's relativity theories of time, in addition to modern research in psychology and neuroscience, shatter Newtonian views of time, providing a much more compelling and transformational approach to time.

Einstein time is *subjective, qualitative, non-linear,* and *flexible,* not fixed. Put simply, time is *not the same* from one situation to another, nor from one perspective to another.[4]

No two people are having the same experience of time.

Twenty-four hours for me and 24 hours for you are *not the same.*

Time expands or contracts based on the speed and distance an object moves through space in a given direction. The faster an object moves, the *slower the times goes* for that object relative to other objects. *Time dilation* is the term describing the "slowing down" of time as an object increases in velocity through space.

The more you can experience in a given amount of time, the further you've traveled and the more your time has dilated or stretched. As entrepreneur and innovator Peter Diamandis said, "The faster you go, the slower time passes, the longer you live."

In the 1800s, many pioneers spent *8-12 months* walking across the plains pulling handcarts to get from the East to the West of the United States. Today, you can *cover the same distance in 4-6 hours* on an airplane. Thus, we have essentially dilated time by multiples in the thousands by covering the same distance in a fraction of the time.

The ancient Greeks had two words for time: *kairos* and *chronos*.[5,6] While *chronos* refers to chronological or sequential time, *kairos* signifies a period or season, a moment of indeterminate time in which an event of significance happens.

Chronos is quantitative.

Kairos has a *qualitative*, permanent nature.

Kairos is an ancient Greek word meaning the right or opportune moment. *Kairos* is what many philosophers and mystics would refer to as "deep time" or "alive time." In *kairos*-time, the world seems to stop entirely. It can be measured in long exhales, a shared laugh, a colorful sunset, a courageous moment. It is qualitative time where you move forward in the present, untethered by any moving clock or calendar.

A transformation has occurred.

Distance of either meaning or progress occurred.

When you embrace *kairos* or relative time, you stop drawing fine lines of separation between the past, present, and future. Rather than time being sequential and literal, time becomes wholistic, flexible, and transformative.[7] As Einstein is attributed with writing, "People like us who believe in physics know that the distinction between past, present, and future is only a stubbornly persistent illusion."[8]

If you're in *kairos*, you can tap into higher levels of being, connection, and inspiration. If you're in *chronos*, time will pass you by. You'll be caught in paralysis-by-analysis or busyness but not real movement.

The University of Chicago professor and theologian William Schweikert described *kairos* as "A moment in which we can deploy our greatest powers to humane purposes or allow this moment to swallow hopes and ideals."[9]

Chronos-time passes whether you're conscious or not. But *kairos*-time can only be experienced when you're fully absorbed in the moment. The more you live in *kairos*, the more in flow you'll be. The more peak experiences you'll have. The more awe, self-expansion, and meaning you'll experience.

A few moments in *kairos* will advance and transform you more than a lifetime of *chronos*.

For the remainder of this chapter, you'll learn to approach time qualitatively. You'll learn a *kairos*-based time system Dan developed years ago to enable entrepreneurs to stretch and transform their experience of time and achieve *time freedom*.

You'll learn to transform yourself more in a day than you previously did in a decade.

Your time will slow down, and you'll become more still and present. Your time will also slow down because you'll advance toward your 10x dreams far more quickly while being far less busy.

Advancement is *kairos*.

Busy is *chronos*.

Let's begin.

Become a 10x Performer: Free Days, Focus Days, Buffer Days

"Most people don't have boundaries in their time system. The majority of entrepreneurs have the attitude that any one of the 365 days in a year can be a workday if there's an opportunity. Their mindsets practically guarantee that work is always going to be favored over anything in their lives—and everyone in their lives. But when you structure your time according to The Entrepreneurial Time System of Free, Focus, and Buffer Days, you have the freedom to make and carry out all your commitments, personal and professional."

—DAN SULLIVAN

In his 20s, Dan was an actor working in the entertainment business. He learned that the actors and entertainers designated a different type of task to complete each day. For example, on *performance days*, entertainers gave 100 percent energy and effort into their performance—such as acting in a play, shooting the scenes of a movie, or as an athlete, playing the actual game.

Every aspect of the entertainer's work and time was to give increasingly valuable performances that people would pay for.

The actual length of a particular performance wasn't very long—maybe 3-4 hours max such as a football game, concert, or filming day.

As the performer develops increasingly rare levels of mastery in their craft, they are paid exponentially higher and higher amounts of money for their performances. Payment is for unique value and performance—i.e., leverage—not time and effort.

Dan found that there are fundamentally three different types of days for entertainers, which enable them to create higher and higher valued performances:

1. Performance days
2. Practice or rehearsal days
3. Rejuvenation days

On *practice or rehearsal days*, the entertainers practice and hone their performances so that they can give increasingly valuable performances when the spotlight turns on.

"We talking bout practice?" the NBA star, Allen Iverson, once asked in frustration to a reporter who questioned his continual absence at team practices.

Yes, Allen, *we talking 'bout practice.*

Those who take full advantage of their preparation days experience dramatic rises in results on their performance days, while those who don't practice plummet in their performances.

Consider the difference between two NBA stars, Denver Nuggets center Nikola Jokić and Los Angeles Lakers center Anthony Davis.

During the 2019–2020 season, both players were ranked among the top 10 players of the entire NBA. That season, the Nuggets played the Lakers in the playoffs and Davis totally outclassed Jokić. The Lakers dominated the Nuggets and went on to win the championship that year. Davis seemed to be ascending to new peaks in his abilities.

Yet, just two years later, it's mind-bending *how much* better Jokić had become and similarly mind-blowing *how much* worse Davis had become.

Jokić developed several sides of his game he previously didn't have, such as his improved shooting ability and defense. He went from already being one of the best players in the world to making a *quantum leap* to another stratosphere of performance, showing that no matter how great you already are, there are several more levels you could go, if you apply the 10x process.

Davis obviously has been caught-up in the 80 percent and became 2x. After winning the championship, it's as though he stopped having a 10x future to stretch him. He stopped applying the power of kairos performance time—wherein he leveraged more practice and performance days and embraced his rejuvenation or recovery days. He was plagued by injuries and a lack of motivation.

His *chronos*-time is speeding up because his *kairos*-progress is slowing down.

When you're not making big progress, time speeds up for you. The years pass by and you aren't really going anywhere. Conversely, when you are transforming and making huge progress, your time dilates and slows down. You advance and transform more in a year than is normal for a decade.

In *kairos*-time, you're operating with different rules than those in *chronos*-time. It's not even comparable.

As a performer, if you utilize your practice and rejuvenation days, your performance days will take on increasingly rare quality and value. Your qualitative time will translate to qualitative Unique Ability and performance. As a result, you will continually 10x your freedom of time, money, relationship, and purpose.

The final type of day for an entertainer is rejuvenation days where the entertainer takes a break to rest and recover. The definition of the word *rejuvenation* is "to make young or youthful again: to give new vigor to." Rejuvenation is about making yourself, your enthusiasm, your excitement, and your ambitions young again.

When new entrepreneurs join Strategic Coach, most are operating on the industrial or 9–5 model of time where they are busy but not productive. They're overly aware of everything going on in their business and overly managing their team. They're in *chronos*-time and they're not making massive progress. They're 2x at best.

They are focused on linear time and effort. They're not continually freeing themselves up to hone their vision, creativity, and results.

Dan helps his entrepreneurs shift to a qualitative and non-linear model of time, where they're focused on creating increasingly powerful results with less time and effort: more *kairos*-time.

In order to create 10x non-linear results, these entrepreneurs need to transform themselves. To help them do that, Dan encourages them to upgrade and segment their time like a world-class entertainer would, where they are continually optimizing around higher and higher performances. The objective is to get increasingly larger checks for the same amount of work.

An entrepreneur may be making $500 per day when they are focused and performing. But over time, they can jump to $5,000 per day, then $50,000, and even $500,000+.

Just think about yourself: *Have you 10xed the value and price of your best performances—even if the amount of time working technically didn't change?*

If you want to 10x the quality and value of your performance, you'll need to transform how you approach your time. Nineteenth-century factory worker and *chronos*-time won't do. Being busy isn't how you become world-class.

You've got to approach time qualitatively and non-linearly—where you're increasingly freeing yourself up to transform yourself, your perspectives, your vision, your insights, and your relationships.

Dan has reframed the three "entertainer days" to the following:

1. Free Days (rejuvenation days)
2. Focus Days (performance days)
3. Buffer Days (organization and preparation days)

Free Days Part 1: Make Recovery Your First Priority

At the beginning of every calendar year, Babs fills in all the Free Days (180 days) on Dan's calendar before anything else. Those are non-negotiable. Nothing gets in the way of that.

The more successful you become, the more recovery takes the front seat to *everything* else. Research shows that recovery is essential for flow and increased high performance.[10,11,12,13,14,15]

For example, LeBron James is notorious for the investment he's put into his body—millions of dollars annually—which has enabled him to play at an elite level for longer than any basketball player in history. He's also known for sleeping at minimum 8-10 hours per day, and often upward of 12 hours per day. Tim Ferriss once interviewed LeBron James and Mike Mancias, LeBron's long-time (over 15 years) athletic trainer and recovery specialist.

The first question Tim asked in the interview, speaking to both LeBron and Mike, but ultimately directed at Mike, focused on recovery:

> "Mike, I'd love to dig into recovery and injury prevention. . . . LeBron, you're a bit of a unicorn in the sense that you've played more than, as I understand it, 50,000 minutes in your career. Most hit a wall and deteriorate after 40,000. So, you're defying all the predictions of player decline. So, Mike, maybe you can give us a window into some of that. Could you walk us through some of the tools of the trade and the approaches that you use to help with recovery in between games?"[16]

Mike replied:

> "I think with any elite athlete the one thing that we all, as trainers and therapists, have to keep

in mind is that recovery never ends. Recovery never stops. If LeBron plays 40 minutes one night, if he plays 28 minutes one night, we're still going to keep recovery as our number one focus, whether that be in nutrition, whether that be in hydration, more flexibility exercises, stuff in the weight room. It's a never-ending process, really. And I think that's the approach that we must take in order for us to be successful and provide longevity for these guys."

Recovery is crucial for being fresh, operating at your best, as well as career and life longevity.

There's now an entire subsection of occupational psychology growing around the importance of work-recovery called *psychological detachment from work.*[17,18,19,20] True psychological detachment occurs when you completely refrain from work-related activities as well as obsessive thoughts during nonwork time.

Research has found that people who psychologically detach from work experience:

- Less work-related fatigue and procrastination.[21]

- Increased physical health and increased *engagement* (vigor, dedication, and flow) at work, especially during highly demanding times.[22]

- Greater marital satisfaction even with a heavy workload.[23]

- Increased overall quality of life.[24]

- Greater mental health.[25]

If you're never fully unplugged, you're also never in the zone.

Your ability to turn 100 percent "on" and work in a flow state is in equal proportion to your ability to turn 100 percent "off" and fully release and let go.

Focus is contraction.

Recovery is expansion.

To achieve flow and higher performance, you want to engage in *active recovery* activities that also generate flow.[26] For instance, LeBron's recovery isn't just sitting on the couch, although I'm sure he does a lot of that as well. Massage, compression, hot tubs, sauna, cold plunges, and other forms of therapy. How you do anything is how you do everything. If you want 10x better flow and performance and work, you'll want 10x better and more restorative recovery.

10x is about *quality*, more than quantity.

Quality in *all things*—your standards in all *important* (i.e., 10x) things evolve. The nutrition and food in your body. The quality of your sleep and environment. The quality of your recovery. The quality of your experiences—including peak and novel experiences that are purely for fun and connection.

The ultimate form of healing and therapy is healthy and close relationships. Creating more meaningful and playful connections with those who are most important to you.

Given that my work is mostly mental and relational—reading books, having conversations, and writing—physical activity, such as heavy weight-training and even long walks are amazing active recovery for me. Not only does it give my mind a rest, but increasing my fitness increases the blood flow to my brain. The quality of my work always increases after active recovery.

Free Days Part 2: Higher Stakes Means You Need More Space

With growing success and mastery, recovery becomes increasingly important because the decisions you make at higher levels have 10x or 10,000x the impact and consequence your previous decisions did. As Naval Ravikant said, "In an age of infinite leverage, judgement is the most important skill."

The more leverage and influence behind your actions, the more judgement and discernment matter.

Sound judgment and thinking through bigger and more complex challenges or opportunities require more brain power, more time, more fermentation. You can't do this if you're always busy at work. You can't do this by jumping from task to task.

Being busy is 2x.

It speeds time up with little transformation in between.

One study found that only 16 percent of respondents reported getting creative insight while at work.[27] Ideas generally came while the person was at home or in transportation, or during recreational activity. "The most creative ideas aren't going to come while sitting in front of your monitor," says Scott Birnbaum, a vice president of Samsung Semiconductor.

When you're working directly on a task, your mind is tightly focused on the problem at hand (i.e., direct reflection). Conversely, when you're not working and fully recovering, your mind loosely wanders (i.e., indirect reflection).

While driving or doing some form of recreation, the external stimuli in your environment (like the buildings or landscapes around you) subconsciously prompt memories and other thoughts. Because your mind is wandering both contextually (on different subjects) and temporally between past, present, and future, your brain will make distant and distinct connections related to the problem you're trying to solve (eureka!).

Creativity and innovation are about making unique and sometimes distant connections. This involves new and interesting inputs as well as the indirect reflection and fermentation process that can only happen when you have space and time.

As David Keith Lynch explained in his book *Catching the Big Fish: Meditation, Consciousness, and Creativity*, ideas and opportunities are like fish.[28] If you stay at the surface level, you will only be aware of the small fish. It is only by going deep into the water that you catch the big fish.

Being busy is staying at the surface.

To find big ideas, you need lots of free time. But also, higher quality time.

Lots of time where you're rested, relaxed, and open.

This is one fundamental reason why recovery is so essential. Your best and most innovative ideas will occur while you're unplugged from the busyness of work and able to really expand and contract your thinking—going hyper-micro and hyper-macro—expanding the vision, coming up with new ideas, etc.

This is how Bill Gates famously got most of the big ideas that led to Microsoft's exponential growth in the 1990s and early 2000s. He would take "Think Weeks" where he'd totally disappear for a few weeks, totally unreachable by anyone and without distraction, and just read countless articles and books.[29] He'd then just think, reflect, ponder, visualize, and ultimately get incredible ideas and breakthroughs. Doubtlessly involved in this process were a select few people he could bounce his ideas back-and-forth with, which was essential to iterating his thinking and ideas.

Dan teaches, "Tightly scheduled entrepreneurs cannot transform themselves."

There are two modes of experimentation: *Explore* and *Exploit*

To go 10x, you'll want both.

Exploring happens on Free Days. It's when you're detached from the stress and strain of work, and have the freedom and openness of mind to relax, think, and *explore*. I call this recovery-flow or *kairos*-recovery. Exploring is about learning new things via reading books or studying ideas way outside your discipline. But also, in exploring, you can look for new opportunities beyond what you're currently doing. You're testing and exploring new things that you'll eventually commit to and exploit.

Exploiting happens on Focus Days. This is when you're in focus-flow or *kairos*-focus and getting stuff done. You're totally in the focus cave and executing on what you're fully committed to.

By giving yourself more space to recover, think, and innovate—you increase the value of your own time. You transform yourself enormously, while others are on the *chronos-hamster wheel.*

10x entrepreneurs understand this, and 2x entrepreneurs don't.

2x entrepreneurs think they need to get all their ducks in a row before they can start taking more time off. They believe they need to have the perfect team in place.

Even when there were only three employees, Dan and Babs would schedule and take their 180 rejuvenation days each year. During those Free Days, their team was not to contact them in any way.

It's counterintuitive, but in order to go 10x, you need to work less, not more.

10x is easier than 2x.

10x is about innovation and results. It's a qualitative and non-linear approach to time.

2x is about busyness and effort. It's a quantitative and linear approach to time.

Free Days Part 3: Your Team Can't Grow and Evolve Unless They Manage Themselves

Increased "free time" isn't just about you.

By taking more time away from work, you also improve your team, your process, and systems.

Most entrepreneurs learn this lesson way too late: *You never know how good your team is until you go away.*

But also, *they'll never know* how good they can be if you're constantly managing them.

It is by freeing yourself up and being away from the team that your team evolves, takes full ownership, and learns to manage the ship without you. This is what Dan calls a *Self-Managing Company,* and it's essential to 10x growth.

As Dan explains:

> "Expanding your freedom of time is essential to having a Self-Managing Company. The more you're freed up to concentrate totally on what fascinates and motivates you, the more your company can grow."[30]

Your company and vision won't grow 10x if you're too busy dealing with daily fires. Going 10x requires having 10x better ideas and innovations, which requires depth of focus-flow and depth of recovery-flow.

You can't focus if you're always at work.

But also, if you're too afraid to step away from the team, then you're overly managing them. You're actually slowing them down. You're stopping them from self-determination and you're stopping yourself from evolving.

You've got to step away and give the reins of the ship to someone else.

That's not your role anymore.

Attempting to stay in that role keeps not only you 2x, but your entire team and company.

Chapter 6 of this book is entirely focused on showing you how to become a transformational leader and build a self-managing and self-expanding team.

Focus Days and Buffer Days: How to Structure Your Day for 10x Transformation and Results

For years, Dan's Focus Days and Buffer Days were pretty equal—approximately 90 to 95 days each. However, as Dan has increasingly applied Who Not How[31] and grown his team, the majority of his workdays—around 150—are now Focus Days. On Focus Days, he's coaching his entrepreneur clients, creating new tools and models, or collaborating on his podcasts or other projects. His team increasingly handles the preparation.

Even still, Buffer Days are super important. Dan still has around 35 Buffer Days per year where he's meeting with his team, organizing, and planning. These keep everyone on the same page and feeling connected to each other.

For each person, Focus Days and Buffer Days will be different.

Your Buffer Days are for any form of preparation or organization—whether that be meeting with key collaborators, working with consultants or coaches, meeting with your team, or preparing notes or resources you'll later use on your Focus Days.

Focus Days, conversely, are all about creating results. On Focus Days, entrepreneurs do nothing outside their 20 percent most high impact tasks. Focus Days are for the highest paying activities, which continually go up as you go 10x in your Unique Ability.

To structure your Focus and Buffer Days for the biggest bang for your buck:

Structure your week for high performance and stack similar activities and meetings next to each other on the same day. Switching from different types of tasks, such as creative tasks to administrative tasks, is ineffective.

Stop running around like a chicken with your head chopped off.

Rather than trying to do several different activities each day during your week, have days solely focused for specific types of activities. By simply having a meeting later in your day, your mind will continually think about it. You'll use it as an anchor to everything you're doing. It will distract and derail your ability to go into the focus cave because you know you'll have to come out prematurely.

If you're going to have meetings in your week, stack them together on one or two days of the week. Leave several work days in your week wide open for your most important work.

This has been massive for me. In the past I'd have meetings scattered everyday throughout my week. Now, I only allow meetings on Fridays except rare and important exceptions. My Mondays through Thursdays are meeting free so I can concentrate on writing, learning, connecting with important people, thinking, and whatever I want.

Your schedule and role will likely be totally different than mine as a writer. Your Unique Ability and 10x objective are different than mine. Apply the principle to yourself and your situation. Stack similar activities and meetings together on the same days. Don't scatter meetings throughout your week. Open more of your days for doing your best work and getting *10x better* at your craft. Do this for even a short period of time and others will be shocked by how radical your progress and transformation are.

Most people are not giving themselves the space to 10x their flow and craft. They're living 2x, caught up in the 80 percent, and are living a linear and busy model of time.

The Philadelphia Eagles quarterback Jalen Hurts is a brilliant example of tapping into kairos-time and 10xing his skills and results in a *very short time*. He's a total 10x person and will likely become one of the most elite quarterbacks in the NFL.

At the current writing in November of 2022, we are nine weeks into the 2022–2023 NFL season. It's Jalen's third year in the league and second as a starter. The Eagles are currently undefeated and Hurts is the leading MVP candidate.

In a recent interview, sports commentator Colin Cowherd asked Super Bowl Champion quarterback Trent Dilfer "What am I seeing in Jalen Hurts?" Trent replied,

"I think you're seeing the product of a lot of lonely work. Jalen Hurts, I remember when he was 17 years old, he was mature like a 25-year-old. He's an old soul. He's also an incredibly hard worker and he's done a lot of the lonely work—the boring, monotonous stuff that no one gets credit for. You don't post it on Instagram. You don't post it on Twitter. You don't pat yourself on the back and say, 'Look at me working hard.' You just go to work, and you work on the nuance of your game. You work on the technique. You work on film-study. You lock yourself in because you could be doing a lot of other things. You have a lot of money and a lot of fame. Instead, you decide to do the hard thing, which is lock yourself in a room and study yourself, study your opponent, work on every aspect of your game. I talked to Quincy Avery (the quarterback developer) about Jalen's off-season regimen. It was intensive. He did say 'No' to a lot of the luxuries of life so he could get better. And you're seeing the payoff of that right now. He's playing at as high of a level as anybody and he's not just doing it as a great athlete like everyone thought he would do it. He's doing it as a true nuanced quarterback in the NFL. My hat's off to him because I think of all the people in the NFL, you've got to look at Jalen Hurts as the guy who's made the biggest stride from last year to this year and he's become a bonafide superstar."[32]

Jalen Hurts proves that with serious focus and commitment, even at the highest level such as the NFL, you can completely elevate yourself and grow to totally ridiculous levels in a seemingly short span of time. But not if you're living 2x.

You've got to have a 10x future and you've got to be continually transforming yourself.

You've got to spend increasing amounts of time in *kairos*—where you're evolving at quantum level. *Kairos*-focus and *kairos*-recovery is a way of life.

Create bigger blocks of open space for deep work. To get 10x better at what you're doing, adopt what Y Combinator cofounder Paul Graham calls a "Maker Schedule."[33] Here's how he explains it:

> "There are two types of schedules, which I'll call the manager's schedule and the maker's schedule. The manager's schedule is for bosses. It's embodied in the traditional appointment book, with each day cut into one-hour intervals. You can block off several hours for a single task if you need to, but by default you change what you're doing every hour. When you use time that way, it's merely a practical problem to meet with someone. Find an open slot in your schedule, book them, and you're done. But there's another way of using time that's common among people who make things, like programmers and writers [and performers]. They generally prefer to use time in units of half a day at least. You can't write or program well in units of an hour. That's barely enough time to get started. When you're operating on the maker's schedule, meetings are a disaster. A single meeting can blow a whole afternoon, by breaking it into two pieces each too small to do anything hard in. Each type of schedule works fine by itself. Problems arise when they meet."

Tim Ferris suggests creating blocks of space of at least four hours when you're working on and trying to solve a massive challenge or creative task.[34] If you're going 10x, your time will need to be far less segmented. Far less thinly-sliced. More wide-open days and more blocks of increasing size, like four or more hours without meetings or distractions.

Taking Ferris' advice a step further, the important work happens in kairos-time: not only do you create bigger blocks of time to either explore or exploit—either focus or recover—you actually expand that outward in your weeks and months. You have focus weeks and recovery weeks, focus months and recovery months. You're taking on bigger projects that require high attention. Yet, you also slip away for weeks or months at a time for *kairos* recovering and exploring—expanding and transforming.

Kairos-focus and *kairos*-recovery are how you live decades of experience and growth in a single year. It's how you slow time while everyone else's time is accelerating.

This is how you become the David. This is how you develop extreme Unique Ability. This is how you do and create things that others could never imagine, because others are up closer to the surface—busy, distracted, linear, segmented, *2x*.

It's also crucial to note that if you're going 10x, *you're not a manager.* . . Managers don't go 10x. You're a visionary and Transformational Leader. Leaders don't manage. They build teams of leaders that manage themselves.

No more than three personal objectives each day (important and designed for flow). Former United States president Dwight Eisenhower said,

> "I have two kinds of problems: the urgent and the important. The urgent are not important, and the important are never urgent."

The 20 percent of activities—your Unique Ability—are important but not urgent. The 80 percent of activities are urgent. At this point, you should probably already be weary of the 80 percent.

When it comes to planning your day, you're going for impact and progress, not busyness. You're also going for quality over quantity. If you have 10 items of your to-do list, you're going shallow. You're not going 10x.

Each day, go for no more than three important results. Once you're done with those three, call it a day. Celebrate and recover. Make sure those three activities are 10x, not 2x. They are the highest and most enjoyable use of your time.

Research shows that there are three essential pre-conditions of being in a flow state:

1. Clear and specific goals.

2. Immediate feedback.

3. The challenge and/or risk of the activity is beyond your current skill or knowledge level.[35]

Make sure your three daily goals are clear and specific, so that you can know where to focus. Make sure your three goals involve some form of feedback, which is, to use Seth Godin's language, "a collision between your work and the outside world."[36]

Feedback has consequences.

It takes courage and vulnerability to get direct and quality feedback. You've got to be completely honest that "this" is where you're currently at. There's risk in getting feedback, but only if you need to *be right*. If you're more interested in *getting it right*, then you'll regularly seek feedback as a forcing function to produce and transform your thinking.

Finally, have your three daily activities be beyond your current skill or knowledge level, so that you're exercising commitment and courage. This is how you grow and transform yourself, developing new capabilities and confidence (think Dan's 4 Cs). This is how you get one or more percent better every day. No repetition or autopilot.

Completely unplug when you're done and actively recover. Don't work longer than is necessary, unless you're on some extreme deadline like a *kairos*-focus week or month. Achieve your core objectives. Be bold. Then, when it's time to be done, let it go.

Unplug.

Psychologically detach from work.

Go actively recover and expand the other important areas of your life, because how you do anything is how you do everything. If you're going 10x in one area, you'll 10x all other *important* areas of your life as well. Emphasis on the word "important."

The simplest evening routine for transformation. In *The Gap and The Gain*, Dan and I dedicated an entire chapter to mastering the final hour of your day, which also happens to be the highest-impact hour of your day.[37]

The final hour of your day determines the quality of your sleep as well as the quality of your next day. Over 90 percent of people are 2x at night, where they fall to unhealthy habits and consumption, especially random Internet scrolling.[38]

For 10x sleep, put your phone on airplane mode at least 30-60 minutes before bed. Pull out your journal for 3-5 minutes and write down three wins you had that day. These wins will be *any* forms of learning or progress you had, even if they weren't planned.

Then, after you've framed the day as a "win"—which is how you want your entire past framed—choose and commit to the three goals or "wins" you'll get tomorrow. Pray and or meditate and then commit to sleep. Be excited and happy to fully shut it down.

Chapter Takeaways

- The public education system and traditional corporate structure are based on a quantitative and linear model of time, which is focused on busyness and effort, not flow, creativity, and results.

- To go 10x, you approach time qualitatively and non-linearly.

- Entertainers have different segments of time, which are optimized for helping them develop higher levels of mastery in their increasingly valuable performances.

- To go 10x, adopt an entertainer or performance model of time, which is focused on quality, not quantity. It's also focused on you becoming 10x better in your craft, which involves hyper-focused days, preparation days, and recovery days.

- The more you go 10x, the more recovery and large blocks of open time for novelty, relaxation, fun, and connection are essential.

- Commit to scheduling Free Days throughout your week, month, and year. Choose the number of Free Days that scares you a little bit. You'll be surprised that you achieve more and better results by doing less.

- Working less is essential to making more money and going 10x.

- Freeing yourself up is a purpose of your team, especially when you evolve to a self-managing company.

- You'll never know how good your team is until you go away. Also, they'll never know how good they can be until you let them manage themselves.

- Structure your week for high performance and flow. Stack and schedule similar activities like meetings on the same day. Only have meetings on various days of the week. Have several days per week where nothing is scheduled.

- Adopt a maker schedule, where you have huge time blocks dedicated for deep work and innovation. This is how you'll get 10x better. Apply focus-flow and recovery-flow at an even higher level, where you not only have focus and Free Days, but you have focus and free weeks, and even focus and free months.

- Stop working when you've completed your three important tasks. Don't work longer than is necessary. Productive and busy are opposites. Be in the gain, not the gap.

- Optimize your evening routine for increasingly quality sleep.

- To get additional resources on utilizing Dan's time system, visit www.10xeasierbook.com.

CHAPTER 6

BUILD A SELF-MANAGING COMPANY

Evolve from Micromanager to Transformational Leader

"As soon as I remove myself as a bottleneck, profits increase by 40 percent. What on earth do you do when you no longer have work as an excuse to be hyperactive and avoid the big questions? Be terrified and hold on to your ass with both hands apparently."

—Tim Ferriss[1]

In early 2017, Susan Kichuk was five months into a year-long sabbatical when she got an unexpected phone call from a headhunter.

The headhunter had been struggling to find someone for this particular gig, because it was the most specific job description he'd ever seen. He was telling a friend of his

199

about the impossibility of finding the right person for this particular job, and the friend immediately thought of Susan and made the introduction.

The problem was Susan wasn't looking for a job.

She was, frankly, fried from working non-stop for nearly 30 years—from getting a PhD in business administration in her early 20s, to raising kids, to spending over 25 years helping structure and scale multiple large organizations.

She'd just spent the previous 17 years as a senior executive for a global organization. Hers was the job of continually developing and improving the organization and ensuring the completion of endless high priority projects.

But as she listened to the headhunter explain the particulars of the job being offered, she was surprised by how interesting and exciting the prospect seemed. It was so interesting that she immediately wanted to get to work and end her sabbatical pre-maturely.

It was a life insurance brokerage called Targeted Strategies Limited that was based on an innovative and brilliant idea. At the time, Targeted Strategies Limited was making millions per year, but it wasn't sustainable. The CEO and founder, Garnet Morris, had finally reached his wits end. He realized that in order to go 10x, he'd need the right Who—someone other than himself—to run and build the company.

Before getting interviewed, Susan went through a battery of testing and was selected as one of a few candidates for the CEO position. During her interview with Garnet and his board of directors, Susan was bold and direct. She spoke straight to Garnet and said, "I know what you're trying to do and I can help you do it. I've done it many times before. What scares you about hiring me?"

Garnet began listing 4-5 concerns he had about Susan. For starters, she had no experience in the life insurance business. As Susan clearly and boldly dismantled each of his concerns, Garnet eventually turned to his board and said, "I like her the best. Let's hire her."

Susan's job was neither simple nor easy. She had the two-fold task of:

- Gaining Garnet's trust so that he would get out of her way and focus on his Unique Ability: innovating financial solutions for their clients.

- Structuring, optimizing, and scaling a business that had stagnated for years.

During the first month on the job, Susan carefully assessed the situation top-to-bottom.

She dug into the finances.

How much money are we making?

Are we receiving all the money we should be?

Where does all the money go?

She dug into the life insurance policies they sold, trying to figure out where they came from and where they were located. "Not surprisingly," she told me, "they were not all in one place."

She dug into the systems and processes, trying to figure out what had yet to be systemized to free up the people from redundant tasks.

After better understanding the current state of the business and organization, she critically assessed which roles and tasks were actually needed, and who the right people were to fill those tasks.

She found that Garnet was the sole person on the team generating sales for the company.

She also found that many of the current team were legacy people who either weren't filling what the company truly needed, or weren't the best for the job. Many of these legacy team members fit the definition of 2x, meaning they wanted things to mostly remain how they were. They didn't want the 10x changes Garnet wanted and that ultimately Susan was in the process of creating.

Of course, Susan was a rate-buster. She was actually hired by Garnet to be a rate-buster, shattering the 2x-problems keeping the business stuck. She was raising the standard and structuring the business and team to go 10x.

Some of her initial and simple questions were:

What needs to be done?

Who is doing it now?

Is this this right Who?

For the next four years—from 2017 to 2021—Susan went through her 4-step process that ultimately led Targeted Strategies Limited to achieve 10x results. They are are currently posed for another 10x jump over the next 4-5 years. Susan's four steps are:

1. Stabilize

2. Optimize

3. Grow

4. Transform

Stabilizing was about making the business functional and compliant. This required Susan to scrutinize the business so she could better understand how it actually makes money. She assessed the policies the company sold, sales, money, the team, and all of the company's gaping holes.

Optimizing was about standardizing key processes and diversifying revenue, so that Garnet was no longer the only person selling. Susan went to the insurance companies and banks that did business with Targeted Strategies and found that all of them *hated* doing business with Targeted. The reason was simple: There were no clear processes or systems in place.

Growing was about building relationships and connections with other parties who would sell Targeted Strategies policies, based on Garnet's innovative structuring and perspectives. Garnet's brilliance is creating radically innovative solutions to life insurance, removing all the undesired aspects and simplifying life insurance to become a valuable and growing asset you can utilize while you're alive, not just when you're dead. He's constantly coming up with incredible intellectual property (IP), which Susan helps him filter and execute.

Susan began nurturing relationships with several Principals who were senior members of accounting firms that worked with ultra-high-net-worth individuals, who were the types of people Targeted Strategies also worked with. She recruited many of these Principals to join their team and become the primary sales people, because these Principals understood the business, had the networks, and could speak the language of those they were selling to.

Structuring and organizing the business and then getting the best Whos possible was Susan's objective. As she increasingly got more and better Whos, they continually found more avenues and referrals for selling life insurance policies in the innovative way Garnet had structured them.

After four years, Susan and Garnet grew Targeted Strategies 10x together.

Now that they've gone 10x, they've reached Susan's fourth stage: *Transformation*. To go 10x again, a few things have changed. First, Garnet has left Targeted Strategies and even the entire Canadian insurance business. He has gone on to start a new company that adds value to clients in other ways.

Susan and Garnet still situationally and strategically collaborate together. However, at this point, Susan controls Targeted Strategies and owns it with a few other key people.

Susan told me that if they're going to go 10x again, it's not going to happen working with Principals, as the last 10x did. "To go 10x from here," Susan told me, "we're going to need to capitalize on our amazing insurance service platform."

To get to this point, Garnet created a *Self-Managing Company* led by Susan. For Garnet to be his best, he had to free his mind of everything going on in the day-to-day of the organization. Susan freed him up and then utilized her skills and passion to stabilize, optimize, and grow the company 10x. All the while, Garnet was free to focus on his Unique Ability and passion of learning, growing, and innovating.

Every time you go 10x, your freedom of purpose and sense of calling or mission also expand, *exponentially.*

If you're going to go 10x again and again—meaning you become 10x better and more innovative in your Unique Ability—then it's essential you create a Self-Managing Company.

Having a Self-Managing Company is exactly what it sounds like. It's a company and team that manages themselves. You're no longer involved in the day-to-day. You have a team that works for you—without being dependent on you. Again, this doesn't mean you're not the visionary and leader. But you're leading in your proper sphere, where you're innovating and transforming yourself—and continually exploring and exploiting radically new and exciting opportunities.

You're no longer the bottleneck, involved in or managing the team, system, or structure of the business. Instead, you've brought on world-class Whos that are better suited for managing the affairs of the system, processes, and team.

You set the vision, your team makes it happen.

As you continually evolve and transform yourself, your thinking, mindset, and identity are always upgrading. You translate your upgrades to your leadership team and they translate that to the rest of the team.

In this chapter, you'll learn the fundamentals of building a Self-Managing Company, and even going beyond that to where you have a self-expanding Unique Ability Team.

There is a progression every entrepreneur goes through of being a rugged individual who does everything themselves, to one who *becomes a leader* applying Who Not How in all aspects of their life and business. Eventually, you go from being the leader to replacing yourself with even more capable leaders who run your company for you, freeing you up to go all-in on your Unique Ability and the next exciting evolutions beyond.

Specifically, there are four levels you'll evolve through as an entrepreneur if you continue going 10x to 10x, which this chapter will walk you through. The four levels are as follows:

1. **Level 1 to Level 2 Entrepreneurship:** Level one entrepreneurship is being a rugged individual who either does everything themselves or micromanages the few Whos they have. Level two entrepreneurship is where you evolve beyond How-focused rugged individualism to Who-focused leadership, applying Who Not How in all areas of your life and business.

2. **Level 2 to Level 3 Entrepreneurship:** Going from level two entrepreneurship of being a leader applying Who Not How to level three entrepreneurship means you've replaced yourself with better-fit leaders who run your Self-Managing Company. You're now freed-up from the day-to-day operations to fully focus on exploring new possibilities, innovating the best 20 percent of what you're now doing, expanding vision, and collaborating within your Unique Ability.

3. **Level 3 to Level 4 Entrepreneurship:** Going from level three entrepreneurship of having a Self-Managing Company to level four entrepreneurship means everything happening around you, including in your business, operates as Self-Multiplying Unique Ability Teamwork. In a Self-Multiplying Unique Ability Team, all individuals are encouraged to continually and autonomously refine their own roles down to their 20 percent. All right-fit Whos embrace the freedom of being intrinsically motivated and transforming their Unique Ability toward the shared 10x vision that excites them. As each Who more fully embraces their Unique Ability, they continually let go of their 80 percent and replace themselves with a new and better-fit Who to take on that 80 percent. The team continually multiplies itself and everyone is getting exponentially better and more valuable.

Now, let's dive into these stages.

Level 1 to Level 2 Entrepreneurship: From Rugged Individual to Leader Applying Who Not How

"You can't have an innovative, increasingly more profitable company unless you have a Self-Managing Company. With the day-to-day activities of running your business managed by your team, you're free to look at the big picture vision, continually innovate greater and greater value, and even transform your marketplace."

—DAN SULLIVAN[2]

In 1997, Tim Schmidt was a young mechanical engineer from West Bend, Wisconsin, who started a small business with three employees. As a business, they lacked clarity. In Tim's words, "We would do anything people would pay for." One thing they did was take designs of in-store displays, such as a PlayStation console display in a toy store, and convert the design to make the physical construction possible to complete.

By 2007—10 years later—Tim's company still had three employees and was doing about $300,000 in revenue, not much more than when he started it a decade earlier.

Tim barely experienced 2x growth between 1997-2007, even though he was "working his ass off."

Compare that decade to the last 10 years—2011 to 2022—wherein his current company, U.S. Concealed Carry Association (USCCA), went from $3-4 million in revenue to now over $250 million in revenue, with over 615 employees throughout the United States, and over 700,000 renewing members. Rather than "working his ass off" in 2x-mode, Tim increasingly adds leaders and teams to accelerate the growth of USCCA.

Yes, it's been hard work.

But it's also been a fun and transformational adventure of increased freedom and success.

What was the difference in those two decades?

What was the difference in Tim?

How did he go from starting a new organization to now impacting literally millions of lives annually?

Let's explore Tim's story. It will help you better understand the progression of going from rugged individual to becoming a *Transformational Leader*.

In 1998, Tim held his newborn first child, Timmy Jr., for the first time. In that moment, he thought to himself, "It's my job to protect and defend this guy, and I don't know what I'm doing."

Despite having grown up around guns, and his dad having taught him to shoot a gun when he was 12 years old, at that point Tim was 28 years old and didn't own a firearm.

Holding his newborn son spurred Tim to learn about self-defense. In this process, he was a bit shocked by his initial reception to the fire arm industry.

Being the engineer and researcher he was, Tim spent a ton of front-end time researching different types of guns until he felt confident about the first handgun he wanted to buy. He drove to the Gun World Gander Mountain store in Germantown, Wisconsin, walked into the store, and went to the back where all the glass cases filled with guns were. He walked up to the glass counter and there was a big rough dude standing behind the counter staring at him, who didn't say a word.

He just stared at Tim.

"Excuse me, sir, can I look at *that* gun right there?" Tim said, pointing to one of the guns.

Folding his arms, the man looked Tim up and down, then impolitely and cynically asked, "What would a guy like you want with a gun like that?"

Startled, Tim replied, "I don't know, dude! That's why I'm asking for help."

Needless to say, it wasn't a positive experience.

This led Tim down the rabbit hole of gun ownership, education, and protection. He studied these topics intensely on the side for a few years while he was running his engineering business.

In 2003, Tim started USCCA from his kitchen table. His idea was to publish a print magazine, *The Concealed Carry Magazine*, sharing gun ownership and defense education and stories.

It took him six months to create the initial magazine. He took out a $100,000 business line of credit out of his engineering business, without asking the bank, and invested all of it into printing and mailing 30,000 copies of his magazine.

He got the addresses from a company that provided list referrals of various demographics.

Within that first magazine was a call to action to join USCCA for ongoing education, which at that time was essentially a subscription to get a new magazine every six weeks.

Out of those initial 30,000 copies mailed, 1,000 people subscribed to USCCA for $47 annually.

Now Tim had put himself into a sticky situation. He now had 1,000 people who expected him to create a new magazine *every six weeks*, which was a ton of work and required a lot of capital!

From 2003 to 2007, growth was linear and fairly slow for USCCA. Tim wasn't yet much of a leader. He didn't know how to apply Who Not How. He was controlling and mostly did everything himself, because he didn't trust other people and thought they would screw everything up. Whenever he'd hire someone, they'd become miserable.

Despite Tim's lack of trust and leadership, the U.S. Concealed Carry Association was growing steadily, and by 2007, the company was profitable, doing nearly $1 million in annual revenue with $200,000 in profits. There were four to five employees, half of whom were disgruntled. Yet, USCCA was starting to gain traction.

Seeing that the company was showing strong signs of growth, Tim had a few realizations. Firstly, he knew that USCCA was exactly what he wanted to dedicate himself to. Secondly, he realized that in order for the company to grow, "Tim would have to work on Tim" and become a true leader.

He sold his engineering company and went all-in on USCCA.

They purchased a small office building.

Tim began reading lots of business and leadership books and began getting coaching from the *Entrepreneurial Operating System (EOS)*—a global entrepreneurial training program that also collaborates with Strategic Coach—where he learned how to systemize and operationalize a business and to develop cultural aspects like core values.

From 2007 to 2011, the company went from just under $1 million revenue to $4 million, with 20 employees. The business was still basically built around the magazine, which provided education but also, being a member of an "Association," provided status and identity.

The year 2011 marked the next crucial inflection point for Tim and USCCA. It was at this point that Tim became committed to building a truly world-class team. He got committed to taking the magazine to the next level, making it more powerful, interesting, and useful.

Tim also came to a really important insight during a private business coaching session he was having, wherein he considered adding self-defense liability insurance as an integral benefit for being a part of USCCA. Rather than just being an organization focused on defense education and training, they would also provide insurance and protection as part of membership.

This was unique, since at the time and even still today for many people, the legalities of self-defense aren't popular nor embraced.

Thus, Tim began to develop a core philosophy and framework for membership in the USCCA, which is an association for responsible gun-ownership. The three pillars of USCCA are:

1. **Mental Preparation:** Focused on education and training.

    a. They are provided mental training, plus members get the *Concealed Carrier Magazine* every six weeks.

    b. They get access to thousands of hours of online training in the Protector Academy, "the Netflix for gun training."

    c. They also get access to hundreds of guides, checklists, and eBooks that have been created over the years.

2. **Physical Preparation:** Focused on physical training and actual gun use.

    a. There are over 5,000 active USCCA-certified instructors throughout the United States who provide tangible gun use training for members.

    b. USCCA has an official partnership with 1,500+ gun ranges nationwide, which have banners saying "Official partner of USCCA."

    c. As a member, you also get all sorts of discounts on ammo and gear.

3. **Legal Preparation:** Insurance and training about the legalities and preparation for the aftermath of gun use, whether in self-defense or otherwise.

    a. USCCA offers a 24/7 legal response team to answer any questions, challenges, or situations.

    b. They have a team of 1,000+ criminal defense attorneys that is available on call 24/7.

    c. You get an up to $2 million annual liability insurance policy to protect yourself.

With his increasing clarity, direction, and commitment, Tim decided to do something bold.

Since 2003 when he initially launched the magazine, the price of annual membership had remained $47. But with the improved team and customer service; the three-pillared focus of education and training mentally, physically, and legally; and the added benefit of self-defense liability insurance, Tim decided to increase the price nearly 4x for membership in USCCA. It was approximately $200 annually for membership.

Immediately half of the members left.

USCCA went from 50,000 renewing members to 25,000 in a single day.

"It felt great," Tim told me, about cutting his customer base in half and focusing on quality over quantity.

Even after cutting their clients in half, the business was now making more than double what it was before and was far more profitable.

Higher quality, less quantity.

Laser focus and clarity of mission and purpose.

Rather than trying to be everything for a large group of people, USCCA narrowed in on a niche, targeted group of people. As Tim explained to me, "Go for the fringes of the bell curve. Going for the middle is death to growing a culture, community, and business."

Since 2011 when they added the insurance, clarified the mission and focus of USCCA, and focused on quality over quantity members, the company has skyrocketed, going from $3-4 million to over $250 million in annual revenue.

Over these past 10-11 years, Tim has focused on developing himself as a leader, as well as developing everyone in his organization. He's continually getting coaching and educating himself, and he now spends a large portion of his time educating and training his team.

It was terrifying for Tim initially taking on that $100,000 line of credit from his engineering business and pouring all of it into the initial shipment of 30,000 magazines.

It was terrifying raising the price 4x within a short period of time, knowing he'd lose a huge chunk of his customers.

Tim has faced his fears again and again—letting go of the 80 percent to go all-in on his 10x vision and purpose.

He had to let go of needing to control how everything got done in his business.

He invested in tons of coaching, education, and support to improve his thinking to the level where he could build out USCCA into something unique and innovative. He worked with speaking coaches to help him improve his communication and speaking so he could better get the message out there.

He grew himself as a leader and visionary, and continually expands the vision and mindsets of everyone involved with USCCA. To this day, his number one focus is evolving and improving himself such that he can transfer that mindset and growth to his team and the entire population of now 700,000+ USCCA members.

Tim's goal is growing the association to over four million members by 2030.

In a recent talk Tim gave at Joe Polish's Genius Network group, Tim provided seven principles he's applied to grow USCCA as he has. These principles reflect much of the science on *Transformational Leadership theory*.[3] Therefore, I'll share Tim's seven principles and also distill connections to the science of Transformational Leadership.

In posing the question, "Why do people join the USCCA?" Tim initially pointed to the three pillars—mental, physical, and legal preparation and training—and all the benefits of being a member. But then he continued:

> "Let me be clear, people *do not* join USCCA because of all these benefits. Sure, these benefits are amazing. But they aren't the real and deeper reason people become members. The truth is, most people

don't directly want all of the benefits we offer. They just want an easy-button that provides those for them. The reason people join any organization or association is *psychographic alignment.* All humans have a deep desire to feel a sense of belonging and connection to a group of people with shared beliefs and culture."

This has been the backbone to everything Tim has developed over the past 20 years at USCCA. Everything they do, from publishing the magazine to having large events, is to create psychographic alignment and a sense of belonging and community among their members. Thus, Tim's seven principles are centered around building psychographic alignment and belonging. These seven principles are:

1. **The Story:** Your organization, association, or business needs a powerful origin story. "Ideally a true story," Tim added, laughing. Tim loves the story of the reluctant hero who nervously advances toward what they believe to be a calling or mission. They're continually stretching themselves to fulfill that mission, facing and overcoming obstacles, and getting their butt kicked along the way. This reflects Joseph Campbell's *hero's journey,*[4] and every good organization or association centers the client *as the* hero of the story.

2. **An Ideology:** "There needs to be a mission and purpose in your organization that gives people goose bumps," Tim said. Timeless ideologies are based on *principles,* not politics. The definition of *principle* is "a fundamental truth or proposition that serves as the foundation for a system of belief or behavior or for a chain

of reasoning." The definition of *politics* is, "the debate or conflict among individuals or parties having or hoping to achieve power." Despite being an organization focused on guns and gun safety, nearly 40 percent of USCCA members are Democrat, because the organization isn't focused on politics, but instead principles, which are relevant to people of all political backgrounds.

3. **A Symbol:** The organization or association needs a strong-sounding and clear name, as well as a symbol or logo people can associate with the organization, like the Nike swoosh symbol. When Tim first started USCCA when he was the only employee and had zero customers, he called it the *United States Concealed Carry Association* (USCCA). It sounded official and important from the beginning. The symbol should be professionally created, look amazing, and be wearable. A good logo and brand is something that some people are even willing to tattoo on themselves, like Harley-Davidson's or Apple's.

4. **Shared Rituals:** A ritual can be any activity that is unique and consistent, which triggers a sense of meaning and belonging. These rituals strengthen the individual's commitment to the organization and its ideology. At their annual expo, 15-20 thousand USCCA members converge at a specific location, where there are booths, trainings, and other forms of community events. To be admitted into the events, and several times throughout the events, the members are required to show their USCCA membership card. This is one of the

rituals they've created at USCCA: the pulling out and proudly showing of your membership card. One way to spread and enhance the rituals is to regularly publish content, whether by a blog, YouTube videos, a magazine, etc., highlighting stories of the members engaging in the rituals of the organization and the benefits they get out of that.

5. **The Enemy:** "You have to have an enemy," Tim said. Interestingly, it's often easier for people to bond on what they don't like than what they do. This taps into in-groups and out-groups, where you can clearly point to something and say, "That's not us." The enemy, whether a group of people, a set of behaviors, etc., is an inherent aspect of the ideology. At Strategic Coach, one of the "enemies" is the idea of retirement. In this book, the enemy is *2x thinking*, which is where you've stopped betting your present (the 80 percent) on a bigger future which excites you (going all-in on your 20 percent Unique Ability).

6. **The Language:** Every sticky organization has a shared *insider language*, with unique words, acronyms, and shared meanings which are continually used in conversation and presented in education materials. When you go to a Strategic Coach meeting, you'll hear people talking about Who Not How, VOTA, DOSS, Gap and Gain, etc. You can tell someone is an insider and part of the group when they speak the language and understand the intricacies of the shared meanings.

7. **The Leader:** Every organization, association, or movement has a leader. This leader is seen

as an attractive character and a servant. They are not the hero of the story; each individual member is the hero. The leader is simply there to serve, guide, and support all the members. The leader takes the customer or member along the journey, helping them through the transformation and process of their own hero's journey, which the association provides.

Tim's story shows someone who went from rugged individual to a *Transformational Leader*. As a transformational leader, he began investing in and developing himself. He expanded his own vision and sense of purpose for himself and the cause he was leading, USCCA.

Rather than stifling his team as he previously had, micromanaging and overcontrolling, he applied *Transformational Leadership* principles of expanding and elevating his team. Some of the core principles of Transformational Leadership, which is the most studied and science-based theory and application of leadership, include:

1. **Idealized Influence:** Transformational leaders are role models who, through their actions and values, inspire those who follow them. They take risks and commit to chosen values and display convictions that create a sense of confidence in those they lead.

2. **Inspirational Motivation:** Transformational leaders inspire inspiration and a sense of purpose in those they lead. They articulate a vision and communicate expectations and confidence in the team. They communicate with clarity and conviction and shift seemingly negative or challenging circumstances into opportunities for gains and growth. They are gain oriented, not gap minded.

3. **Intellectual Stimulation:** Transformational leaders value creativity and autonomy among each team member. The leader involves members in the decision-making process and stimulates creative thinking. They challenge assumptions and create an environment where healthy conflict can arise. They change how their followers think about and frame problems and obstacles, empowering them to take ownership of decisions and results.

4. **Individualized Consideration:** Transformational leaders know that each member of the team is a unique individual, with unique goals and a Unique Ability. Transformational leaders remove friction and anxiety and provide an environment where each unique individual feels free and autonomous to be their best selves and to openly and honestly communicate their challenges, wishes, and perspectives.[5,6,7,8]

In addition to growing into a Transformational Leader, Tim also began enabling the Whos on his team to operate autonomously—leading themselves, taking ownership, and deciding how they would fulfill their individual roles and responsibilities, rather than being helicoptered over by a manager, not a leader.

Tim also developed his own philosophy and ideology—and put it into a clear framework—which not only guided the direction and vision of the company and team but also provided psychographic clarity and alignment for the end customer and community.

As a Transformational Leader, Tim provided principles, training, language, rituals, and community for people who want to responsibly own guns. He provided a culture for people to attach and build as a part of their identity.

He also provided a *maturity model,* including an initial level that ascends as the client learns, evolves, and applies USCCA.

Tim consciously and humbly went from rugged individualist to Transformational Leader. He stopped needing to control the Hows and instead began investing in himself by getting increasingly high-quality Whos. He let those Whos operate in their Unique Ability and increasingly manage themselves, rather than control their every movement.

He became a leader, evolving and expanding himself, his vision, his philosophy, and the unique value he brought to his team and clients.

At each stage of Tim's development, he had to let go of the 80 percent that got him there, which was now holding him back from making his next 10x jump.

With Tim's story now behind us, I will go into some of the core "Who Not How" principles and applications. These are also the core areas people get stuck attempting to apply Who Not How, which stop them from going 10x and keep them stuck in 2x-mode.

WHO NOT HOW FAQ

Question: Who is the first "Who" that young entrepreneurs should get?

Get an administrative assistant of some sort, whether in-person or digital. Another word for this, using the language of Gino Wickman and the Entrepreneurial Operating System (EOS), is "integrator." Susan Kichuk is an extremely high-level application of this role, though you can also start small by simply getting a digital assistant who immediately frees-up 20+ hours of your time, the "80 percent" including scheduling, email, logistics, etc.

Their job is to *organize you*, make your life easy and simple, and handle mundane and daily tasks. The goal is that your mind is increasingly freed to focus on what you do best, whatever that may be. As the popular saying goes, "Frank Sinatra doesn't move his own pianos."

Similarly, Dan advises his entrepreneurs to "Never show up on your own and without a team supporting you." To be blunt, you simply don't look high-level if you're the one answering your own emails and inquiries, and seemingly handling the operations side of your work. You look like a one-person show, which calls into question the level of service and quality, as well as professionalism and results, you can provide.

Never show up without a team.

Whenever you're facing a client or prospect, have that outward facing initial contact and systemized process be handled by a Who, not you. Let your Who organize you and set the stage for you so that you can show up and perform your best work. Not only does this enable you to focus on what you do best, but it also positions you far better for those you serve.

In addition to having your Who "set the stage" for the actual work you do, enabling you to just show up, they can and should set the stage for everything else in your life, making it increasingly easier. For example, they can set the stage for your day and week—helping you know where to focus your best energy and efforts and filtering out all the noise so you can keep your mind and attention on the highest-leverage Unique Ability activities.

Question: What if I'm scared of being a jerk and bossing someone else around?

Clarity in the beginning about what your standards and success criteria are is crucial. However, you can always reconnect and reclarify your standards anytime. If it's a strong relationship, and if you're constantly learning and growing, then your standards and processes will always be updating and improving. It should be a continuous and iterative *process*.

For example, as someone who regularly goes on podcasts to promote my books, I'm regularly communicating to Chelsea, my assistant and implementer, about the standards for the podcasts I go on. It's never a one-time thing, but an ongoing process of tightening up the filter, which she helps me apply to achieve desired results.

The more you apply Who Not How and empower your Whos to take ownership, and the more you experience the freedom of being in your 20 percent, the less you'll feel like a jerk.

You're a leader.

They have a job they are excited to support you in. This is *their* job. Get people who *want* to work, and who want to be successful. As Jim Collins stated in *Good to Great,*

"If you have the right people on the bus, the problem of how to motivate and manage people largely goes away. The right people don't need to be tightly managed or fired up; they will be self-motivated by the inner drive to produce the best results and to be a part of creating something great.[9] "

Question: What if you can't afford a Who?

You can't afford *not* to get Whos. *Don't see them as a cost.* Getting a Who is an investment in yourself and your results. The longer you wait to get a Who, the more of your time and energy will be sucked up in the 80 percent that only produces 20 percent of your results. Moreover, by being overly spread thin and busy, you're experiencing very little flow and depth, which is how you produce 10x higher quality results.

When you invest in a Who, not only will you free yourself up by dozens of hours, hours you can spend on the 20 percent of activities that are 10x more valuable, but you'll flow and focus while you're doing that 20 percent. All the while, your new Who will be more focused on their role and will more consistently produce the desired results of their role, which you were lackluster and inconsistently producing before. Everything immediately gets better, especially your own psychology and focus, which are foundational to going 10x.

Question: How do you find the right Whos?

Who Not How is a continuous process that you'll progressively get better at with time. It's like any other skill. In the beginning, you won't be that great at it. You won't have the best clarity and filters you'll use to find highly specific Whos.

You'll also probably not have the funds to get the most specialized and capable Whos you can. As with all things, start small. But just start.

Get your first assistant to take 20 hours of logistical and operational work off your plate. You can find a digital assistant overseas or even a person in the United States for less than $15 per hour to take this role, and you'll actually be surprised at the level of talent you can find for this role.

As you start seeing the power of Who Not How, you'll stop resisting it so much. You'll feel the power of having someone handle a ton of work for you, and you'll have more bandwidth to produce more in your 20 percent, which is the unique value you bring to the market place, which also brings you energy, flow, and joy.

There are limitless places you can find a Who—even social media. I found my first two assistants asking my Facebook friends if they knew anyone who wanted a part-time job as my personal assistant. I literally got dozens of applications and both of the women I hired were amazing for that stage of my career.

Eventually, I stopped finding my own Whos, enabling my assistant to do that for me. I just give her clear directions on the type of results I'm looking for (i.e., my vision and standards) and let her find and interview the Who she feels best about.

The more specialized you become, the more specific the Whos you'll need to help you get your desired results, which actually makes them *easier* to find since there are far fewer of them. As an example, to get this book where I wanted it, I knew I needed an editor that *really* knew business books. It took me less than an hour to think of Helen, who is a top-tier editor of business books like these and has worked on huge titles with household-name-level authors.

Question: What happens if I get the wrong Who and waste tons of money?

This happens regularly. Get in the gain, not the gap. Everything happens *for* you, not *to* you. The reason you got the wrong Who is because you weren't clear on what you wanted, and you weren't being a great "Buyer," using Dan Sullivan's language. When you're a "Buyer" rather than a "Seller," you're very clear on the results you want to create, you have high standards for everything you do, and you only work with increasingly high-impact players who are proven and committed.

Even still, this is a progression we all go through, and even after you've built an amazing team and group of collaborators, there's never a time you'll arrive and be completely free of the wrong Whos. The main thing is having a system in place where you filter out the wrong people faster and also course correct faster once you've realized the wrong Who is in place.

Often, you'll "lose money" on the wrong Whos. Even writing this book, I went through multiple editors and consultants who couldn't get me and this book where I wanted it to go. But I'm in the gain, not the gap. Therefore, I'm turning my experiences into growth and learning, wherein I'm clearer and clearer, and my system is better in the future for finding Whos than it was in the past.

Who Not How is not a skill set you're taught even in business school. Stay in the gain and keep getting better. Over time, the Whos around you will blow you away, and the system will be increasingly self-managing.

Question: Is it possible to overdo Who Not How?

Not really. The more you place your focus and energy into your 20 percent Unique Ability and get more consistent at producing 10x quality results, the more valuable your time and results will become. Your revenue and income will go 10x again and again, enabling you to get more Whos in all areas of your life.

10x is about depth and quality. To become a master at what you do, you can't have a million things on your mental plate sapping your cognitive load. Focus on higher quality and less quantity of things. This also applies in your personal life. If you can get someone to come and clean your house, do various tasks like laundry and dishes, run errands, etc., the higher the quality and depth you'll have with your family.

The personal side can be a big jump mentally for people. But again, this is about leadership and depth. It took years to convince my wife to get a "Mother's Helper" for 20 hours per week. But Cony has become a crucial member of our family. She watches our little kids—4-year-old twin girls and 2-year-old boy—so Lauren can focus on the older kids who are getting homeschooled. Cony also helps keep our house clean. More so, she also brings a calming and peaceful energy to our home.

Level 2 to Level 3 Entrepreneurship: From Leader Applying *Who Not How* to Self-Managing Company

"Taking your business 10x is only possible by ensuring that you and everyone on your team is operating as quickly as possible within a Self-Managing Company."

—DAN SULLIVAN

When the 19th-century American religious leader Joseph Smith was building up the city and community of Nauvoo, Illinois—approximately 20,000 people—he was approached by a member of legislature. The government official was keen to understand how Mr. Smith was able to govern such a large group of people, and how he was able to maintain such "perfect order." The official further remarked that it was impossible for them to govern the people and maintain order in the rest of Illinois.

Mr. Smith commented that it was *very easy* to do that.

"How?" responded the gentleman. "To us it is very difficult."

Mr. Smith replied, *"I teach them correct principles, and they govern themselves."*[10]

Joseph Smith's statement about governing a large and zealous religious community is applicable to building a Self-Managing Company.

It's not that hard.

It's actually the easiest way to lead and govern a group.

You let them *govern themselves.*

However, in order to do that, there must be a clear vision, standards, and culture. When you have a clear vision and culture—meaning you know who you are and what you're about—the right Whos will be *attracted to you* and what you're doing. These "right Whos" won't need you to motivate and govern them.

On the contrary, these right Whos will be intrinsically motivated to bring their best skills (and more) to the table. Actually, a concept connected with Transformational Leadership is what is known as *organizational citizenship behaviors* or *perceived role breadth.*[11,12,13] Organizational citizenship behaviors (OCB) are altruistic activities and behaviors that support the team and organization that are "above and beyond" the specifics of their role. This could be doing whatever is required to complete a project, providing support to others, bringing positive energy, etc. It's actions that are done out of want, not need. Done for the sake of doing, not for any particular reward.

Perceived role breadth is what an individual perceives as their role, and research shows that Transformational Leaders build trust and commitment in people, such that they expand their perceived role to include OCBs.[14,15,16] They see that as part of being on the team, wherein they go above and beyond, not because they have to but because they want to.

As part of my dissertation research, I found that Transformational Leaders inspire those they lead to expand their role to go far above and beyond by gaining their followers' trust and commitment.[17]

Trust in leader is a highly researched concept and is a crucial aspect of Transformational Leadership.[18] Without trust, there is no Transformational Leadership. It's the mediating force that enables leaders to inspire those they lead to elevate and transform themselves to create results and reach the new standard.

Recent meta-analytic research has shown that trust in leader, as well as *emotional organizational commitment,* facilitates the relationship between Transformational Leadership and expanded role breadth and OCBs.[19] Basically, Transformational Leaders gain the trust of those they lead, and help those they trust get highly emotionally committed to the cause and vision by which they are all involved. Through that trust in the leader and emotional commitment to the organization and mission, people do amazing things. They do things they never otherwise would have or could have.

When the "why" is strong enough, you find the "how."

In this case, when the "why" is strong enough, because the team trusts the leader and is emotionally committed to the cause, there is nothing they can't do to achieve the objective.

There's one final layer to this equation, which shows how Transformational Leaders get the most out of people and ultimately enable them to govern themselves as Joseph Smith described to the Illinois government official.

In his book *The Speed of Trust: The One Thing that Changes Everything*, Stephen M.R. Covey explains that to gain trust, you don't earn it. Instead, to gain trust, *you give trust*.[20] This is what building high quality relationships as well as a Self-Managing Team is all about. Rather than micromanaging and governing people, you give them vision, clarity, culture, and standards to live by. You also respect and value their own evolving and growing standards, which they hold for themselves as individuals. You trust the right Whos to manage themselves. You trust them to expand and clarify their role and to go above and beyond the call of duty.

When you trust people, they show up in amazing ways.

When you trust the right people, they expand that trust. Not only that, but this is the only way to get the best out of people, and it taps into the essence of human motivation. According to one of the most science-backed motivational theories ever, *self-determination theory*, there are three crucial components of high-levels of intrinsic motivation:

1. **Autonomy:** You have freedom to do what you want, how you want, when you want, and with whom you want.

2. **Mastery:** You have the freedom to continually elevate and evolve the artistry and skill of your Unique Ability.

3. **Relatedness:** You have the freedom to create transformational relationships with the 10x individuals you want to collaborate and transform with.[21,22]

In order for people to be highly motivated in what they do, these three pieces are essential. The more autonomy they have in what they do, the more motivated and empowered they will be. As I wrote in *Who Not How*:

"If you're going to apply higher levels of team-work in your life, you'll need to relinquish control over how things get done. . . Not only must the Who fully own the How, but they must have complete permission to do so."[23]

Nearly all of the entrepreneurs throughout this book whose stories I've highlighted have built a Self-Managing company.

In Chapter 1, I told the stories of Carson Holmquist and Linda McKissack.

Carson realized that he was the bottleneck of his company, Stream Logistics, and was stalling its ability to go 10x. He was involved in literally every aspect of the decision-making process. He raised up the leadership in Stream Logistics such that he entirely freed up his time and focus to explore everything happening in his business, as well as to better understand his best clients and customers.

This led him to realize that his best customers, the High Stakes Freight customers, only made up 5 percent of their clients but over 15 percent of their profits. With his Self-Managing team, Carson was freed up to be in his Unique Ability, expand his vision and leadership, and ultimately redirect the entire ship of the company, which has now 4x'd its profits in the past few years while maintaining the same size of team.

Linda created various iterations of a Self-Managing Company. First, she hired a personal assistant to manage everything logistical and organizational. Then she hired another assistant and eventually other agents to handle the rest. But even still, at this point she was mostly just applying Who Not How.

It wasn't until she hired her brother-in-law, Brad, to fully manage her businesses that she had a Self-Managing Team. Once she had that in place, she could focus on growing the Keller Williams regions in Ohio, Indiana, and Kentucky.

With her Self-Managing Company in place, she did grow two regions, which now have 28 offices and over 5,000 active real estate agents working within them. Her business now does over $14 billion in annual revenue.

None of this would have happened if Linda didn't go from a rugged individualist to a leader applying Who Not How, to a Transformational Leader of a Self-Managing and Self-Expanding Company.

In Chapter 2 of this book, I told the story of Chad Willardson, the financial advisor who left his fancy gig at Merrill Lynch to start his own private fiduciary, Pacific Capital. Chad's progression has followed the same pattern, wherein he went from rugged individualist doing everything himself to eventually applying Who Not How in all aspects of his life and business.

Eventually, Chad made his company entirely Self-Managing. He is no longer involved in the day-to-day, though he is still leading the overall vision and strategy of Pacific Capital. Now Chad comes into the office maybe 30 days per year to connect with the team, update them on the ongoing vision and focus they have, and support them in any ways they need.

Chad is fully freed up to have peak experiences with his family, travel the world, continually upgrade and elevate his thinking, and expand his growing network of collaborators, co-investors, and clients.

Earlier in the chapter, I told the story of Garnet Morris and Targeted Strategies Group, who is a brilliant innovator and strategist who grew his business into a multimillion-dollar company by applying Who Not How where he could. Yet, it wasn't until he made his company Self-Managing, by hiring Susan Kichuk, that his company's growth skyrocketed to totally different levels. Now, Targeted Strategies Group sells more life insurance than any other company in all of Canada, by a factor of 10.

What about you?

- Are you a rugged individualist or are you a leader applying Who Not How?

- Let's be real: Are you a true leader or are you still a bottleneck manager?

- Do you trust your Whos or do you only trust yourself?

- Can you imagine what it would be and feel like to have a Self-Managing Company, where you've freed yourself up to explore, expand, innovate, learn, and create?

- Are you ready to become a *transformational leader*?

Level 3 to Level 4 Entrepreneurship: From Self-Managing Company to Self-Expanding Unique Ability Teamwork

"Having a Unique Ability Team means working out a deal whereby each person is freed up to focus on their own area of Unique Ability. It means hiring people with diverse skills and talents, including in areas where you're lacking, so that each task and responsibility in your business is covered by someone who loves doing it and is best at it. Your team members will only work this way, though, once they've gotten permission to do that from your example. They can't give themselves any more permission than you demonstrate. Just as it's true that your team won't feel they have permission to free themselves up to focus on their areas of Unique Ability without your leadership example, it's also the case that you won't be able to focus on your Unique Ability and

achieve a Self-Managing Company unless your team members are also freed up to focus on what they love to do and do best—those things that give them energy, and therefore, energize the entire organization. To give this kind of freedom to your team requires a profound shift in your thinking, but you'll increasingly enjoy greater creative and collaborative support for your own Unique Ability as more of your team members are able to focus entirely on theirs. My presence isn't required for my team to do their best work, and this continual development and expansion of everyone's Unique Ability Teamwork automatically creates a Self-Managing Company."

—DAN SULLIVAN

Having a *self-multiplying team* is a natural extension of having a self-managing team.

As a leader, you set the tone for everything that happens in your organization and team. When you take seriously your own Unique Ability, and when you're living the 10x process of going all-in on your 20 percent and continually eliminating the 80 percent, you encourage your team to do the same.

You encourage your team to take seriously their own Unique Ability. They are encouraged to double down into their own 20 percent that both excites and scares them, and to continually refine their role as they see fit. Jim Collins explained in *Good to Great* that it's not just about having the right people on the bus, you want the right people in the right seats.[24] What Collins didn't explain is that the "right seat" is ultimately hand-crafted by the right Whos themselves.

In a Self-Managing Company operating with Unique Ability Teamwork, each individual member continually refines their own role so that they're only working in a few areas that excite and energize them. As they do this, they form new roles with their old 80 percent and bring on right-fit people who excitedly want that 80 percent. This is when a team begins expanding itself in an autonomous way.

Take my company, for example.

When I first started writing books professionally, I did a lot of editing myself. However, over time, as I've homed in on 20 percent, I've gotten more Whos around me to support and elevate the work I do. This includes strategists, marketing people, publicist, better editors, etc.

All of these Whos have allowed me to increase my commitment to my 20 percent. Now, whenever I collaborate or work with someone, such as Dan Sullivan and Strategic Coach, on these books, they don't just get me and my Unique Ability. Instead, they get my growing and self-multiplying team that comes with me, which now includes multiple editors, marketers, publishers, administrative assistants, soon-to-be publicists, etc.

My assistant, Chelsea, recently went through this process herself. When she became my assistant around two years ago, her role involved a great deal of responsibility, including managing my schedule, calendar, etc. Increasingly, I threw more and more at Chelsea, and for a time, she handled it quite well, despite being a mom at home and raising three beautiful kids.

However, as my goals grew bigger and the projects I threw at Chelsea to lead and delegate got more intensive, she began dropping important balls. It became obvious that she was spread far too thin.

Her role had grown far too much. She also had become much clearer on the aspects of her job that excited and fascinated her—her own Unique Ability. She clarified the 20 percent of her role she wanted to focus on as well as the 80 percent of her role that she wanted to pass off to a new Who.

Chelsea's 80 percent revolved around organizational development and the follow-up and completion of big projects. Her superpower 20 percent was in supporting and keeping me organized, as well as supporting the team when they were executing big projects.

Chelsea then went out and found Kaytlin, an unbelievably talented person to take over her old 80 percent. Kaytlin loves organizing systems and processes. She's also extremely high in her follow-through and completion of big tasks and projects. She loves solving problems and getting things done. Now that Kaytlin is around, Chelsea's job is 10x more enjoyable and she's 10x better and more focused on the few areas she loves.

Eventually, Chelsea and Kaytlin will identify their own 20 percent, and thus multiply their roles and teams around them autonomously and organically.

A word of caution. One thing that Dan talks about is that when you enable people to autonomously operate in their Unique Ability, they will become increasingly valuable and brilliant at what they do. In fact, they will become so valuable that they will have many options to leave and work for other organizations.

As Dan explains in his book *The Self-Managing Company*:

> "The corporate, bureaucratic attitude is that everybody is replaceable, and you never want to become dependent on people. But the only way you can actually make an extraordinary organization, that in fact you've grown people's Unique Ability to such extent that they virtually are irreplicable. If something were to happen that they were to leave, you wouldn't be able to replace them. You'd have to create something new. We have many people that, if something were to happen to them, there would be a permanent hole in terms of what they were doing. Now, we'd move on to other things and make other people irreplaceable in other ways, but it's a risk that you take. I don't

think greatness comes without that risk of having people who are so uniquely good at what they do that they're irreplaceable. It's the only way you get greatness in an entrepreneurial organization."[25]

This is the "risk" you have to take to become great. When you provide an environment of freedom and 10x vision that's so big that being a part of it transforms people, you risk creating Unique Ability people that are utterly amazing at what they do.

However, there are very few organizations that take Unique Ability seriously. Very few founders and leaders take even their own Unique Ability seriously, let alone becoming Transformational Leaders with a Self-Managing Company, rather than being bottleneck micromanagers.

Therefore, it's a worthwhile risk to take. You create an environment of freedom where the right Whos continually craft their own role and niche.

A connected risk to developing incredibly brilliant people with insanely valuable Unique Abilities is not having a 10x vision. If you stop having a 10x vision, your best people will leave you. The best people to team up with are not those interested in 2x, only 10x.

Is your vision compelling enough that your best people see a 10x future and growth for themselves in it?

Does being a part of what you're doing excite, energize, and transform your best people?

Just as true, when you're operating toward a 10x vision, the 2x people who simply want a "job" will leave. They don't want to transform at the level your vision requires all involved to be a part of.

If you're serious about 10x, then freedom is the language and operating system that will get you there. Your own freedom as well as the freedom of everyone else who joins you on your 10x adventure.

What about you?

- Do you take your Unique Ability seriously enough to free yourself from the 80 percent?

- Do you lead by example and create a culture of freedom where those on your team are given permission to take their Unique Ability seriously as well?

- Does your self-managing team have the confidence to go all-in on their Unique Ability, honing their own roles and bringing on additional Whos to handle their former 80 percent?

Core Applications

- Start getting Whos immediately to handle the 80 percent of tasks you're currently doing.

- The first Who you'll likely want is an administrative assistant of some form to take most of the logistical and procedural tasks off your plate, enabling you to focus where you're best. Get a Who that *organizes and systemizes you*, so you can stop having to continually organize yourself. The more dedicated you are to your creativity and craft, the less bandwidth and cognitive load you'll be able to give to procedural and organizational tasks. Get Whos to happily and successfully handle that stuff for you. Remember, Frank Sinatra didn't move his own pianos. Neither should you—whatever that means for you.

- Begin investing in Whos in all the key areas of your life. This will enable greater depth, quality, and flow in all aspects of your life. Every Who you get is an investment in *you*, your life, and your results.

- Before you feel ready, train up leadership to replace you from being the organizational leader of the business. Create a Self-Managing Company that operates and runs without you involved in the day-to-day. The leader(s) you hire or develop will be better than you at leading the organization and team, unless that is 100 percent your Unique Ability. Even still, your best contribution is continually expanding yourself as a person and leader, expanding your vision, and increasing the quality and impact of your Unique Ability for increasingly niche people.

- Create a culture of freedom wherein all team members are encouraged to clarify and expand their own Unique Ability. Each member increasingly specifies what excites them—their own 20 percent—and they are encouraged to pass off their own 80 percent to a new Who, whom they help find and train.

Chapter Takeaways

- There are at least four core levels of entrepreneurship that you'll need to pass through to go 10x again and again. The faster you go up these levels, the faster and easier each following 10x jump will be.

- Level one entrepreneurship is being a solopreneur or micromanager, where you're a rugged individual who either does all the How yourself, with very little Who. Or, if you do have Whos, you micromanage them, stunting your own freedom and growth, and stunting their autonomy and growth. This is where Tim Schdmit, the founder and CEO of the U.S. Concealed Carry Association (USCCA), was for over a decade until he shifted to level two entrepreneurship.

- Level two entrepreneurship is evolving beyond the rugged individual to becoming a leader who applies Who Not How. By applying Who Not How, you begin operating far more in the 20 percent of your 10x process—which is your Unique Ability. You fully trust the Whos to handle the Hows of their various roles, and you don't micromanage them. You give them autonomy and trust with clear vision and standards.

- Level three entrepreneurship goes beyond applying Who Not How in all aspects of your life to creating a Self-Managing Company. In a Self-Managing Company, you're no longer managing or leading the day-to-day aspects of the business. Instead, you've trained up or hired leaders to lead the team and business for you. You're still a visionary and leader of the business as a whole, and you're not entirely disconnected. However, increasingly more, the business manages itself without you, freeing you entirely to be in your Unique Ability— where you're exploring, expanding, innovating, and collaborating. You're transforming yourself 10x, and, as a result, the vision and freedom in all of your company expands 10x continuously as well.

- Level four entrepreneurship is where, in your Self-Managing Company, everyone is increasingly encouraged to operate in their own Unique Abilities—their own 20 percent of the 10x vision. When people are autonomously operating in their Unique Ability, they become incredibly skillful and valuable at what they do. They become self-managing and self-governing leaders themselves, continuing to go above and beyond the call of duty and to focus on *results*, not being busy. They take responsibility for being as valuable to themselves and the team as they can. They feel trusted to go all in on their Unique Ability and become as valuable and powerful as possible. As a result, they multiply themselves by getting others to take over their 80 percent. They do this again and again, and now you have a self-multiplying unique ability team.

- The biggest risk of Unique Ability Teamwork is that the people involved in your 10x vision develop such incredible Unique Abilities that they become attractive to other organizations. However, few places offer them the 10x vision you do, and few offer them the freedom to continue transforming themselves and their Unique Ability as you do. Even still, it's a true risk that the people you develop will become so good you cannot replace them, and if they leave you won't find someone like them. That's the risk of becoming great.

- The final risk of becoming great is not going 10x. If you're not going 10x, then the best people will not be attracted to working with you. 2x isn't exciting or motivating to the best Whos. If you go into 2x mode, you'll be left with a lot of people working with you who simply want a job. They don't want 10x transformation and growth. They certainly won't be expanding their role and going above and beyond. They won't have the trust in you as their leader or emotional commitment to their organization. They won't go 10x beyond the call of duty. Instead, they'll do as little as possible.

CONCLUSION

10x Is Easier Than 2x

◆ ◆ ◆

"In the end we will only be transformed when we can recognize and accept the fact that there is a will within each of us, quite outside the range of conscious control, a will which knows what is right for us, which is repeatedly reporting to us via our bodies, emotions, and dreams, and is incessantly encouraging our healing and wholeness."

—DR. JAMES HOLLIS[1]

In the book *Power versus Force*, Dr. David Hawkins developed what he calls the *Map of Consciousness*, which conveys where a person is in their spiritual and emotional development. The scale goes from 20 (shame) all the way to 1,000 (enlightenment).[2]

Everything below 200 (courage) on the scale is operating from a negative emotion, such as guilt (30), apathy (50), fear (100), or anger (150).

The higher emotional energies include acceptance (350), love (500), joy (540), and peace (600).

According to Dr. Hawkins—who spent decades developing and studying this map and testing it on *millions of people*—the average person only advances *five points up* this scale in their entire life.

As he explains in *Power versus Force*:

"The average advance in the level of consciousness throughout the global population is little more
than five points during a lifetime. Apparently, from
untold millions of individual experiences in one's
life, usually, only a few lessons are ever learned. The
attainment of wisdom is slow and painful, and few
are willing to relinquish familiar, even if inaccurate,
views; resistance to change or growth is considerable.
It would seem that most people are willing to die
rather than alter those belief systems which confine
them to lower levels of consciousness."

According to Dr. Hawkins' research, over 80 percent of
the global population operate between 100 (fear) and 150
(anger) in terms of their individual level of consciousness and
emotional development.

Given that most people only grow by *five points* on this
scale in their entire lifetimes, most people never make it
beyond being driven by fear or anger.

Even still, there are some people *who grow hundreds of
points* up this scale, even in a relatively short period of time.
It's available to everyone, though few choose it.

It takes commitment and courage (200) to begin transforming your life.

All progress starts by telling the truth.

Once you make commitment and courage toward 10x
dreams, you can and will evolve to the higher dimensions
on Hawkins' map. You can reach a place of acceptance, love,
peace, and even enlightenment.

You do this by stripping more and more layers of the
David away.

As you develop your Unique Ability to unfathomable levels, and as you consciously choose a life of freedom, you will

have increasing power in your life. You'll stop operating out of brute-force emotions or energy.

You'll stop forcing yourself to do anything you don't want to do. You'll accept and live by what psychologists call *pull motivation*, rather than push motivation.[3],[4] When you're pulled by what you want and what excites you, that's freedom and intrinsic motivation.

You'll no longer operate based on need, but want. *You're free.*

You'll also stop forcing others to do anything they don't want to do and create a 10x culture of freedom and transformation for all around you. Increasingly, you *only* operate with people who are fully committed to freedom within their Unique Ability as well. Everyone around you is transforming themselves 10x.

Hawkins found that the higher up his map a person goes, the bigger and more profound the ripple effects throughout the world they will have. Here's how Dr. Hawkins breaks it down:

- One person living and vibrating to the energy of optimism and a willingness to be nonjudgmental of others (310) will counterbalance the negativity of 90,000 people who calibrate at the lower weakening levels.

- One person living and vibrating to the energy of pure love and reverence for all of life (500) will counterbalance the negativity of 750,000 people who calibrate at the lower weakening levels.

- One person living and vibrating to the energy of illumination, bliss, and infinite peace (600) will counterbalance the negativity of 10 million people who calibrate at the lower weakening levels.

- One person living and vibrating to the energy of grace, pure spirit beyond body, in a world of nonduality or complete oneness (700–1,000), will counterbalance the negativity of 70 million people who calibrate at the lower weakening levels.[5]

Whether Dr. Hawkins' exact measurements are correct is less important than the central message he's conveying, as well as the message of this book.

By going 10x and stripping away the layers of the David, your life will become increasingly focused and simple. Your Unique Ability will become increasingly rare and valuable. To use author Cal Newport's language, your "rare and valuable skills" will produce work that's "so good it can't be ignored."[6] Thus, despite you becoming simpler and more focused, the ripple effects of everything you do will have higher leverage and impact.

There's a Chinese saying, "Si liang bo qian jin," which roughly translates to "Defeat a thousand pounds with four ounces."

As you go deeper into your Unique Ability, you apply less and less pressure yet produce 10x, 100x, 1,000x and more the impact and leverage.

You can defeat a thousand pounds with four ounces of leverage.

There's a fictional story of an operational problem at a nuclear power plant. The malfunction was slowing energy generation down and reducing the efficiency of the entire plant. It became an extreme bottleneck.[7]

The plant's engineers spent months and months trying to solve the problem but couldn't figure it out. Consequently, they brought in one of the nation's top consultants on nuclear powerplant engineering. For the next several hours, he looked around at every little detail of the plant—studying the hundreds of dials and gauges and taking notes and making calculations.

After nearly a full day's work, he pulled a marker out of his pocket, climbed up a ladder, and put a big "X" on the one of the gauges. "This is the problem," he said, pointing to the big X. "Replace this and everything will be back to functioning properly."

This specialist then left the plant and flew home.

Later that day, the plant manager got an email from the consultant's assistant with an invoice of $50,000.

Despite the fact that this single problem was costing the plant hundreds of thousands of dollars every week, the manager was still shocked by the fee. He replied to the assistant, "How is it possible for less than a day's work to be valued at $50,000? All he did was write an X with a marker."

The assistant replied, "$1 for the X, and $49,999 for knowing where to put the X."

In the words of author and speaker Brian Tracy, "Knowing where to put that X is your focal point."

Your "focal point" is the concentrated energy of your Unique Ability.

The more you evolve your Unique Ability by going 10x again and again, the more powerful and impactful the focal point of all you do will be, because you'll be increasingly operating by power and not force.

You'll have extreme leverage and flow.

All the while, you'll continuously be expanding your four freedoms:

1. Freedom of Time

2. Freedom of Money

3. Freedom of Relationship

4. Freedom of Purpose

Each of these four freedoms is *qualitative* and individual. They are based far more on quality and value than on quantity and comparison.

As you go 10x, the quality and value of your time will expand, as will the quality and value of your money and how you get paid, as well as the quality and value of those you spend time and work with, and finally the quality and value of your overall purpose and mission in life.

As I'm wrapping up this book and our time together, it's crazy looking at my life now, in November of 2022, and attempting to compare it to where I was at the beginning of this year. My life is profoundly and qualitatively different *and better* in so many ways.

Certainly, I could compare the differences, and it's good to be *in the gain* and measure those differences explicitly.

Yet, at the same time, who I am now and what my life is like versus even 10–12 months ago is incomparably and non-linearly different. There was no obvious and linear path from where I was to where I'm at now. The whole system and context of my life, relationships, attention, and focus is entirely evolved from where I was before.

The world is entirely different.

My trajectory is non-linear, yet better.

I'm freer to live in and cultivate my Unique Ability.

My team is self-managing, and we're continually improving and systemizing our minimum standards of excellence.

Recently, I had the opportunity to take these concepts into a unique and personally meaningful environment. I'd been asked by the mission leader of my church in Ft. Lauderdale to come and train the leadership of his mission on these concepts.

The mission leader had a spreadsheet of the mission's numbers over the previous 12 months. As a mission of around 200 missionaries, they'd baptized 430ish people in the past 12 months. Part of the report broke down the different "finding" activities into three core categories: 1) working with members of the church, 2) finding people to teach in their own way such as knocking on doors, and 3) using social media.

Forty percent of the baptisms came from working with the members of the church and getting referrals from those members of people to teach.

Thirty-four percent of the baptisms came from the missionaries' own finding efforts. One of these activities accounted for a huge portion of these finding efforts—13 percent overall—which was getting referrals from those they were teaching.

Finally, 26 percent of the overall baptisms came from finding and teaching people via social media.

During the training, and while going over these numbers, I asked the missionaries how much time they worked during a regular day.

"Eight hours," they responded.

"How many of those eight hours are spent working with members?" I asked.

"Maybe one," they replied.

"What about working on social media?" I asked.

"Maybe 15-30 minutes," they replied.

"So let me get this straight. You spend 1.5 hours of your day engaged in activities that account for 66 percent of your baptisms?"

One-and-a-half out of eight hours is 18.75 percent, less than 20 percent.

If you include the simple activity of the missionaries asking the people they're teaching for referrals, which takes just a few minutes and accounts for 13 percent more of their baptisms, then we're talking about almost exactly *20 percent* of their time yielding *80 percent* of results.

According to constraint theory, every unit or system has a core goal or objective. That core objective also highlights the core constraint or bottleneck that must be solved in order for the goal to be achieved.

Without solving the bottleneck, you won't achieve the goal, no matter how much energy and effort you're putting in.

The bottleneck is the 20 percent.

Everything else is the 80 percent, which doesn't meet the filter of the goal.

In most businesses, the majority of energy and resources are put toward activities in the 80 percent, not the bottleneck, which is why most business are growing linearly not exponentially. Most businesses are 2x at best, not 10x.

To go 10x, you let go of the 80 percent and put your energy, attention, and resources into the bottleneck, which is the 20 percent.

The missionaries keep dedicated records of every person they contact and teach in a digital "Area Book." When they contact a person and teach them a simple lesson, the person gets a colored dot on the digital map of their Area Book—such as grey. As that person advances with the missionaries, such as wanting more lessons or coming to church, the color of their dot changes.

I explained to the missionaries the concept of *fitness function* and that as a person or group, you *are* what you're optimizing *for*.

"If you want to double your baptisms as a mission, you'll have to get half the dots you're now getting. Are you okay with that?"

This was mind-blowing to them.

They were beginning to see that individually and collectively, they'd been *optimizing for dots*—contacting and teaching people—when *baptizing individuals and families* was their stated and true goal.

10x is about higher quality and less quantity.

Most of their "dots" were people who were never going to get baptized, found through low-quality activities that had a low conversion rate (one percent or less) such as knocking on doors.

Not all dots are created equal.

Not all activities are created equal.

You could get thousands of "dots" or contacts but get only a handful of actual baptisms.

If they wanted to baptize more, they'd need their "dots"—the people they're teaching—to come from the highest-yielding 20 percent of activities: working with members, getting referrals from the people they're already teaching, and social media.

"If you want quick wins, you can keep your 80 percent and keep collecting dots," I told them. "If you want to go bigger and elevate your standards and baseline, then you'll need to let go of the 80 percent and stop optimizing for dots."

One sister missionary asked, "But we've been taught to keep 'all of our lines' out in the water. This feels like we're pulling many of our lines out of the water."

I replied, "What if your lines are in the wrong ponds, and there are no fish where you're fishing?"

Another sister missionary raised her hand and said, "This reminds me of the story of Peter and his brothers fishing all night and catching nothing. Then Jesus came and told them to put their nets on the other side of the boat and immediately there were so many fish the boat almost sank."

When you insist on doing what you've been doing, 10x is essentially impossible.

Only when you expand your vision and focus on the 20 percent can immediate and transformative results be yours.

The mission leader felt inspired that God wanted them to double their minimum standard from 50 baptisms as a mission per month, which they'd recently been getting, to 100 baptisms per month. The missionaries now understood that it would be unlikely for them to realize that new standard if they kept their 80 percent.

However, if they focused on the 20 percent—and got 10x better and more skilled in the 20 percent—then they'd realize and systemize the new standard in a short period of time. Actually, they'd blow way past the new standard.

Indeed, if they got serious about the 20 percent, and getting 10x better in the few things that matter, as well as letting go of the 80 percent that is keeping them stuck—then they'd be able to go 10x.

What about you?

- What is your 10x vision?

- What is your 20 percent?

- What is your Unique Ability?

- Are you committed to going 10x and creating a Self-Managing Company?

- Are you playing the infinite game or stuck in a finite one?

- Are you ready for 10x freedom and purpose?

- Are you going to let go of your 80 percent again and again, devoting your time to an ever-shrinking 20 percent within 20 percent within 20 percent, becoming the most powerful, unique, and optimized version of yourself?

10x is easier than 2x.

2x is doing the same thing, only more of it. It's brute force, not intelligent, not transformational, not an upgrade in thinking.

10x is an entirely different way of doing things, based on an entirely different future. To go 10x, you can't avoid the bottleneck—the 20 percent. Instead, you fully embrace and transform it, knowing all the while that the bottleneck has always been *yourself.*

ADDITIONAL RESOURCES FROM STRATEGIC COACH

To take your personal 10x thinking to the next level visit www.10xeasierbook.com for additional tools and resources.

ENDNOTES

Epigraph

1. Ferriss, T. (2018). *Astro Teller, CEO of X – How to Think 10x Bigger (#309)*. The Tim Ferriss Show.

Introduction

1. Stone, I. (2015). *The Agony and the Ecstasy*. Random House.

2. Stone, I. (2015). *The Agony and the Ecstasy*. Random House.

3. Holroyd, C. Michael Angelo Buonarroti, with Translations of the Life of the Master by His Scholar, Ascanio Condivi, and Three Dialogues from the Portuguese by Francisco d'Ollanda. London, Duckworth and Company. P. 16. X111. 1903. http://www.gutenberg.org/files/19332/19332-h/19332-h.html#note_20

4. Condivi, A. *The Life of Michelangelo*. Translation: Baton Rouge, Louisiana State University Press, F1976. Quotations from Condivi's *The Life of Michelangelo* are paraphrased based upon the Wohl text and other readings of Michelangelo.

5. Hercules drawing. Retrieved from Michelangelo.net on August 17, 2022, at https://www.michelangelo.net/hercules/.

6. Doorley, J. D., Goodman, F. R., Kelso, K. C., & Kashdan, T. B. (2020). Psychological flexibility: What we know, what we do not know, and what we think we know. *Social and Personality Psychology Compass, 14*(12), 1–11.

7. Kashdan, T. B., & Rottenberg, J. (2010). Psychological flexibility as a fundamental aspect of health. *Clinical Psychology Review, 30*(7), 865–878.

8. Bond, F. W., Hayes, S. C., & Barnes-Holmes, D. (2006). Psychological flexibility, ACT, and organizational behavior. *Journal of Organizational Behavior Management, 26*(1–2), 25-54.

9. Kashdan, T. B., Disabato, D. J., Goodman, F. R., Doorley, J. D., & McKnight, P. E. (2020). Understanding psychological flexibility: A multimethod exploration of pursuing valued goals despite the presence of distress. *Psychological Assessment, 32*(9), 829.

10. Godbee, M., & Kangas, M. (2020). The relationship between flexible perspective taking and emotional well-being: A systematic review of the "self-as-context" component of acceptance and commitment therapy. *Behavior Therapy, 51*(6), 917–932.

11. Yu, L., Norton, S., & McCracken, L. M. (2017). Change in "self-as-context"("perspective-taking") occurs in acceptance and commitment

therapy for people with chronic pain and is associated with improved functioning. *The Journal of Pain, 18*(6), 664–672.

12. Zettle, R. D., Gird, S. R., Webster, B. K., Carrasquillo-Richardson, N., Swails, J. A., & Burdsal, C. A. (2018). The Self-as-Context Scale: Development and preliminary psychometric properties. *Journal of Contextual Behavioral Science, 10*, 64–74.

13. De Tolnay, C. (1950). *The Youth of Michelangelo*. Princeton University Press; 2nd ed. pp. 26–28.

14. Coughlan, Robert (1966). *The World of Michelangelo*: 1475–1564. et al. Time-Life Books. p. 85.

15. Stone, I. (2015). *The Agony and the Ecstasy*. Random House.

16. Fromm, E. (1994). *Escape from Freedom*. Macmillan.

17. Sullivan, D., & Hardy, B. (2020). *Who Not How: The formula to achieve bigger goals through accelerating teamwork*. Hay House Business.

18. Carse, J. (2011). *Finite and Infinite Games*. Simon & Schuster.

19. Hardy, B. (2016). Does it take courage to start a business? (Masters' thesis, Clemson University).

20. Hardy, B. P. (2019). Transformational leadership and perceived role breadth: Multi-level mediation of trust in leader and affective organizational commitment (Doctoral dissertation, Clemson University).

21. Hardy, B. (2018). *Willpower Doesn't Work: Discover the hidden keys to success*. Hachette.

22. Sullivan, D. & Hardy, B. (2020). *Who Not How: The Formula to Achieve Bigger Goals through Accelerating Teamwork*. Hay House Business.

23. Sullivan, D. & Hardy, B. (2021). *The Gap and The Gain: The high achievers' guide to happiness, confidence, and success*. Hay House Business.

24. Greene, R. (2013). *Mastery*. Penguin.

25. Eliot, T. S. (1971). *Four Quartets*. Harvest.

Chapter I

1. Koch, R. (2011). *The 80/20 Principle: The secret of achieving more with less: Updated 20th anniversary edition of the productivity and business classic*. Hachette UK.

2. Wided, R. Y. (2012). For a better openness towards new ideas and practices. *Journal of Business Studies Quarterly, 3*(4), 132.

3. Snyder, C. R., LaPointe, A. B., Jeffrey Crowson, J., & Early, S. (1998). Preferences of high- and low-hope people for self-referential input. *Cognition & Emotion, 12*(6), 807–823.

4. Chang, E. C. (1998). Hope, problem-solving ability, and coping in a college student population: Some implications for theory and practice. *Journal of Clinical Psychology, 54*(7), 953–962.

5. Charlotte Law, M. S. O. D., & Lacey, M. Y. (2019). How Entrepreneurs Create High-Hope Environments. *2019 Volume 22 Issue 1* (1).

6. Vroom, V., Porter, L., & Lawler, E. (2005). Expectancy theories. *Organizational Behavior, 1*, 94–113.

7. Snyder, C. R. (2002). Hope theory: Rainbows in the mind. *Psychological Inquiry, 13*(4), 249–275.

8. Landau, R. (1995). Locus of control and socioeconomic status: Does internal locus of control reflect real resources and opportunities or personal coping abilities? *Social Science & Medicine, 41*(11), 1499–1505.

9. Kim, N. R., & Lee, K. H. (2018). The effect of internal locus of control on career adaptability: The mediating role of career decision-making self-efficacy and occupational engagement. *Journal of Employment Counseling, 55*(1), 2–15.

10. Holiday, R. (2022). *Discipline Is Destiny: The power of self-control (The Stoic Virtues Series).* Penguin.

11. Sullivan, D. (2019). *Who Do You Want to Be a Hero To?: Answer just one question and clarify who you can always be.* Strategic Coach, Inc.

12. Csikszentmihalyi, M., Abuhamdeh, S., & Nakamura, J. (2014). *Flow.* In Flow and the foundations of positive psychology (pp. 227–238). Springer, Dordrecht.

13. Heutte, J., Fenouillet, F., Martin-Krumm, C., Gute, G., Raes, A., Gute, D., ... & Csikszentmihalyi, M. (2021). Optimal experience in adult learning: conception and validation of the flow in education scale (EduFlow-2). *Frontiers in Psychology, 12*, 828027.

14. Csikszentmihalyi, M., Montijo, M. N., & Mouton, A. R. (2018). Flow theory: Optimizing elite performance in the creative realm.

15. Kotler, S. (2014). *The Rise of Superman: Decoding the science of ultimate human performance.* Houghton Mifflin Harcourt.

16. Collins, J. (2001). *Good to Great: Why some companies make the leap and others don't.* HarperBusiness.

17. Sullivan, D. (2015). *The 10x Mind Expander: Moving your thinking, performance, and results from linear plodding to exponential breakthroughs.* Strategic Coach Inc.

18. Hardy, B. (2016). Does it take courage to start a business? (Masters' thesis, Clemson University).

19. Snyder, C. R. (2002). Hope theory: Rainbows in the mind. *Psychological Inquiry, 13*(4), 249–275.

20. Feldman, D. B., Rand, K. L., & Kahle-Wrobleski, K. (2009). Hope and goal attainment: Testing a basic prediction of hope theory. *Journal of Social and Clinical Psychology, 28*(4), 479.

21. Baykal, E. (2020). A model on authentic leadership in the light of hope theory. *Sosyal Bilimler Arastirmalari Dergisi, 10*(3).

22. Bernardo, A. B. (2010). Extending hope theory: Internal and external locus of trait hope. *Personality and Individual Differences, 49*(8), 944-949.

23. Tong, E. M., Fredrickson, B. L., Chang, W., & Lim, Z. X. (2010). Re-examining hope: The roles of agency thinking and pathways thinking. *Cognition and Emotion, 24*(7), 1207–1215.

24. Chang, E. C., Chang, O. D., Martos, T., Sallay, V., Zettler, I., Steca, P., ... & Cardeñoso, O. (2019). The positive role of hope on the relationship between loneliness and unhappy conditions in Hungarian young adults: How pathways thinking matters!. *The Journal of Positive Psychology, 14*(6), 724–733.

25. Pignatiello, G. A., Martin, R. J., & Hickman Jr, R. L. (2020). Decision fatigue: A conceptual analysis. *Journal of Health Psychology, 25*(1), 123–135.

26. Vohs, K. D., Baumeister, R. F., Twenge, J. M., Schmeichel, B. J., Tice, D. M., & Crocker, J. (2005). Decision fatigue exhausts self-regulatory resources—But so does accommodating to unchosen alternatives. Manuscript submitted for publication.

27. Allan, J. L., Johnston, D. W., Powell, D. J., Farquharson, B., Jones, M. C., Leckie, G., & Johnston, M. (2019). Clinical decisions and time since rest break: An analysis of decision fatigue in nurses. *Health Psychology, 38*(4), 318.

28. Sullivan, D. & Hardy, B. (2020). *Who Not How: The formula to achieve bigger goals through accelerating teamwork*. Hay House Business.

29. Dalton, M. (1948). The Industrial "Rate Buster": A Characterization. *Human Organization, 7*(1), 5-18.

30. Drew, R. (2006). Lethargy begins at home: The academic rate-buster and the academic sloth. *Text and Performance Quarterly, 26*(1), 65–78.

Chapter 2

1. Koomey, J. (2008). *Turning Numbers into Knowledge: Mastering the art of problem solving*. Analytics Press.

2. McKeown, G. (2020). *Essentialism: The disciplined pursuit of less*. Currency.

3. McAdams, D. P. (2011). *Narrative identity. In Handbook of identity theory and research* (pp. 99–115). Springer: New York, NY.

4. Berk, L. E. (2010). *Exploring Lifespan Development (2nd ed.)*. Pg. 314. Pearson Education Inc.

5. Sitzmann, T., & Yeo, G. (2013). A meta-analytic investigation of the within-person self-efficacy domain: Is self-efficacy a product of past performance or a driver of future performance?. *Personnel Psychology, 66*(3), 531–568.

6. Edwards, K. D. (1996). Prospect theory: A literature review. *International Review of Financial Analysis, 5*(1), 19–38.

7. Haita-Falah, C. (2017). Sunk-cost fallacy and cognitive ability in individual decision-making. *Journal of Economic Psychology, 58*, 44–59.

8. Strough, J., Mehta, C. M., McFall, J. P., & Schuller, K. L. (2008). Are older adults less subject to the sunk-cost fallacy than younger adults?. *Psychological Science, 19*(7), 650–652.

9. Knetsch, J. L., & Sinden, J. A. (1984). Willingness to pay and compensation demanded: Experimental evidence of an unexpected disparity in measures of value. *The Quarterly Journal of Economics, 99*(3), 507–521.

10. Kahneman, D., Knetsch, J. L., & Thaler, R. H. (1990). Experimental tests of the endowment effect and the Coase theorem. *Journal of political Economy, 98*(6), 1325–1348.

11. Morewedge, C. K., & Giblin, C. E. (2015). Explanations of the endowment effect: an integrative review. *Trends in Cognitive Sciences, 19*(6), 339–348.

12. Festinger, L. (1957). *A Theory of Cognitive Dissonance*. Stanford University Press.

13. Heider, F. (1946). Attitudes and cognitive organization. *Journal of Psychology, 21*, 107–112.

14. Heider, F. (1958). *The Psychology of Interpersonal Relations*. New York: John Wiley.

15. Doorley, J. D., Goodman, F. R., Kelso, K. C., & Kashdan, T. B. (2020). Psychological flexibility: What we know, what we do not know, and what we think we know. *Social and Personality Psychology Compass, 14*(12), 1–11.

16. Kashdan, T. B., Disabato, D. J., Goodman, F. R., Doorley, J. D., & McKnight, P. E. (2020). Understanding psychological flexibility: A multimethod exploration of pursuing valued goals despite the presence of distress. *Psychological Assessment, 32*(9), 829.

17. Harris, R. (2006). Embracing your demons: An overview of acceptance and commitment therapy. *Psychotherapy in Australia, 12*(4).

18. Blackledge, J. T., & Hayes, S. C. (2001). Emotion regulation in acceptance and commitment therapy. *Journal of Clinical Psychology, 57*(2), 243–255.

19. Hayes, S. C., Strosahl, K. D., & Wilson, K. G. (2011). *Acceptance and Commitment Therapy: The process and practice of mindful change*. Guilford Press.

20. Gloster, A. T., Walder, N., Levin, M. E., Twohig, M. P., & Karekla, M. (2020). The empirical status of acceptance and commitment therapy: A review of meta-analyses. *Journal of Contextual Behavioral Science, 18*, 181–192.

21. Hawkins, D. R. (2013). *Letting Go: The pathway of surrender*. Hay House, Inc.

22. Ferriss, T. (2009). *The 4-Hour Workweek: Escape 9–5, live anywhere, and join the new rich*. Harmony.

23. MrBeast. (2016). *Dear Future Me (Scheduled Uploaded 6 Months Ago)*. MrBeast YouTube Channel. Accessed on August 22, 2022 at https://www.youtube.com/watch?v=fG1N5kzeAhM

24. MrBeast. (2020). *Hi Me in 5 Years*. MrBeast YouTube Channel. Accessed on August 22, 2022 at https://www.youtube.com/watch?v=AKJfakEsgy0

25. Rogan, J. (2022). *The Joe Rogan Experience: Episode #1788 – Mr. Beast*. Spotify. Retrieved on March 15, 2022, at https://open.spotify.com/episode/5lokpznqvSrJO3gButgQvs

26. Gladwell, M. (2008). *Outliers: The story of success*. Little, Brown.

27. Jorgenson, E. (2020). *The Almanack of Naval Ravikant*. Magrathea Publishing.

28. Charlton, W., & Hussey, E. (1999). *Aristotle Physics Book VIII (Vol. 3)*. Oxford University Press.

29. Rosenblueth, A., Wiener, N., & Bigelow, J. (1943). Behavior, purpose and teleology. *Philosophy of Science, 10*(1), 18–24.

30. Woodfield, A. (1976). *Teleology*. Cambridge University Press.

31. Baumeister, R. F., Vohs, K. D., & Oettingen, G. (2016). Pragmatic prospection: How and why people think about the future. *Review of General Psychology, 20*(1), 3–16.

32. Suddendorf, T., Bulley, A., & Miloyan, B. (2018). Prospection and natural selection. *Current Opinion in Behavioral Sciences, 24*, 26–31.

33. Seligman, M. E., Railton, P., Baumeister, R. F., & Sripada, C. (2013). Navigating into the future or driven by the past. *Perspectives on Psychological Science, 8*(2), 119–141.

34. Schwartz, D. (2015). *The Magic of Thinking Big*. Simon & Schuster.

35. Godin, S. (2010). *Linchpin: Are you indispensable? How to drive your career and create a remarkable future*. Penguin.

36. Clear, J. (2018). *Atomic Habits: An easy & proven way to build good habits & break bad ones*. Penguin.

37. Hoehn, C. (2018). *How to Sell a Million Copies of Your Non-Fiction Book*. Retrieved on October 5, 2022, at https://charliehoehn.com/2018/01/10/sell-million-copies-book/

38. Berrett-Koehler Publishers. (2020). *The 10 Awful Truths about Book Publishing*. Steven Piersanti, Senior Editor. Retrieved on October 5, 2022, at https://ideas.bkconnection.com/10-awful-truths-about-publishing

39. Clear, J. (2021). 3-2-1: *The difference between good and great, how to love yourself, and how to get better at writing*. Retrieved on November 2, 2022, at https://jamesclear.com/3-2-1/december-16-2021

40. Clear, J. (2014). *My 2014 Annual Review*. Retrieved on October 5, 2022, at https://jamesclear.com/2014-annual-review

41. Clear, J. (2015). *My 2015 Annual Review*. Retrieved on October 5, 2022, at https://jamesclear.com/2015-annual-review

42. Clear, J. (2016). *My 2016 Annual Review*. Retrieved on October 5, 2022, at https://jamesclear.com/2016-annual-review

43. Clear, J. (2017). *My 2017 Annual Review*. Retrieved on October 5, 2022, at https://jamesclear.com/2017-annual-review

44. Ryan, R. M., & Deci, E. L. (2017). *Self-Determination Theory. Basic psychological needs in motivation, development, and wellness.*

45. Deci, E. L., Olafsen, A. H., & Ryan, R. M. (2017). Self-determination theory in work organizations: The state of a science. *Annual Review of Organizational Psychology and Organizational Behavior, 4*, 19–43.

46. Clear, J. (2018). *My 2018 Annual Review*. Retrieved on October 5, 2022, at https://jamesclear.com/2018-annual-review

47. Clear, J. (2019). *My 2019 Annual Review*. Retrieved on October 5, 2022, at https://jamesclear.com/2019-annual-review

48. Godin, S. (2007). *The Dip: A little book that teaches you when to quit* (and when to stick). Penguin.

49. Collins, J. (2001). *Good to Great: Why some companies make the leap and others don't.* HarperBusiness.

50. David Bowman, N., Keene, J., & Najera, C. J. (2021, May). *Flow encourages task focus, but frustration drives task switching: How reward and effort combine to influence player engagement in a simple video game.* In Proceedings of the 2021 CHI Conference on Human Factors in Computing Systems (pp. 1-8).

51. Xu, S., & David, P. (2018). Distortions in time perceptions during task switching. *Computers in Human Behavior, 80*, 362-369.

52. Sullivan, D. (2015). *Wanting What You Want: why getting what you want is incomparably better than getting what you need.* Strategic Coach Inc.

53. Sullivan, D. (2015). *Wanting What You Want: why getting what you want is incomparably better than getting what you need.* Strategic Coach Inc.

54. Graham, P. (2004). *How to make wealth*. Retrieved on October 11, 2022, at http://www.paulgraham.com/wealth.html

Chapter 3

1. Sullivan, D. (2015). *Wanting What You Want: why getting what you want is incomparably better than getting what you need.* Strategic Coach Inc.

2. Ferriss, T. (2022). *Brian Armstrong, CEO of Coinbase — The Art of Relentless Focus, Preparing for Full-Contact Entrepreneurship, Critical Forks in the Path, Handling Haters, The Wisdom of Paul Graham, Epigenetic Reprogramming, and Much More (#627).* The Tim Ferriss Show.

3. Armstrong, B. (2020). *Coinbase is a mission focused company.* Coinbase .com. Retrieved on October 10, 2022, at https://www.coinbase.com/blog/coinbase-is-a-mission-focused-company

4. Covey, S. R., & Covey, S. (2020). *The 7 Habits of Highly Effective People.* Simon & Schuster.

5. Carter, I. (2004). Choice, freedom, and freedom of choice. *Social Choice and Welfare, 22*(1), 61–81.

6. Fromm, E. (1994). *Escape from Freedom.* Macmillan.

7. Frankl, V. E. (1985). *Man's Search for Meaning.* Simon & Schuster.

8. Canfield, J., Switzer, J., Padnick, S., Harris, R., & Canfield, J. (2005). *The Success Principles* (pp. 146–152). Harper Audio.

9. Sullivan, D. (2017). *The Self-Managing Company. Freeing yourself up from everything that prevents you from creating a 10x bigger future.* Strategic Coach Inc.

10. Rodriguez, P. (2022). *Paul Rodriguez | 20 and Forever.* Paul Rodriguez YouTube Channel. Retrieved on October 10, 2022, at https://www.youtube.com/watch?v=xUEw6fSlcsM

11. Stephen Cox (April 11, 2013). *"Paul Rodriguez Interrogated."* The Berrics. Archived from the original on April 13, 2013. Retrieved April 13, 2013.

12. "City Stars Skateboards." Skately LLC. Archived from the original on March 26, 2018. Retrieved April 8, 2018.

13. Sigurd Tvete (July 31, 2009). *"Paul Rodriguez Interview."* Tackyworld. Tacky Products AS. Archived from the original on April 9, 2014. Retrieved September 27, 2012.

14. Transworld Skateboarding, (2002). *In Bloom.* Transworld Skateboard Video.

15. Greene, R. (2013). *Mastery.* Penguin.

16. Rodriguez, P. (2022). *Paul Rodriguez | 20 and Forever.* Paul Rodriguez YouTube Channel. Retrieved on October 10, 2022, at https://www.youtube.com/watch?v=xUEw6fSlcsM

17. Quoted in Howard Gardner, *"Creators: Multiple Intelligences,"* in The Origins of Creativity, ed. Karl H. Pfenninger and Valerie R. Shubik (Oxford: Oxford University Press, 2001), 132.

18. Hall, D. T., & Chandler, D. E. (2005). Psychological success: When the career is a calling. Journal of Organizational Behavior: *The International Journal of Industrial, Occupational and Organizational Psychology and Behavior, 26*(2), 155–176.

19. Duffy, R. D., & Dik, B. J. (2013). Research on calling: What have we learned and where are we going?. *Journal of Vocational Behavior, 83*(3), 428–436.

20. Dobrow, S. R., & Tosti-Kharas, J. (2012). Listen to your heart? Calling and receptivity to career advice. *Journal of Career Assessment, 20*(3), 264–280.

21. Duke, A. (2022). *Quit: The power of knowing when to walk away.* Penguin.

22. Sullivan, D. (2019). *Always Be the Buyer: Attracting other people's highest commitment to your biggest and best standards.* Strategic Coach Inc.

23. Sullivan, D. (2019). *Always Be the Buyer: Attracting other people's highest commitment to your biggest and best standards.* Strategic Coach Inc.

24. Carse, J. (2011). *Finite and Infinite Games.* Simon & Schuster.

25. Jorgenson, E. (2020). *The Almanack of Naval Ravikant.* Magrathea Publishing.

Chapter 4

1. Jobs, S. (2005). *Steve Jobs' 2005 Stanford Commencement Address.* Stanford University YouTube Channel. Retrieved on August 26, 2022, at https://www.youtube.com/watch?v=UF8uR6Z6KLc

2. Sullivan, D., & Hardy, B. (2021). *The Gap and The Gain: The high achievers' guide to happiness, confidence, and success.* Hay House Business.

3. Perry, M. (2022). *Friends, Lovers, and the Big Terrible Thing: A Memoir.* Flatiron Books.

4. Sullivan, D., & Hardy, B. (2021). *The Gap and The Gain: The high achievers' guide to happiness, confidence, and success.* Hay House Business.

5. Fredrickson, B. L. (2004). The broaden–and–build theory of positive emotions. Philosophical transactions of the royal society of London. *Series B: Biological Sciences, 359*(1449), 1367–1377.

6. Garland, E. L., Fredrickson, B., Kring, A. M., Johnson, D. P., Meyer, P. S., & Penn, D. L. (2010). Upward spirals of positive emotions counter downward spirals of negativity: Insights from the broaden-and-build theory and affective neuroscience on the treatment of emotion dysfunctions and deficits in psychopathology. *Clinical Psychology Review, 30*(7), 849–864.

7. Vacharkulksemsuk, T., & Fredrickson, B. L. (2013). *Looking back and glimpsing forward: The broaden-and-build theory of positive emotions as applied to organizations.* In Advances in positive organizational psychology (Vol. 1, pp. 45–60). Emerald Group Publishing Limited.

8. Thompson, M. A., Nicholls, A. R., Toner, J., Perry, J. L., & Burke, R. (2021). Pleasant Emotions Widen Thought–Action Repertoires, Develop Long-Term Resources, and Improve Reaction Time Performance: A Multistudy Examination of the Broaden-and-Build Theory Among Athletes. *Journal of Sport and Exercise Psychology, 43*(2), 155–170.

9. Lin, C. C., Kao, Y. T., Chen, Y. L., & Lu, S. C. (2016). Fostering change-oriented behaviors: A broaden-and-build model. *Journal of Business and Psychology, 31*(3), 399–414.

10. Stanley, P. J., & Schutte, N. S. (2023). Merging the Self-Determination Theory and the Broaden and Build Theory through the nexus of positive affect: A macro theory of positive functioning. *New Ideas in Psychology, 68*, 100979.

11. Chhajer, R., & Dutta, T. (2021). Gratitude as a mechanism to form high-quality connections at work: impact on job performance. *International Journal of Indian Culture and Business Management, 22*(1), 1-18.

12. Park, G., VanOyen-Witvliet, C., Barraza, J. A., & Marsh, B. U. (2021). The benefit of gratitude: trait gratitude is associated with effective economic decision-making in the ultimatum game. *Frontiers in Psychology, 12*, 590132.

13. Sitzmann, T., & Yeo, G. (2013). A meta-analytic investigation of the within-person self-efficacy domain: Is self-efficacy a product of past performance or a driver of future performance?. *Personnel Psychology, 66*(3), 531–568.

14. Tong, E. M., Fredrickson, B. L., Chang, W., & Lim, Z. X. (2010). Re-examining hope: The roles of agency thinking and pathways thinking. *Cognition and Emotion, 24*(7), 1207–1215.

15. Peterson, S. J., & Byron, K. (2008). Exploring the role of hope in job performance: Results from four studies. *Journal of Organizational Behavior: The International Journal of Industrial, Occupational and Organizational Psychology and Behavior, 29*(6), 785–803.

16. Sullivan, D. (2016). *The 10x Mind Expander: Moving your thinking, performance, and results from linear plodding to exponential breakthroughs.* Strategic Coach Inc.

17. Utchdorf, D. (2008). *A Matter of a Few Degrees.* April 2008, General Conference. The Church of Jesus Christ of Latter-day Saints.

18. Johnston, W. A., & Dark, V. J. (1986). Selective attention. *Annual Review of Psychology, 37*(1), 43–75.

19. Treisman, A. M. (1964). Selective attention in man. *British Medical Bulletin, 20*(1), 12–16.

20. Kiyosaki, R. T., & Lechter, S. L. (2001). *Rich Dad Poor Dad: What the rich teach their kids about money that the poor and the middle class do not!.* Business Plus.

21. Lorenz, E. (2000). The Butterfly Effect. *World Scientific Series on Nonlinear Science Series A, 39*, 91–94.

22. Shen, B. W., Pielke Sr, R. A., Zeng, X., Cui, J., Faghih-Naini, S., Paxson, W., & Atlas, R. (2022). Three kinds of butterfly effects within Lorenz Models. *Encyclopedia, 2*(3), 1250-1259.

23. Shen, B. W., Pielke Sr, R. A., Zeng, X., Faghih-Naini, S., Shie, C. L., Atlas, R., ... & Reyes, T. A. L. (2018, June). *Butterfly effects of the first and second kinds: new insights revealed by high-dimensional lorenz models.* In 11th Int. Conf. on Chaotic Modeling, Simulation and Applications.

24. Hilborn, R. C. (2004). Sea gulls, butterflies, and grasshoppers: A brief history of the butterfly effect in nonlinear dynamics. *American Journal of Physics, 72*(4), 425-427.

25. Waitzkin, J. (2008). *The Art of Learning: An inner journey to optimal performance.* Simon & Schuster.

26. Moors, A., & De Houwer, J. (2006). Automaticity: a theoretical and conceptual analysis. *Psychological Bulletin, 132*(2), 297.

27. Logan, G. D. (1985). Skill and automaticity: Relations, implications, and future directions. *Canadian Journal of Psychology/Revue Canadienne De Psychologie, 39*(2), 367.

28. Graham, P. (2004). *How to make wealth.* Retrieved on October 11, 2022, at http://www.paulgraham.com/wealth.html

29. Adabi, M. (2017). *The Obamas are getting a record-setting book deal worth at least $60 million.* Business Insider. Retrieved on October 11, 2022, at https://www.businessinsider.com/obama-book-deal-2017-2

Chapter 5

1. Brown, B. (2010). *The Gifts of Imperfection: Let go of who you think you're supposed to be and embrace who you are.* Simon & Schuster.

2. Godin, S. (2014). *The wasteful fraud of sorting for youth meritocracy: Stop Stealing Dreams.* Retrieved on September 29, 2022 at https://seths. blog/2014/09/the-shameful-fraud-of-sorting-for-youth-meritocracy/

3. Slife, B. D. (1995). Newtonian time and psychological explanation. *The Journal of Mind and Behavior,* 45–62.

4. Slife, B. D. (1993). *Time and Psychological Explanation.* SUNY press.

5. Murchadha, F. Ó. (2013). *The Time of Revolution: Kairos and chronos in Heidegger (Vol. 269).* A&C Black.

6. Smith, J. E. (2002). Time and qualitative time. Rhetoric and kairos. *Essays in History, Theory, and Praxis,* 46–57.

7. Slife, B. D. (1993). *Time and Psychological Explanation.* SUNY press.

8. Einstein, A. (2013). *Relativity.* Routledge.

9. Tompkins, P. K. (2002). Thoughts on time: Give of yourself now. *Vital Speeches of the Day, 68*(6), 183.

10. Malhotra, R. K. (2017). Sleep, recovery, and performance in sports. *Neurologic Clinics, 35*(3), 547-557.

11. Neagu, N. (2017). Importance of recovery in sports performance. *Marathon, 9*(1), 53–9.

12. Kellmann, M., Pelka, M., & Beckmann, J. (2017). Psychological relaxation techniques to enhance recovery in sports. *In Sport, Recovery, and Performance* (pp. 247–259). Routledge.

13. Taylor, K., Chapman, D., Cronin, J., Newton, M. J., & Gill, N. (2012). Fatigue monitoring in high performance sport: a survey of current trends. *J Aust Strength Cond, 20*(1), 12–23.

14. Sonnentag, S. (2012). Psychological detachment from work during leisure time: The benefits of mentally disengaging from work. *Current Directions in Psychological Science, 21*(2), 114–118.

15. Karabinski, T., Haun, V. C., Nübold, A., Wendsche, J., & Wegge, J. (2021). Interventions for improving psychological detachment from work: A meta-analysis. *Journal of Occupational Health Psychology, 26*(3), 224.

16. Ferriss, T. (2018). *The Tim Ferriss Show Transcripts: LeBron James and Mike Mancias (#349)*. The Tim Ferriss Show. Retrieved on September 30, 2022, at https://tim.blog/2018/11/30/the-tim-ferriss-show-transcripts-lebron-james-and-mike-mancias/

17. Karabinski, T., Haun, V. C., Nübold, A., Wendsche, J., & Wegge, J. (2021). Interventions for improving psychological detachment from work: A meta-analysis. *Journal of Occupational Health Psychology, 26*(3), 224.

18. Sonnentag, S. (2012). Psychological detachment from work during leisure time: The benefits of mentally disengaging from work. *Current Directions in Psychological Science, 21*(2), 114–118.

19. Sonnentag, S., Binnewies, C., & Mojza, E. J. (2010). Staying well and engaged when demands are high: the role of psychological detachment. *Journal of Applied Psychology, 95*(5), 965.

20. Fritz, C., Yankelevich, M., Zarubin, A., & Barger, P. (2010). Happy, healthy, and productive: the role of detachment from work during nonwork time. *Journal of Applied Psychology, 95*(5), 977.

21. DeArmond, S., Matthews, R. A., & Bunk, J. (2014). Workload and procrastination: The roles of psychological detachment and fatigue. *International Journal of Stress Management, 21*(2), 137.

22. Sonnentag, S., Binnewies, C., & Mojza, E. J. (2010). Staying well and engaged when demands are high: the role of psychological detachment. *Journal of Applied Psychology, 95*(5), 965.

23. Germeys, L., & De Gieter, S. (2017). Psychological detachment mediating the daily relationship between workload and marital satisfaction. *Frontiers in Psychology*, 2036.

24. Greenhaus, J. H., Collins, K. M., & Shaw, J. D. (2003). The relation between work–family balance and quality of life. *Journal of Vocational Behavior, 63*(3), 510–531.

25. Shimazu, A., Matsudaira, K., De Jonge, J., Tosaka, N., Watanabe, K., & Takahashi, M. (2016). Psychological detachment from work during nonwork time: Linear or curvilinear relations with mental health and work engagement?. *Industrial Health*, 2015–0097.

26. Kotler, S. (2021). *The Art of Impossible: a peak performance primer.* HarperCollins.

27. Culley, S. et al., (2011). Proceedings Volume DS68-7 IMPACTING SOCIETY THROUGH ENGINEERING DESIGN VOLUME 7: *HUMAN BEHAVIOUR IN DESIGN*. Human Behaviour in Design, Lyngby/

Copenhagen, Denmark. Retrieved on September 30, 2022, at https://www.designsociety.org/multimedia/publication/1480c22e7a4a2eb7016 0bfd90471ac2d.pdf

28. Lynch, D. (2016). *Catching the big fish: Meditation, consciousness, and creativity.* Penguin.

29. Reservations. *How to do a Think Week Like Bill Gates.* Retrieved on September 30, 2022, at https://www.reservations.com/blog/resources/think-weeks/

30. Sullivan, D. (2017). *The Self-Managing Company. Freeing yourself up from everything that prevents you from creating a 10x bigger future.* Strategic Coach Inc.

31. Sullivan, D., & Hardy, B. (2020). *Who Not How: The formula to achieve bigger goals through accelerating teamwork.* Hay House Business.

32. Cowherd, C. (2022). *The Herd | Colin "crazy on" Jalen Hurts led Philadelphia Eagles beat Commanders to prove 3-0. YouTube.* Retrieved on September 30, 2022, at https://www.youtube.com/watch?v=ETu6-P-KRMg

33. Graham, P. (2009). *Maker's Schedule, Manager's Schedule.*

34. Kotler, S. (2021). *The Art of Impossible: a peak performance primer.* HarperCollins.

35. Csikszentmihalyi, M., Abuhamdeh, S., & Nakamura, J. (2014). Flow. *In Flow and The Foundations of Positive Psychology* (pp. 227–238). Springer, Dordrecht.

36. Godin, S. (2010). *Linchpin: Are you indispensable?* Penguin.

37. Sullivan, D. & Hardy, B. (2021). *The Gap and The Gain: The high achievers' guide to happiness, confidence, and success.* Hay House Business.

38. Albaugh, N., & Borzekowski, D. (2016). Sleeping with One's cellphone: The relationship between cellphone night placement and sleep quality, relationships, perceived health, and academic performance. *Journal of Adolescent Health, 58*(2), S31.

Chapter 6

1. Ferriss, T. (2009). *The 4-Hour Workweek: Escape 9-5, live anywhere, and join the new rich.* Harmony.

2. Sullivan, D. (2017). *The Self-Managing Company. Freeing yourself up from everything that prevents you from creating a 10x bigger future.* Strategic Coach Inc.

3. Bass, B. M., & Riggio, R. E. (2006). *Transformational Leadership.* Psychology Press.

4. Campbell, J. (2003). *The Hero's Journey: Joseph Campbell on his life and work (Vol. 7).* New World Library.

5. Bass, B. M. (1999). Two decades of research and development in transformational leadership. *European Journal of Work and Organizational Psychology, 8*(1), 9–32.

6. Siangchokyoo, N., Klinger, R. L., & Campion, E. D. (2020). Follower transformation as the linchpin of transformational leadership theory: A systematic review and future research agenda. *The Leadership Quarterly, 31*(1), 101341.

7. Turnnidge, J., & Côté, J. (2018). Applying transformational leadership theory to coaching research in youth sport: A systematic literature review. *International Journal of Sport and Exercise Psychology, 16*(3), 327–342.

8. Islam, M. N., Furuoka, F., & Idris, A. (2021). Mapping the relationship between transformational leadership, trust in leadership and employee championing behavior during organizational change. *Asia Pacific Management Review, 26*(2), 95–102.

9. Collins, J. (2001). *Good to Great: Why some companies make the leap and others don't.* HarperBusiness.

10. Taylor, J. (1851). "The Organization of the Church," *Millennial Star, Nov. 15, 1851*, p. 339.

11. Organ, D. W. (1988). A restatement of the satisfaction-performance hypothesis. *Journal of Management, 14*(4), 547–557.

12. Lam, S. S. K., Hui, C. & Law, K. S. (1999). Organizational citizenship behavior: comparing perspectives of supervisors and subordinates across four international samples. *Journal of Applied Psychology, 84*(4), 594–601.

13. Morrison, E. W. (1994). Role definitions and organizational citizenship behavior: the importance of the employee's perspective. *Academy of Management Journal, 37*(6), 1543–1567.

14. Vipraprastha, T., Sudja, I. N., & Yuesti, A. (2018). The Effect of Transformational Leadership and Organizational Commitment to Employee Performance with Citizenship Organization (OCB) Behavior as Intervening Variables (At PT Sarana Arga Gemeh Amerta in Denpasar City). *International Journal of Contemporary Research and Review, 9*(02), 20503–20518.

15. Engelbrecht, A. S., & Schlechter, A. F. (2006). The relationship between transformational leadership, meaning and organisational citizenship behaviour. *Management Dynamics: Journal of the Southern African Institute for Management Scientists, 15*(4), 2–16.

16. Lin, R. S. J., & Hsiao, J. K. (2014). The relationships between transformational leadership, knowledge sharing, trust and organizational citizenship behavior. *International Journal of Innovation, Management and Technology, 5*(3), 171.

17. Hardy, B. P. (2019). Transformational leadership and perceived role breadth: Multi-level mediation of trust in leader and affective

organizational commitment (Doctoral dissertation, Clemson University).

18. Schaubroeck, J., Lam, S. S., & Peng, A. C. (2011). Cognition-based and affect-based trust as mediators of leader behavior influences on team performance. *Journal of Applied Psychology, 96*(4), 863–871.

19. Nohe, C., & Hertel, G. (2017). Transformational leadership and organizational citizenship behavior: a meta-analytic test of underlying mechanisms. *Frontiers in Psychology, 8*, 1364.

20. Covey, S. R., & Merrill, R. R. (2006). *The Speed of Trust: The one thing that changes everything.* Simon & Schuster.

21. Deci, E. L., & Ryan, R. M. (2012). *Self-Determination Theory.*

22. Ryan, R. M., & Deci, E. L. (2019). Brick by brick: The origins, development, and future of self-determination theory. *In Advances in Motivation Science* (Vol. 6, pp. 111–156). Elsevier.

23. Sullivan, D., & Hardy, B. (2020). *Who Not How: The formula to achieve bigger goals through accelerating teamwork.* Hay House Business.

24. Collins, J. (2001). *Good to Great: Why some companies make the leap and others don't.* HarperBusiness.

25. Sullivan, D. (2017). *The Self-Managing Company. Freeing yourself up from everything that prevents you from creating a 10x bigger future.* Strategic Coach Inc.

Conclusion

1. Hollis, J. (2005). *Finding Meaning in the Second Half of Life: How to finally, really grow up.* Penguin.

2. Hawkins, D. R. (1994). *Power Versus Force: An anatomy of consciousness.* Hay House, Inc.

3. Gódány, Z., Machová, R., Mura, L., & Zsigmond, T. (2021). Entrepreneurship motivation in the 21st century in terms of pull and push factors. *TEM J, 10*, 334–342.

4. Uysal, M., Li, X., & Sirakaya-Turk, E. (2008). Push-pull dynamics in travel decisions. *Handbook of Hospitality Marketing Management*, 412, 439.

5. Hawkins, D. R. (2013). *Letting go: The pathway of surrender.* Hay House, Inc.

6. Newport, C., (2012). *So Good They Can't Ignore You: Why skills trump passion in the quest for work You love.* Grand Central Publishing.

7. Tracy, B. (2001). *Focal Point: A proven system to simplify your life, double your productivity, and achieve all your goals.* Amacom.

INDEX

Dan's
Acknowledgments

My greatest gratitude always goes first to Babs Smith whose lifetime wisdom about entrepreneurial growth always guides me to choose wisely. She is 10x in every way and makes everything possible.

And, here in our third book, I feel profoundly fortunate having Ben Hardy's masterful thinking and writing. A marvelous upward journey we're on together.

A special shout-out to Shannon Waller, Julia Waller, Cathy Davis, Eleonora Mancini, and Serafina Pupillo (who between them have been indispensable Coach team members for over 125 years) for jumping in to contribute their unique talents in a myriad of ways to ensure the best, most accurate result.

Heartfelt thanks to our dedicated group of associate coaches who have contributed many years of expertise, wisdom, and stories to bring these concepts to life for our Strategic Coach community. Your commitment to continually deepen and expand our program is so important to keeping us on the forefront of entrepreneurial growth. I treasure our collaboration.

All of our 10x concepts and strategies derive entirely from the 50 thousand hours of discussion about the extraordinary creative success of more than 22 thousand talented and innovative entrepreneurs we've been privileged to collaborate with in the many growth levels of the Strategic Coach Program since 1974.

I'm deeply grateful for the unique learning opportunity that continues to grow in ways that always surprise and delight me.

Ben's Acknowledgments

Wow, this book has been a complete doozy to write. It's been a thrill ride that has changed my life in so many ways. As I look at the holistic system of my life—inside and out—now, versus when I started writing this book in late 2021, it's shocking. My inside and outside feel and look non-linearly and qualitatively different from when I started this book.

My wife and I have reframed what matters to us, and how we want to live. We've dramatically improved our own connection, as well as the climate and culture of our family, and how we relate to our six kids. We live far more based on want, not perceived need.

I have a different office, one that resonates much more deeply with my vision and desired lifestyle. I drive a different car. I've shed many of my former biases, weaknesses, distractions, and people who were keeping me at 2x, not 10x. My schedule is completely different, and how I approach my time. Rather than being busy, my time is much slower and simpler—with bigger blocks for creativity and focus, and full days and even weeks dedicated to either flow-based focus or flow-based recovery. My identity and standards are totally evolved, and are much clearer and more committed than they've ever been. The structure and focus of my business are different, much simpler and focused on the 10x I'm committed to, and thus I've shed several degrees of 80 percent I was holding on to just 3 to 12 months ago, including some of the most lucrative aspects of my business the past five years.

I say all of this to say, I'm totally humbled and transformed personally by the ideas and stories presented in this book. It changed my life to write it, and it also changed how I write. I did everything I could in writing this book to provide the best possible path for every reader to get 10x qualitative and quantitative transformations in their lives, even and especially those who have already gone 10x many times before.

There are many people who were essential and integral for me being able to understand the concepts of this book, and to put it on paper in a way I believe the concepts, stories, and ideas deserve.

Firstly, I thank Dan and Babs for trusting me with Dan's concepts and ideas, as well as with the amazing coaches and members at Strategic Coach, who provided insights and stories that brought Dan's ideas and this book to life. I'm lucky and blessed to have such a close connection with Dan and Babs, and to be able to have multiple Zoom calls with Dan for each book we write together. It's a true pleasure, one I don't take for granted, and one that was genuinely a dream come true.

I'd also like to specifically thank Cathy Davis, Shannon Waller, and Julia Waller of Strategic Coach. You all treat me like family and support me so much! Thank you!

A special thanks to Howard Getson, for having many conversations with me throughout the years on these topics. Howard, you are brilliant at 10x-thinking and this book would not have been as clear or powerful without your thoughtful words, encouragement, and insights.

Big, big thanks to all the Strategic Coach coaches who have given me not only their time, stories, and insights, but their emotional support. Specifically, Chad Johnson, Adrienne Duffy, Kim Butler, Lee Brower, and Colleen Bowler. But also, to the other coaches who invested time, feedback, and any forms of support. You have no idea how much it helped and how much I rely on you to comprehend and express the ideas you all embody and teach masterfully.

Also, huge thanks to all of the Strategic Coach members and entrepreneurs I interviewed for this book. Whether your story ended up in the book or not, you helped me so much. Thank you for your love for and brilliant application of these ideas. Hearing your stories helped me more fully comprehend what 10x, Unique Ability, Free Days, and having a Self-Managing Team means. Thanks for your generosity, passion, and love.

Appreciation to Hay House for yet again trusting me to do another book. Since 2020, this is our fourth book published together, and hopefully there are many, many more to come. Specific thanks to Reid Tracy, Patty Gift, and Melody Guy for working directly with me, and being patient with my growing pains as a writer and professional. Particular thanks to Melody for being my editor for my past four books, including all three of my co-authored books with Dan and Babs. Melody, thanks for supporting me in the unique and sometimes difficult ways I write these books. Your patience, support, and insight are incredible. Thank you again. I'm grateful for all of you.

To those who helped me put the words on the page, thanks to Tucker Max for his friendship, emotional support, words of wisdom, and important perspectives to make these books solid and continually improving. Tucker, thanks for helping me continue to evolve as a person and as a writer. To PeggySue Wells, for going through the book with me a few times and providing your amazing editorial insights and supports. To Helen Healey, for jumping into the project during the last stages and helping me get the book from *good* to closer to *great* (from a "five" to a "nine" in your words). Thanks for your brilliance, availability, and insights. Finally, to my mom, Susan Knight, for always being there for me, for having countless conversations on the phone with me about my life, writing, and the books. And thanks for reading through really nasty drafts with me on Zoom and helping me clarify and make the books solid. Love you, Mom!

For my team who supports my work, our clients, and readers! Specifically, Chelsea Jenkins, Natasha Schiffman, Jenessa Catterson, Alexis Swanson, Kateyln Chadwick, Kara Avey, Kirsten Jones, and Kaytlin Mortensen. Thank you so much for all you do. You keep the business floating while I go into the writing and creation cave. Thanks for taking ownership, being Self-Managing, and for the passion and purpose you bring to all we do!

To my beautiful and supportive wife, Lauren, and our six kids. I love you so much! Thanks for being the most exciting and purposeful aspect of my life. You all help me become 10x better every single day. I'm humbled and grateful for the life we have together, and for the experiences we create. Thanks for your patience with me as I continue growing and evolving as a husband, father, professional, and provider.

Also, shout-out to my dad, Philip Hardy, and my brothers, Trevor and Jacob Hardy, for being essential emotional support for me. To Daniel Amato, Chad Willardson, Nate Lambert, Richie Norton, Draye Redfern, Wayne Beck, and Joe Polish, for being close friends and emotional support in my life, as a person, and as a professional.

Finally, to God, my Heavenly Father. Thank you for my life. Thank you for this amazing and transformational experience. Thank you for always being there for me, and enabling me with expanded vision and abilities. Thank you for the agency to choose how I live and direct my life.

About Dan Sullivan

Dan Sullivan is the world's foremost expert on entrepreneurship and has personally coached more successful entrepreneurs than anyone else living. He's the founder and president of The Strategic Coach Inc., the premier entrepreneurial coaching company in the world, which over the past 40+ years has provided teaching and training to more than 30,000 entrepreneurs. Dan's innovative and counterintuitive perspectives enable already successful entrepreneurs to get 10x bigger and better results in their business and personal lives, while creating enormous freedom of time, money, relationships, and overall sense of purpose. Dan is the author of more than 55 publications, including the *Wall Street Journal* bestsellers, *Who Not How* and *The Gap and The Gain*, co-authored with Dr. Benjamin Hardy. Dan is married to Babs Smith, his partner in business and in life. They jointly own and operate The Strategic Coach Inc., which has offices in Toronto, Chicago, U.K., Los Angeles, and Vancouver. Dan and Babs reside in Toronto.

www.strategiccoach.com

About
Dr. Benjamin Hardy

Dr. Benjamin Hardy is an organizational psychologist and is the world's leading expert on the psychology of entrepreneurial leadership and exponential growth. His PhD research focused on entrepreneurial courage and transformational leadership. Before completing his PhD, he wrote for Medium where his blogs were read by over 100 million people, published his first major book, *Willpower Doesn't Work*, and ran a seven-figure online training business. Since finishing his PhD in 2019, Dr. Hardy has published five additional books, including three co-authored with the legendary entrepreneurial coach, Dan Sullivan. His books have sold hundreds of thousands of copies and he is a sought-after teacher and speaker at corporate and entrepreneurial events as well as Fortune 500 companies. He and his wife, Lauren, are the parents of six children and live in Orlando, Florida.

www.benjaminhardy.com
www.futureself.com

We hope you enjoyed this Hay House book. If you'd like to receive our online catalog featuring additional information on Hay House books and products, or if you'd like to find out more about the Hay Foundation, please contact:

Hay House, Inc., P.O. Box 5100, Carlsbad, CA 92018-5100
(760) 431-7695 or (800) 654-5126
(760) 431-6948 (fax) or (800) 650-5115 (fax)
www.hayhouse.com® • www.hayfoundation.org

———

Published in Australia by: Hay House Australia Pty. Ltd.,
18/36 Ralph St., Alexandria NSW 2015
Phone: 612-9669-4299 • *Fax:* 612-9669-4144
www.hayhouse.com.au

Published in the United Kingdom by: Hay House UK, Ltd.,
The Sixth Floor, Watson House, 54 Baker Street, London W1U 7BU
Phone: +44 (0)20 3927 7290 • *Fax:* +44 (0)20 3927 7291
www.hayhouse.co.uk

Published in India by: Hay House Publishers India,
Muskaan Complex, Plot No. 3, B-2, Vasant Kunj, New Delhi 110 070
Phone: 91-11-4176-1620 • *Fax:* 91-11-4176-1630
www.hayhouse.co.in

———

Access New Knowledge.
Anytime. Anywhere.

Learn and evolve at your own pace
with the world's leading experts.

www.hayhouseU.com